1001
Business Letters
for All Occasions

1001
Business Letters
for All Occasions

From Interoffice Memos and Employee Evaluations
to Company Policies and Business Invitations—
Templates for Every Situation

COREY SANDLER and JANICE KEEFE

Avon, Massachusetts

Published by Adams Media, a division of F+W Media, Inc.
57 Littlefield Street, Avon, MA 02322. U.S.A.
www.adamsmedia.com

ISBN 10: 1-59869-454-5
ISBN 13: 978-1-59869-454-3

Printed in the United States of America.

10 9 8 7 6 5 4 3 2

Library of Congress Cataloging-in-Publication Data
is available from the publisher.

This publication is designed to provide accurate and authoritative information with regard to the subject matter covered. It is sold with the understanding that the publisher is not engaged in rendering legal, accounting, or other professional advice. If legal advice or other expert assistance is required, the services of a competent professional person should be sought.

—From a *Declaration of Principles* jointly adopted by a
Committee of the American Bar Association and a Committee of Publishers and Associations

Many of the designations used by manufacturers and sellers to distinguish their product are claimed as trademarks. Where those designations appear in this book and Adams Media was aware of a trademark claim, the designations have been printed with initial capital letters.

This book is available at quantity discounts for bulk purchases.
For information, please call 1-800-289-0963.

Dedication

To our fathers, Herb and Dan, who conducted their business in style.

❧

Dear Reader,

Thank you for your patronage. We're glad to have you as a customer and we look forward to meeting your needs now and in the future.

We are pleased to provide you with this book, which includes 1,001 business letters and e-mails that you can use in whole or in part, or as the model for your own communication.

Some of you may be familiar with another book we've written, *1001 Letters for All Occasions*, (Adams Media) which concentrates on personal letters to friends with a smattering of basic letters to employers, schools, and government agencies.

This new book is strictly business.

What does that mean? A personal letter is intended to convey feelings, deliver news, or deal with matters within the family or amongst friends. You can be chatty, you can be deeply informal, and you can even write for no other purpose than to say hello.

On the other hand, a business letter is designed with a specific goal: to sell something, to buy something, to inquire about an available job, to send information on a company policy, or to address a community need.

When you get down to business, your writing should be direct and to the point: here is why I am writing, here are the specifics of my request or my offer, and here is what I am asking you to do.

That doesn't mean that you have to write like a lawyer or a bureaucrat. Business communication can (and should) be clear and easy to comprehend. And there's nothing wrong with being polite and friendly in most communications.

In general, the best letters are written versions of what you might say to a person if you were sitting across the table from him or her. When you are seeking to communicate directly with someone, you can refer to yourself as "I" and to your reader as "you." That's engaging and natural.

If you are committing your company or organization to a policy or an offer, it is usually best to use "we" or the name of the business entity.

Here is an example that includes all of these voices:

"I am writing on behalf of Consolidated Intergalactic to offer you the position of executive vice president for transportation services. In addition to the salary offer we discussed when you visited our offices, we offer a generous range of benefits.

"I'm hoping you will accept the job and join our team soon. Please contact me at (727) 555-0101 soon to discuss your plans."

And please don't refer to yourself as "one." Over time, one has found this to be a very weak way to construct a phrase. It's an archaic and distracting construction.

It is also important to find an active voice. "You have violated our policy on vacation time" is straight and to the point and gets a lot more attention than, "It has been determined that company policy on vacation time has not been followed."

Again, imagine that the addressee of your letter is sitting across the table from you. Be direct and polite, but don't hide information behind inactive or reflexive phrases.

In this book we have created a very fictional company called Consolidated Intergalactic, a maker of geegaws, doodads, and thingamabobs located in metropolitan Lumbertown. What are geegaws, doodads, and thingamabobs and where is Lumbertown?

It doesn't matter. Even with 1,001 letters, there is no way we could possibly include every type of product or service as well as small towns, huge cities, and everything in between. Instead, we have written this book with the idea that readers can easily modify them to apply to real products or services in their own place of work or residence.

We've also kept to a minimum the salutations, address lines, and closing lines for letters. There are very many choices here. In our opinion, though, you can never go wrong by erring on the side of propriety and politeness. Let your letter put your best foot forward.

You can use the index to find a letter that fits your needs most closely, or you can read the book from cover to cover; Consolidated Intergalactic and its suppliers, partners, employees, and customers are a pretty interesting lot. You can think of *1001 Business Letters for All Occasions* as an epistolary novel—a story told in the form of letters—and absorb and use the phrases and terms in your own work.

Oh, and feel free to send us a letter with your comments and suggestions. We prefer e-mails: send them to us at *letters@econoguide.com* or visit our Web site at *www.econoguide.com.*

Thank you.
Corey Sandler and Janice Keefe

Contents

Acknowledgments

We thank our publishing partners at Adams Media, including Gary Krebs, Andrea Norville, and Katrina Schroeder.

Thanks once again to Ed Claflin for charting the course.

And as always, thanks to you, our reader. We are gathered together in hopes of a successful and fulfilling business relationship.

Introduction

Who Writes Letters Anymore?

Almost all of us put pen to paper—or more likely, fingers to keyboard—all the time. Although we have entered into an era where verbal communication by telephone is very common, there are still many areas where the formalities of recorded words are required.

We need to write or respond to legal notices from employers, government agencies, and other entities. And in many situations we need to put it down in writing when we challenge an order or seek confirmation of an important action.

The fact that the medium may have changed from a handwritten or typed letter to a computer-generated printout or a totally electronic exchange of e-mails does not mean that our business communication should be any less precise or clear.

In this book, we do not make many distinctions between letters and e-mails. Most letters can also be sent as e-mails, following the same rules and styles. When it comes to e-mails, we recommend that writers take great care not to be too informal in their communication; forget about the medium and concentrate instead on the content.

One other thing: when you write an e-mail, a great danger arises from the ease of communication and the speed at which it is delivered. When you write a letter, you can (and should) take the time to read over your work before you print it or sign it, and if you change your mind you can always pull the envelope out of the outgoing tray on your desk.

With an e-mail, you should teach yourself to stop and read your message carefully before pressing the SEND button. As we pointed out in the original book in this series, the biggest danger to letter writers is a process that goes like this: *Ready? Fire! Aim.*

A minute spent reading and editing a letter—and especially an e-mail—may save you hours of explanation, correction, and apology.

All of the letters in this book can be found on the enclosed CD-ROM.
All you need to do is insert the CD-ROM and click through the various folders and subfolders to find the letter that you want to use. Feel free to manipulate the letters to suit your needs.

1 The Executive Office: Intraoffice

Notification of calendar for coming year

From Executive Office, Office Services, or Human Resources to employees

Attached please find a spreadsheet copy of the company calendar for 2009. The enterprise calendar, shared amongst all employees for scheduling appointments and meetings, has also been updated.

The annual open enrollment periods for the company health plan will be January 5 through 16, and again July 6 through 17.

One point to note: Christmas of 2009 and New Year's Day of 2010 both occur on a Friday, which creates two consecutive three-day weekends. Because of the need to maintain staff during the holiday period there will be only a limited number of available vacation slots during that time; all requests for time off during that period must be on file before August 1, and approval will be made on the basis of seniority and staffing needs.

If you have any questions about the calendar, please contact Human Resources.

Announcing company-wide meeting

From Executive Office to employees

Our annual company-wide update meeting is scheduled for Wednesday, June 1, from 2 to 5 P.M., at the Marriott Hotel in Lumbertown.

This long-time tradition at Consolidated Intergalactic is an important part of our commitment to keeping all employees updated on every facet of our business and our plans for the future. President and chief Executive Officer Daniel Keyes will open the session, and there will be presentations from each division of the company.

Attendance at the meeting is strongly encouraged, but staffers who have appointments or assignments that conflict with the schedule (including those asked to cover phones and other essential assignments at headquarters) will be able to view a videotape of the session on our company intranet beginning June 2.

As you know, the Marriott Hotel is within walking distance of our offices. We will also offer a shuttle bus, beginning at 1:15 P.M., for those needing special assistance.

We look forward to seeing you at the meeting.

Soliciting suggestions for topics for company-wide meeting

From Executive Office to employees

Here at Consolidated Intergalactic, we are committed to an open exchange of ideas and concerns with all employees. In preparation for the June 1 company-wide meeting, Human Resources encourages submission of general-interest questions or suggestions for topics to be covered at the meeting.

We ask that you submit your suggestions to wylie@hr.consolidatedintergalactic.com before May 25.

If you have a specific question that relates to any personal concerns, please call Human Resources directly.

Introducing Employee of Month program

From Executive Office or Human Resources to employees

Beginning August 1, Consolidated Intergalactic will honor one employee each month for exceptional performance or other special contributions to the company or our community.

Any supervisor or departmental manager is eligible to nominate an employee by sending an e-mail to employee_of_the_month@benefits.consolidatedintergalactic.com

Please describe the reasons for your nomination in a short message. A committee in the benefits department will choose each month's honoree. The deadline for the first Employee of the Month nomination is July 15; after then, supervisors or managers can send their recommendations at any time.

Announcement of Employee of Month

From Executive Office or Human Resources to employees

Percy Vander Zoot, a quality inspector in the mainframe Manufacturing Department, has been named Employee of the Month for August.

According to the nomination submitted by Henry Silver, manager of the manufacturing unit, Percy discovered a design flaw in our new 6SJ7 Enhanced Transmogrifier that would likely have caused expensive and dangerous failures after a short period of time. "This was a great catch," Silver wrote. "Even with the best designers, engineers, and computer-aided design it took a trained eye like Percy's to find a potential problem and protect our customers and our company."

In recognition, Percy will receive a $500 bonus and be given a pass to park in the Employee of the Month parking space at the entrance to the building for all of August. In addition, he will be eligible for selection as Employee of the Year, an honor that will be announced at the annual holiday party in December.

Please join me in congratulating Percy on his excellent service.

Congratulations to Employee of Month

From Executive Office or Human Resources to employee

I am most pleased to tell you that you have been chosen as Employee of the Month for August.

You were nominated by Henry Silver, manager of the manufacturing unit, who praised your discovery of a design flaw in our new 6SJ7 Enhanced Transmogrifier before it had been shipped to customers. I will be including details of your fine work in an e-mail that will be sent to all employees.

Henry will be presenting you with your bonus check and the golden parking pass to the Employee of the Month space at the front of the parking lot. (It's a better spot than I've got . . .)

Again, congratulations, and thanks for your good work.

Response to widespread rumor, closing of plant

From Executive Office, Human Resources, or department head to employees

It is not our usual practice to respond to rumors, but we do feel it necessary to make an exception in this case: There is no truth to the rumor that Consolidated Intergalactic plans to close its Lumbertown plant.

There are no such plans, and in fact we have begun soliciting bids for equipment for a new assembly line—which may be the source of the rumor. At this time we are not prepared to make an announcement about the expansion, but we do want to bring an end to a completely incorrect rumor that has upset some of our valued employees here.

Response to widespread rumor, sale of company

From Executive Office, Human Resources, or department head to employees

(NOTE: Check with your legal department or investor relations department before sending a letter of this type.)

A small item in this morning's *Lumbertown Gazette* has caused some concern amongst employees about a possible sale of the company.

Although it is not our usual practice to respond to rumors, we do feel it necessary to make an exception in this case: The article is incorrect, and we have no plans to make any substantial changes to the ownership or operation of the company.

The article notes than an outside investor has increased its ownership of shares in the company. That is correct, and we always welcome investments; our share price has risen by 5 percent in the past several months, which is a benefit to all investors.

However, even with this new investment, no single outside entity will own more than about 8 percent of the shares of the company. The biggest single owner of shares in Consolidated Intergalactic will continue to be employees and executives who participate in our ESOP (employee stock ownership program). These shares currently represent about 62 percent of the investment in the company and that proportion is likely to increase over time.

Announcement of opening of new sales office

From Executive Office to employees

I am pleased to announce that we expect to open a new sales office in Boston this fall.

This new facility will allow us to better serve our clients in New England, and to improve coordination with our Canadian sales office in Montreal.

Details for the Boston office, including the exact location and the date for start of operations, are not yet finalized, but we are seeking to lease space in or near downtown, and hope for an opening date in September.

The office will operate as an extension of the sales and marketing office here at headquarters. We anticipate the appointment of a regional manager, three Boston-based sales personnel, and two clerical support staffers. Some or all of these jobs may be transfers from the central office.

If you are interested in a possible opening in the Boston office, please feel free to notify John Whalen, executive vice president for sales. We will also post available job positions on Human Resources Job hotline as soon as they are determined.

General announcement to staff of closing of sales office

From Executive Office to employees

We will be closing our sales office in Phoenix on April 15.

We have decided it would be a better use of company resources to consolidate the Phoenix operations with our office in San Diego, which already covers a large portion of the southwest.

Although we realize this consolidation of two offices may be disruptive to some of our valued employees, the savings to the organization will be substantial and should help us expand in other areas.

We hope to be able to offer transfers to San Diego or headquarters for many of the current staffers in Phoenix. Where this is not possible, or where a staffer may choose not to accept reassignment, we will offer all possible assistance to employees in seeking other employment as well as all appropriate benefits.

Harry Jones, vice president for Human Resources, will be meeting with all affected staffers in Phoenix today to discuss options.

Update to employee manual policy on confidential information

From Executive Office, Legal Office, or Human Resources to employees

We are writing to inform all employees of a recent important update to the employee manual regarding the safeguard of company confidential information.

No internal financial information or personnel records are to be disclosed to, discussed with, or provided to any person or organization outside of the company without specific written permission by an executive of the accounting or Human Resources office.

Because of the availability of such information over the Internet on devices including personal computers, laptops, and personal digital assistants (PDAs), the employee manual is amended to include the following new section.

Invitation to anniversary reception

From Executive Office to employees and retirees

As I'm sure you know, Consolidated Intergalactic is about to celebrate its twenty-fifth anniversary, an event that literally would not have been possible without your involvement as one of the first employees of the company.

On behalf of all of us at Consolidated Intergalactic, I would like to invite you and members of your family to a special preview of our anniversary exhibit on Friday, May 2, from 4:30 to 6:00 P.M. The reception will include past and present employees of the company.

The geegaw that launched a company—and an entire industry—will be the centerpiece of the exhibit that will be open to the public throughout the month of May at the worldwide headquarters of Consolidated Intergalactic in Lumbertown.

The Model 1 Involuted Reverser, handcrafted out of original growth betel nut wood by Consolidated Intergalactic founder Harry Simplon Jones in 1983, has been brought out of the vaults for the twenty-fifth anniversary celebration. Model 1, still functional, will be displayed in a temperature and humidity-controlled case in the main lobby along with more than 150 other artifacts.

Please call Maria Martez at extension 4343 to let us know you will be coming.

Announcing a special anniversary bonus to employees

From Executive Office to employees and retirees

On behalf of all of us at Consolidated Intergalactic, I'd like to join in the celebration of our twenty-fifth anniversary with a very special day of your own.

On May 2, our anniversary, we will add an extra personal day to the accrued time account of every full-time employee of the company. Part-time employees will receive person time proportionate to their average weekly hours.

I hope to see all of you at the employee preview reception for our twenty-fifth anniversary collection from 4:30 to 6 P.M. in the lobby of our Lumbertown headquarters building.

Seeking greeters for open house

From Executive Office to employees and retirees

As we prepare to open our exciting twenty-fifth anniversary display in the main lobby, we'd like to invite current and retired employees and members of their family to apply for temporary jobs as greeters for the celebration.

The display will be open to the public throughout the month of May, and we would like to have at least two greeters on duty every day. Current employees will receive compensatory time off for hours volunteered during the celebration; retirees and family members will be paid $12 per hour for their time.

To sign up for this fun and exciting special job, please contact Jay Joblot in the Employment Office at extension 2311.

Announcement of foreign visitors touring company

From Executive Office to department heads

The Board of Directors and senior executives will be hosting a delegation from Japan on August 1. This group of businessmen and women and financiers is touring the United States looking for companies with which they may develop financial and trade partnerships.

We will be contacting a number of individual department heads to set up specific tours and presentations, but we also expect there will be a number of informal excursions throughout our headquarters.

Please alert members of your staff about the visitors, and where appropriate please devote a reasonable amount of time and effort to cleaning and organizing your area.

If you have any questions, please call my assistant, Janice Jean, at extension 1111.

Announcement to general staff about foreign visitors touring company

From Executive Office to employees

The Board of Directors and senior executives will be hosting a delegation from Japan on August 1. This group of businessmen and women and financiers is touring the United States looking for companies with which they may develop financial and trade partnerships.

We're sure that all of our employees will show our guests every courtesy as they tour the company. They will be accompanied by representatives of the public relations staff, and they may have questions about some of our operations; please take your cues from the PR rep about how much detail to put into your answers.

Invitation to lunch with foreign visitors

From Executive Office to specified department heads

The Board of Directors would like to invite you to join us at a special luncheon with a group of Japanese businessmen and women and financiers who are touring the United States looking for companies with which they may develop financial and trade partnerships.

The lunch will be held at the Lumbertown Marriott from 12:30 to 2:30 P.M. on August 1. We will arrange for shuttle bus service from the main entrance to the hotel beginning at 12:15 P.M.

Please contact Janice Jean, at extension 1111 to confirm your attendance.

Policy on accepting gifts

From Executive Office, Procurement Office, or Office Services to vendors and suppliers

At Consolidated Intergalactic we appreciate the good efforts of all of our business partners. We also want to assure that all of our activities are conducted in keeping with the highest ethical standards.

Effective immediately, no Consolidated Intergalactic employee is permitted to solicit or accept a gift of any value from someone with whom we do business or a company or organization seeking to do business with Consolidated Intergalactic. Although we recognize that in nearly all cases such gifts are ordinary pleasantries of a business relationship, the purpose of this policy is to avoid the appearance of a conflict of interest in all of our operations.

If you have any questions about this policy, please contact your account executive or the Procurement Office at extension 4044.

Year-end statement, good year

From Executive Office to employees

I want to express my personal thanks to all of our dedicated team members here at Consolidated Intergalactic as we reach the end of another banner year.

Sales for the past twelve months have exceeded our expectations, and orders already on the books for the first quarter of next year point to a strong start for 2009.

I am proud to work with such a dedicated and capable staff.

I wish each of you and your family and friends a healthy and happy new year.

Year-end statement, difficult year

From Executive Office to employees

As we reach the end of the year, I want to give my personal thanks to all of our family here at Consolidated Intergalactic.

We are all aware that this has been a difficult year, mostly because of events that were completely out of our control: adverse weather in the South Pacific, labor difficulties at our independent suppliers, and a soft economy in our primary markets here in the United States and in Guatemala.

I have never, though, felt that the company has been let down by our dedicated workers. And I am convinced that next year will bring greatly improved financial results; our orders in the past month are indicating a strong first quarter.

Finally, I want to wish each of you and your family and friends a healthy and happy new year.

Statement on death of former executive

From Executive Office to employees

It is with great sadness that I must report the passing of Charles "Bud" Wilson, former director of personnel for Consolidated Intergalactic.

Bud was one of the first employees of CI, working for the company for more than twenty-three years until his retirement last September. He truly was one of the builders of this company—every employee who has come to work in the years following his arrival benefited from the corporate culture he helped develop.

Bud passed away last night at his home here in Lumbertown after a short illness; he had returned only two weeks ago from an around-the-world cruise with his beloved wife Marissa. In addition to Marissa, he is survived by his two sons, Peter (currently deputy director of procurement for Consolidated Intergalactic) and Malcolm.

Details of a memorial service for Bud will be announced within the next day and posted on the Human Resources Web site.

Announcement of memorial for deceased employee

From Executive Office to employees

On Tuesday, September 15, we will be dedicating a park bench and memorial garden to honor the memory of Charles "Bud" Wilson, a valued former employee of Consolidated Intergalactic who passed away a month ago. The garden is located just outside of the southwest employee lobby of our Lumbertown offices.

I invite any friend and colleague of Bud to join me and Marissa Wilson in dedicating the garden in a ceremony at 12:30 P.M.

Announcement of memorial scholarship for deceased employee

From Executive Office to employees

The Board of Directors and members of the family of Charles "Bud" Wilson are honored to be able to announce the creation of a new scholarship to aid children of CI employees with college expenses.

The perpetual endowment of the Wilson Scholarship will award $5,000 toward each year of a four-year college program for two children of employees. Recipients will be selected by a committee consisting of family members and representatives of the company on the basis of academic achievement and community service.

We will be publishing details of the application process for the scholarship in the first week of March of each year.

Letters of Congratulations and Thanks

Holiday greetings to employees

Holiday message:

On behalf of Consolidated Intergalactic, I would like to wish each and every one of our employees and their families a joyous holiday season and a healthy, prosperous, and happy new year.

Letter of thanks for community service

From Executive Office, Human Resources, or department head to employee

I wanted to tell you how much we appreciate your volunteer community service. Your hard work reflects well on you, and on Consolidated Intergalactic.

Your supervisor has informed us of your volunteer work, and has nominated you for a special honors program.

Letter of thanks for appearance at community function

From Executive Office, Human Resources, or department head to employee

Thank you for representing all of us here at Consolidated Intergalactic by your recent appearance at the Lumbertown Cares fundraising luncheon.

As a company, we are committed to service to our community, and we are especially proud of the efforts contributed by our employees.

Thanks for involvement in community campaign

From Executive Office, Human Resources, or department head to employee

We are very proud to learn of the success you had as the leader in a campaign that raised more than $10,000 to help support important medical research at Lumbertown Community Hospital. It is especially gratifying that Consolidated Intergalactic was able to assist your efforts.

Congratulations, and thank you.

Congratulations to employee on publication of book or article

From Executive Office or department head to employee

I have received a copy of the current issue of *Modern Gadget*, and I was very pleased to see an article you wrote about new trends in automated micro repair techniques.

The article was well written, and reflects very well on your expertise. We are proud of the credit you gave to our Research Department here at Consolidated Intergalactic.

Congratulations. Please keep me posted on any future publications.

Compliments to speaker and thanks for presentation

From Sales Department or Executive Office to invited speaker

I wanted to let you know how impressed I was with your recent presentation to the sales force about "The Power of Planned Obsolescence." Your message was right on the mark, and I'm already thinking of ways to make use of your theories in our new line of products.

Thanks again.

Congratulations to recipient of community service award

From Executive Office or Human Resources to employee

On behalf of all of us here, please accept my congratulations on being named Consolidated Intergalactic's Volunteer of the Year.

You have been a superb representative of the company in your fundraising and involvement with Habitat for Humanity; as a result of your personal work, more than a hundred other CI employees have chosen to work with that group here in Lumbertown.

As I always say, the most important contribution we make is not our products or services but our involvement in the community as individuals and as a company.

Congratulations to business acquaintance on publication of book or article

From Executive Offices, department head, or employee to customer or employee

Your article in the current issue of *Gadget News* was very well done. It is a real treat to read something new from a true visionary in our field.

Congratulations.

Thanks for speech, donation in appreciation

From Executive Office to invited speaker

On behalf of Consolidated Intergalactic, I want to thank you again for your inspirational speech at our recent company meeting.

I am aware that your employer prohibits the acceptance of gifts from companies with whom you do business; we have the same policy in place for our staff.

However, I want you to know that we have made a donation in your name to Lumbertown Cares as a token of our appreciation for your time and effort.

Thanks to employee accepting honorary or voluntary position

From Executive Office, Human Resources, or department head to employee

I am very pleased to hear that you have accepted appointment as our representative on the Board of Directors of Lumbertown Cares.

This organization is an important part of our community and we are happy to have you participate on our behalf.

Personal letter of thanks and condolence to family of former employee

From Executive Offices to family of employee

Dear Amelia,

Words cannot express our sadness at your loss. Eugene was a valued member of our team here at Consolidated Intergalactic, and he proved himself to be a true hero.

Nothing we can do can ever erase the pain you have experienced, but you have my word that we will do everything we can to honor your husband's sacrifice. I have instructed our Benefits Office to assign a staffer as your personal contact for any questions about insurance, pension, and other matters.

In addition, we will be making a special announcement at the memorial for your husband later today about CI's commitment to honoring Eugene's memory.

Again, you have our deepest sympathies.

2 The Executive Office: To the Community

Letter of appreciation for assistance from area company

From Executive Office or Medical Office to community organization

On behalf of Consolidated Intergalactic, I would like to express our thanks to the managers and staff of Lumbertown Emergency Services for your prompt and professional response to our urgent call last week after a major water pipe burst in the ceiling of the main lobby.

Your staff took over all of the details, from arranging for emergency repairs to the plumbing system to removal of the water and cleaning services. We could not have received better service.

Nomination of employee for industry or association award

From Executive Office, Human Resources, or department head to organization

On behalf of Consolidated Intergalactic, I am nominating Dr. Linda Donald for the 2009 Researcher of the Year Award from the International Geegaw Association.

Ms. Donald's successful development of a hybrid synthetic replacement for *Casuarina oligodon* has benefited the entire geegaw and doodad industry. Although we all hope for a successful recovery of the oligodon crop, our customers—and those of our partners and competitors who have adopted her research findings—have been saved from significant problems that would have been caused by a complete absence of this important component for advanced widget products.

Nomination of employee for community service award

From Executive Office, Human Resources, or department head to community organization

Please consider Janet Gould for recognition as Consolidated Intergalactic's Volunteer of the Year.

Ms. Gould is a superb representative of the company in her fundraising and involvement with Habitat for Humanity; as a result of her personal work, more than a hundred other CI employees chose to work with that group here in Lumbertown.

Invitation to serve in honorary or voluntary position with community organization

From Executive Office, Human Resources, or department head to employee

We hope you will accept appointment as our company's representative to the Board of Directors of Lumbertown Cares.

Here at Consolidated Intergalactic, we are committed to community service, and we are especially proud of our representatives to important local groups such as this one.

Please consult with your supervisor for details of our policy that grants compensatory time off for employees who are appointed to community boards. We also honor all such volunteers at an annual Chairman's Luncheon in November.

Please advise Marjorie Atled, at extension 6735, if you are willing to accept this appointment.

Policy on matching contributions to community organizations

From Executive Office, Benefits Office, or Human Resources to employees

Consolidated Intergalactic is pleased to participate in a number of matching grant programs with area organizations. In the current quarter, we match contributions to ten area groups, up to a maximum of $100 per employee.

To see the current list of matching grant programs, please visit the Benefits Office Web site and click on the "Matching Grants" icon.

If you would like to suggest a worthy organization for inclusion in the program, please call the Benefits Office. It is CI policy not to make charitable gifts to religious or political groups.

Request for approval of participation in donation matching program

From employee to Executive Office, Benefits Office, or Human Resources

I am writing to request Consolidated Intergalactic add the Broome Country Animal Shelter to the organizations eligible for matching grants by the company. The shelter, which has been serving the needs of area animals and animal-lovers for more than forty years, is embarking on a major fundraising program to allow construction of a new veterinary hospital in Lumbertown.

I have attached a copy of the shelter's current Annual Report. I would be happy to assist Payroll Services in assessing this group and overseeing the publicity for a matching grant program.

Announcement of matching program

From Executive Office and Payroll Office to employees

Consolidated Intergalactic is announcing a matching grant program to support the expansion plans for the Lumbertown Atheneum. Between May 1 and July 1, the company will match 100 percent of direct withdrawal paycheck contributions to the library building fund (up to a maximum of $250 per employee).

For information on the program and to enroll in the automatic paycheck withdrawal program, please contact the Payroll Office at extension 6902.

Announcing criteria for matching grant program

From Executive Office, Human Resources, or Employment Office to community organizations

Consolidated Intergalactic seeks proposals from community organizations for its annual matching grant program.

Each year, CI selects as many as five area nonprofit and charitable organizations and offers to match contributions by its employees of as much as $250 each. Contributions are directly deducted from paychecks over a ten-week period and participating groups receive checks from the company in July of each year.

For details on the criteria necessary for consideration for the program, please contact the Payroll Services Department at CI at extension 2348. Organizations must meet IRS regulations as a nonprofit, and must not be political or religious in nature.

Nomination of former employee for scholarship

From Human Resources, Executive Office, or department head to educational institution

I am pleased to heartily recommend Janet Gould for a Community Service Scholarship to Lumbertown Community College. Ms. Gould has been an exemplary employee here at Consolidated Intergalactic for the past two years, and has extended her good works into involvement with half a dozen important organizations in the community.

She was honored within the company as Volunteer of the Year for her fundraising and involvement with Habitat for Humanity; as a result of her personal work, more than a hundred other CI employees chose to work with that group here in Lumbertown.

It would be a great benefit to the community to assist Ms. Gould in her plans to attend college locally. I am certain that wherever she attends college she will be a local treasure.

Nomination of employee for grant

From Human Resources, Executive Office, or department head to organization

On behalf of Consolidated Intergalactic, I am writing to recommend Linda Donald for the 2008 Advanced Research Grant from the International Geegaw Association.

Ms. Donald has been working on a synthetic replacement for *Casuarina oligodon*, a unique ironwood tree harvested in New Guinea and heavily used in the global geegaw and doodad industry. The oligodon crop has been devastated in recent years by a blight caused by invasive moss.

The results of Ms. Donald's work-in-progress have been widely covered in industry publications, and Consolidated Intergalactic has committed to making the results of her work freely available to the entire industry without patent claims or licensure.

Nomination of employee for internal award

From Human Resources, Executive Office, or department head to Executive Office or department head

I am pleased to nominate Walt Webster for Consolidated Intergalactic's Employee of the Year Award.

As director of purchasing for the company, Walt has completely reorganized procedures to implement a just-in-time supply chain for most of our products. At the same time he has recognized CI's dependence upon certain difficult-to-obtain natural commodities used in the manufacturing process and has worked closely with buyers and growers to maximize our ability to meet the needs of our customers.

Overall, we estimate that CI's cost of goods has decreased by 22 percent over the past two years, even as the price of some commodities has increased.

3 Employment Office: To Applicants and Other Organizations

Letters from the Employment Office

Offers of Employment and Negotiations

Letters from Employment Office to Other Organizations

Letters from the Employment Office

Acknowledging job application

From Human Resources or Employment Office to individual

Thank you for applying for a job with Consolidated Intergalactic. We have received your letter and resume and have sent copies to the search committee.

You can expect to hear from the committee within the next four weeks. Candidates who meet the requirements for the job will be invited to come in for an interview.

We have enclosed a brochure about our company and basic information about the benefits package we offer full-time employees.

Providing information about open job positions

From Human Resources or Employment Office to individual

Thank you for your call inquiring about available jobs at Consolidated Intergalactic.

As we discussed, I am including a copy of the current listing of open positions. Please note the differing deadlines for application for the jobs, and if you choose to apply for more than one job please send separate letters of application and resumes for each.

I have also enclosed a brochure about our company and basic information about the benefits package we offer full-time employees.

We wish you the best of luck in your job search.

Invitation to travel to company for interview

From Human Resources or Employment Office to individual

I am pleased to inform you that the search committee has asked me to invite you to come to our offices for a personal interview.

Because you are coming from out of state, we will be happy to arrange for a prepaid roundtrip airline ticket and two nights in a hotel here in Lumbertown. Please give me a call to discuss your preferred schedule.

I have also enclosed a brochure about our company and basic information about the benefits package we offer full-time employees.

Invitation for job interview and explanation of reimbursement for travel

From Human Resources or Employment Office to individual

Enclosed please find e-tickets for your airline flight and confirmation of your hotel reservation for your job interview here in Lumbertown.

Please obtain receipts for taxis, meals, and other travel-related expenditures. I have enclosed a copy of our corporate policy, which gives guidelines on travel expenses and includes a form to request reimbursement. Once you have completed your trip please send the form and copies of the receipts to my attention.

We look forward to your visit to Consolidated Intergalactic and hope that your interview goes well.

Requesting more information from job applicant

From Human Resources or Employment Office to individual

Thank you for your letter and resume submitted in application for the position of director of public information at Consolidated Intergalactic.

We appreciate your interest. In order for us to proceed with evaluation by the search committee, we ask that you please fill out the enclosed application form. Please note that the form includes a request for current references.

We look forward to receiving this material soon and passing it along to the search committee.

Requesting permission to contact references, employers

From Human Resources or Employment Office to individual

Thank you for your application for the position of senior financial analyst at Consolidated Intergalactic.

We have reviewed your resume and background and have determined that you are a qualified applicant for the position. At this point we would like to request that you provide us with a list of at least three references from current or previous employers or supervisors; if you would prefer that we not contact your current employer or supervisor until after you have been interviewed, please indicate that on the form.

Once we have reviewed your complete application package, we may be in contact with you to arrange for an interview.

Seeking clarification of educational credentials

From Employment Office or Human Resources to individual

Thank you for your application for employment at Consolidated Intergalactic.

As part of your application you granted permission to our Human Resources Office to verify any information included on the form.

In checking your academic credentials, we contacted Lumbertown Community College to verify the M.B.A. degree you listed on the application; the college was unable to confirm that such a degree was granted.

We need clarification of this matter before we can proceed with consideration of your application. If you need to contact the college to correct an error on their part, please do so.

Requesting authorization to verify educational credentials

From Human Resources or Employment Office to individual

Thank you for applying for a position as a benefits manager in the Human Resources Office of Consolidated Intergalactic.

We have reviewed your resume and background and have determined that you are an appropriate candidate for the position. Before we proceed to an invitation for a formal interview, we ask that you sign and return the enclosed form granting us permission to verify your academic credentials with schools of higher education you have attended.

Requesting authorization to verify licensure and certification

From Human Resources or Employment Office to individual

Thank you for your application for a position as a quality control engineer at Consolidated Intergalactic.

On behalf of the search committee, I am writing to request that you sign and return the enclosed permission form allowing us to verify your licensure and certification with appropriate state agencies and professional organizations.

The verification process usually requires about two weeks after we receive the permission form from applicants. For that reason, you can next expect to hear from us about the next stage in the interview process after that period of time has elapsed.

Thank you again for your interest in employment with our company.

Requesting clarification of licensure and certification

From Human Resources or Employment Office to individual

In regard to your application for a position as a quality control engineer at Consolidated Intergalactic, the search committee has asked me to seek clarification about your professional certification.

On your job application you list a "Commercial Class B Engineering Certificate" from the Society of Quality Control Professionals. Such certification is an essential qualification for this job opening.

We have contacted that organization and they cannot confirm issuance of such a certificate in your name.

Can you assist us in clarifying this discrepancy? Please feel free to call me or send documents to my attention.

Requesting job applicant make appointment for interview

From Human Resources or Employment Office to individual

On behalf of the search committee, I would like to invite you to make an appointment for a job interview for the open position of senior financial analyst at Consolidated Intergalactic.

This is the next step in the selection process, and we expect to conduct interviews in the period between June 1 and June 15. Please plan on allowing at least ninety minutes for the interview and screening by Human Resources.

Please call my office to schedule a date and time. Thank you again for your interest in employment with our company.

Notification of required aptitude test for employment

From Human Resources or Employment Office to individual

Thank you for your application for a position as a computer technician at Consolidated Intergalactic. We have reviewed your resume and have determined that you have the proper credentials for the job.

Please call my office within the next two weeks to schedule a required industry-standard aptitude test that will gauge your level of understanding of information technology topics. The test will be administered by a third-party assessment company; you should plan on devoting about two hours to the appointment.

Thank you again for your interest in employment with our company.

Notification of physical aptitude test for employment

From Human Resources or Employment Office to individual

Thank you for your application for a position working on the manufacturing line at Consolidated Intergalactic. We have reviewed your resume and have determined that you have the proper credentials for the job.

We welcome all applicants for this job. However, it is one of a relatively few at the company that require certain levels of strength and coordination.

Please call my office within the next two weeks to schedule a required physical aptitude test that will gauge your ability to lift a reasonable amount of weight and operate certain physically demanding tools and machinery. The test will be administered by a third-party assessment company; you should plan on devoting about one hour for the appointment.

Thank you again for your interest in employment with our company.

Notification of required visual aptitude test for employment

From Human Resources or Employment Office to individual

Thank you for your application for a position working as a quality control engineer at Consolidated Intergalactic. We have reviewed your resume and have determined that you have the proper credentials for the job.

We welcome all applicants for this job. However, the nature of quality control requires a certain level of visual acuity and the ability to visually determine faulty product on a moving assembly line.

Please call my office within the next two weeks to schedule a required computer-based visual acuity test that will gauge your ability to perform the specific tasks of a quality control engineer. The test will be administered by a third-party assessment company; you should plan on devoting about one hour for the appointment.

Thank you again for your interest in employment with our company.

Notification of required criminal record and background check for employment

From Human Resources or Employment Office to individual

We have reviewed your application for the night security guard position currently open with our company. We find your qualifications suitable for the job.

Enclosed please find a form granting Consolidated Intergalactic a one-time permission to obtain a criminal record and background check. Under state law, the results of this investigation may be used only for the purposes of pre-employment verification and will remain confidential.

Please sign and return the authorization form in the enclosed envelope. You can next expect to hear from us within approximately ten days after we receive your completed paperwork.

Thank you again for your interest in employment with our company.

Notification of required drug testing for employment

From Human Resources or Employment Office to individual

Thank you again for your application for a position as a delivery driver for Consolidated Intergalactic.

As part of the pre-employment review process, we require all applicants to submit to a drug test. Our company fully adheres to all federal and state laws, regulations, and recommendations regarding substance abuse in the workplace and such tests may also be administered on an unannounced basis for employees.

Please call the Human Resources Office at the number listed below to make an appointment for the test.

Notification of required physical for employment

From Human Resources or Employment Office to individual

Thank you for your recent visit to Consolidated Intergalactic to be interviewed for a position as a manufacturing supervisor.

Please call the Human Resources Office at the number listed below to arrange for a physical examination, as required for employment in a factory position. The physicals are conducted at a clinic near our offices; plan on allowing at least two hours for the examination.

Follow-up after job interview

From Human Resources or Employment Office to individual

Thank you for coming in for an interview for the open position of senior financial analyst at Consolidated Intergalactic.

On behalf of the search committee, I wanted to advise you that we will begin final review of all applications for the job on May 1. We may make a job offer that week or invite one or more finalists back for another interview.

Again, thank you for your interest.

Offers of Employment and Negotiations

Offer of employment

From Human Resources or Employment Office to individual

(NOTE: Review with your in-house or outside legal counsel, or with your Human Resources)

On behalf of Consolidated Industries, I am pleased to offer you the position of senior financial analyst in the Accounting Department. You will be reporting to William Keys, supervisor of the department.

This job is a full-time exempt position, and the starting salary will be $52,000 per year; paychecks are issued biweekly. Enclosed with this letter is a listing of all health, vacation, retirement, and other benefits offered to salaried employees.

Under federal law you will be required to verify your eligibility to work in the United States; please consult the enclosed list of documents acceptable for this purpose.

The starting date of employment is June 1. Please report to Human Resources at 9 A.M. to fill out necessary employment, tax, and benefit paperwork. You will also view a videotape presentation about our company's mission statement, code of conduct, and benefits.

I have enclosed a copy of the employee manual for you to review before your first day of work. You will be asked to sign a statement acknowledging your understanding of the manual and agreement to its terms.

We are very pleased that you have chosen to apply for a job at Consolidated Intergalactic and hope that you will enjoy great success here.

Please inform us of your acceptance of this job offer by sending a letter of agreement to me, or by signing the enclosed duplicate copy of this letter. We must be in receipt of this notification no later than May 15.

If you have any questions about this job offer please feel free to call me. We look forward to hearing from you soon.

Responding to counterproposal on job offer

From Human Resources or Employment Office to individual

We have received your request for modifications to the offer of employment as a senior financial analyst in the Accounting Department of Consolidated Intergalactic.

We are very pleased that you are excited at working here, and we want to do everything we can to accommodate you and your family in making the move to Lumbertown.

You asked for a starting date of June 1 to make allowances for your children's school calendar, and we are pleased to make that adjustment.

Regarding your request for an increase in the moving and relocation allowance from $10,000 to $17,500 I have consulted our Human Resources Office and they suggest the following: Because we have master contracts with several large moving companies, we should be able to negotiate better terms for your relocation. Therefore, we will amend our job offer to allow as much as $17,500 in moving and relocation expenses provided that you make all arrangements through vendors that have been pre-approved by Human Resources.

Your contact at Human Resources is Mary Swoboda, and she is ready to assist you immediately.

Please inform us of your acceptance of this job offer by sending a letter of agreement to me, or by signing the enclosed duplicate copy of this letter. We must be in receipt of this notification no later than May 1.

Conditional offer of employment

From Human Resources or Employment Office to individual

We are pleased to offer you the position of night security guard at Consolidated Intergalactic, contingent upon the completion of a satisfactory background check.

Based on your grant of permission, the background check is now underway and should be completed within the next ten days. We reserve the right to withdraw this offer of employment if the results of the background investigation are not satisfactory.

Your starting date is tentatively set for June 1, and your initial pay rate will be $15 per hour. The job is considered full-time, nonexempt. Attached to this letter is a list of all applicable health, vacation, and retirement benefits.

We will be in contact with you as soon as we receive the results of the background check. Feel free to call me with any questions before then. You may also contact Human Resources to inquire about benefits and paperwork.

Under federal law you will be required to verify your eligibility to work in the United States; please consult the enclosed list of documents acceptable for this purpose.

Please inform us of your acceptance of this job offer by sending a letter of agreement to me, or by signing the enclosed duplicate copy of this letter. We must be in receipt of this notification no later than May 10.

Cover letter providing employee manual to new hire

From Human Resources or Employment Office to individual

We are very pleased that you will be joining the team here at Consolidated Intergalactic.

Enclosed is a copy of our employee manual. Please review the document before your first day of work.

When you report to Human Resources, you will be asked to sign a statement acknowledging your understanding of the manual and agreement to its terms.

Acknowledgment of receipt of employee manual

From Human Resources or Employment Office to individual

Please read carefully the following information and then sign and return this form to Human Resources no later than your first day of work.

I have received and read a copy of the Consolidated Intergalactic Employee Manual.

I understand that it is my obligation to be aware of all of the policies and goals included in the manual. Further, I acknowledge that policies, goals, and benefits set forth in the employee manual are subject to change at any time at the sole discretion of the company.

| _____ | _____ | _____ |
| Employee Name | Signature | Date |

Rejecting job application, general

From Human Resources or Employment Office to individual

Thank you for your application for a position as senior financial analyst with Consolidated Intergalactic.

Upon review of your resume, however, we do not feel that you presently have the necessary qualifications for this job.

We appreciate your interest and wish you the best of luck in your job search.

Rejecting application, job already filled

From Human Resources or Employment Office to individual

Thank you for your application for a position as a night security guard for Consolidated Intergalactic.

I regret to inform you that this position has already been filled and there are no other security guard openings with the company. We will keep your letter and resume on file for the next twelve months and notify you if a similar job becomes available.

We appreciate your interest and wish you the best of luck in your job search.

Rejecting application, applicant does not indicate required qualifications

From Human Resources or Employment Office to individual

Thank you for your application for a position as a quality control engineer with Consolidated Intergalactic.

The job posting states that all applicants must have a "Commercial Class B Engineering Certificate" from the Society of Quality Control Professionals. Upon review of your resume, we do not see an indication of this essential credential.

For that reason, we are removing your application from our list of qualified candidates. If you have further information to share with us about your background, please send an updated letter to my attention as soon as possible.

We appreciate your interest and wish you the best of luck in your job search.

Responding to job application, no jobs available

From Human Resources or Employment Office to individual

Thank you for your application for a position with Consolidated Intergalactic.

We currently do not have any entry-level jobs available. We will keep your letter and resume on file for the next twelve months and notify you if an appropriate job becomes available.

We appreciate your interest and wish you the best of luck in your job search.

Notification that applicant will not be offered job

From Human Resources or Employment Office to individual

I regret to inform you that we will not be able to offer you the senior financial analyst job you applied for on March 22.

As you may realize, we had a very large number of highly qualified applicants for the job.

We appreciate your interest in Consolidated Intergalactic and will keep your letter and resume on file for the next twelve months and notify you if an appropriate job becomes available. We wish you the best of luck in your job search.

Rejecting job application, but advising of other openings

From Human Resources or Employment Office to individual

I regret to inform you that we will not be able to offer you the senior financial analyst job you applied for on March 22.

Although we have filled that position, I do want to bring to your attention another opening: health benefits account executive in Human Resources. If you would like to apply for that job, please review the attached job description and send a letter of application to my attention as soon as possible.

Response to application for a summer internship

From Employment Office to student

Thank you for your application for a summer internship in the Media Relations Department at Consolidated Intergalactic.

Please call Ferd Rouge in Human Resources at extension 3451 to set up an appointment for an interview between now and April 15. We plan on filling the internship post by May 1, with employment starting on May 15.

As part of the interview process you will be given the details of a product announcement and asked to produce the draft of a press release.

Offer of summer internship job

From Employment Office to student

We are pleased to offer you a job as a summer intern in the Media Relations Department of Consolidated Intergalactic.

Your college record and references show an excellent background for the internship, and we were very impressed with the draft press release you wrote during your visit to our offices.

We would like you to begin work on May 15. You will report to Bill Cummings, assistant director of Media Relations. You will be scheduled for 37.5 hours per week, at an hourly wage of $12.

Please call or write to confirm your acceptance of our offer. We look forward to seeing you this summer.

Declining to offer summer internship job

From Employment Office to student

Thank you for applying for a position as a summer intern in the Media Relations Department of Consolidated Intergalactic.

We were impressed with your background and the quality of the draft press release you wrote during your interview.

Unfortunately, we will not be able to offer you a position this summer. We had a very difficult time choosing from among several very well qualified applicants, but we have decided to offer the job to another student.

Please do not hesitate to apply for other internships or permanent jobs at Consolidated Intergalactic; we will keep your resume, and our positive comments, on file here in the Employment Office.

Advisory of seasonal job openings

From Employment Office to employees

Summer is almost here, and we'd like to give our employees first notice of available seasonal jobs. We're always happy to see members of the family of our employees at work here.

Available jobs include season fill-in jobs in the Shipping Department, landscaping crews, and painter's assistants.

For information on any of these seasonal jobs, please see the postings on the Employment Office Web site.

Letters from Employment Office to Other Organizations

Letter of verification of former employment (general)

From Human Resources or Employment Office to outside company or institution

This letter verifies that William Stafford was employed by Consolidated Intergalactic from April 3, 2001 through June 5, 2007. His job title at the time he left the company was assistant comptroller.

Letter of verification of former employment (detailed)

From Human Resources or Employment Office to outside company or institution

William Stafford was employed by Consolidated Intergalactic from April 3, 2001 through June 5, 2007.

He began his employment as an entry-level accounts payable clerk and received two promotions; his job title at the time he left the company was assistant comptroller.

During the course of his employment he passed all necessary examinations and received accreditation as a Certified Public Accountant.

Policy on letters of verification of former employment

From Human Resources or Employment Office to outside company or institution

In response to your request for confirmation of current job status, it is our policy at Consolidated Intergalactic that you obtain permission from any employee before we can provide any information.

Enclosed please find a copy of an authorization form; please obtain the signature of any person about whom you seek information.

Consolidated Intergalactic retains the right to decline to provide information about its employees for any permitted reason.

Response to request for confirmation of current employment

From Human Resources or Employment Office to outside company or institution

In response to your request for confirmation of current employment, accompanied by a signed authorization form, we can verify the following information:

Employee name:

Date of hiring:

Current job title:

Current monthly salary:

Alerting college placement office of available jobs

From Employment Office to college placement office, list of available jobs

Consolidated Intergalactic currently has twenty entry-level job openings in our Manufacturing, Shipping, and Customer Service Departments.

Attached are the job postings for these positions. We would welcome your assistance in alerting qualified candidates to these full-time permanent positions.

Thank you.

Alerting college placement office of available internships

From Employment Office to college placement office

As summer approaches, we'd like to seek your assistance in filling fifteen seasonal internships at Consolidated Intergalactic.

Now in its twenty-first year, the internship program at CI gives real-world experience to students with an interest in a career in manufacturing. It has also proven to be one of our most valuable recruiting tools for employees of the future.

Available internships include positions in the Media Relations, Benefits, Information Technology, and Office Services Departments. The jobs offer an hourly wage but do not include benefits.

Alerting union apprenticeship program of available jobs

From Employment Office to union apprenticeship program

Consolidated Intergalactic currently has twenty skilled-labor job openings in our Manufacturing department.

We would once again welcome the assistance of the International Brotherhood of Widget Workers in recruiting and training new workers who would be appropriate hires for this bargaining unit.

Attached are the job postings for these positions, including a full list of required skills and necessary certifications.

Thank you.

Announcing job fair

From Human Resources or Employment Office to community organizations

Consolidated Intergalactic will conduct a job fair at its Lumbertown headquarters on Saturday, May 19. The event will be held from 9 A.M. to 3 P.M. in a tent erected in the main parking lot.

Applicants should have a minimum of a high school diploma for entry-level jobs. A full listing of currently available positions at CI can be found on the company Web site at *www.consolidatedintergalactic.com* and in ads that will be published in the *Lumbertown Times* on May 18.

Representatives of Human Resources, Manufacturing, Quality Control, and Office Services Departments will be on hand to discuss current and expected job openings and to accept applications.

CI employs more than 12,000 dedicated workers around the world, including some 6,000 people here in Lumbertown. The company is an equal opportunity employer, dedicated to maintaining diversity in background and skills.

Responding to request for participation in job fair

From Human Resources or Employment Office to community organization

Thank you for your invitation to participate in the Lumbertown Community College Job Fair.

We would be pleased to once again meet with LCC students and graduates at the fair. Based on our experience in previous years, we would request three booths to handle the large number of applicants we will likely receive.

Notice of seasonal job openings

From Employment Office to high school advisor

As summer arrives, we would like to alert juniors and seniors at Lumbertown High School of a number of seasonal jobs that will be available from June 15 through September 1.

We're looking for responsible young men and women to assist as members of our landscaping, maintenance, and Shipping Departments. Preference will be given to applicants who have experience in a related job or job task.

Working hours will vary, including weekday day shifts, night shifts, and weekend hours. Summer hires are paid an hourly rate and are not eligible for benefits.

For information on any of these seasonal jobs, please call the Employment Office at extension 3292.

4 Employment Office: From Applicants

Application for specific job

From individual to Human Resources or Employment Office

I am writing to apply for the position of executive assistant to the vice president for public affairs, as advertised on your company Web site. (Job code 6SJ7.)

I feel that I am very well qualified for this position, and I know that I could more than exceed your expectations.

Enclosed please find a copy of my resume. You will see that I have worked for more than ten years in the public affairs office of a major corporation in another state, and my academic background includes a bachelor's degree in communications.

I would be glad to provide references and am able to come in for an interview at your convenience.

Looking forward to hearing from you soon.

Sincerely yours,

Detailed letter of application for specific job

From individual to Employment Office

Enclosed please find my resume, submitted in application for the position of manufacturing quality control trainee at Consolidated Intergalactic.

I have just completed my associate degree in forestry science at Lumbertown Community College, and I feel that I have the right stuff for a job in quality control at CI.

My professors, including John Fabian—associate director of procurement for Consolidated Intergalactic—have helped me put together my educational program. Professor Fabian is among the references listed on my resume.

I would appreciate the opportunity to schedule an interview for the trainee position.

Thank you.

Cover letter for general application for employment

From individual to Employment Office

Enclosed please find my resume, submitted in application for employment with Consolidated Intergalactic.

Although I am a recent college graduate, I have been working steadily since the age of seventeen at a number of jobs including landscaping, Maintenance, and carpenter's helper. I believe that this background, in combination with my degree in business administration, makes me a very good candidate for positions in CI's Office Services, maintenance, or Manufacturing Departments.

I am available for an interview at your convenience and can provide references from former employers and professors.

Letter to follow up on telephone conversation about employment

From individual to Human Resources or Employment Office

Dear Mr. Russert,

Thank you for your time on the phone today. From what I learned, I am very interested in working for your company.

As we discussed, I would like to apply for the open position of senior sales manager in the international division.

Attached is a copy of my resume. As you can see, I have worked in sales for the past five years and have extensive experience in dealing with foreign clients. And I have received training on customs regulations, international shipping, and other relevant special requirements that are appropriate for this job.

I would be glad to provide references and am able to come in for an interview at your convenience.

Follow-up letter based on meeting at job fair

From individual to Human Resources or Employment Office

Dear Mr. Russert,

I enjoyed meeting with you at the Job Fair at the Convention Center yesterday. I was very impressed with what I learned from you about the opportunities available at your company.

We discussed several available positions, including benefits manager in Human Resources and senior accountant in the Purchasing Department. You said that you would refer my resume to several departments with job openings.

I feel that I am well qualified for these and similar positions. I have worked for the past eight years in a clerical position for a major investment house.

As you requested, enclosed is a copy of my resume. I would be happy to provide references and come in for an interview at your convenience.

Submission of job application based on referral

From individual to Human Resources or Employment Office

Tom Chase, director of investor relations, suggested I contact you regarding a current job opening as a financial analyst in your department. Tom and I worked together at another company ten years ago, and we have stayed in contact through a service organization here in town.

Enclosed is a copy of my resume. I would be happy to provide references and to come in for an interview at your convenience.

Through Tom, I know a great deal about the goals and corporate culture of your organization. I feel that I could make a significant contribution to your future success.

Submission of resume and general inquiry about employment

From individual to Human Resources or Employment Office

Enclosed is a copy of my resume. I would appreciate being considered for any appropriate job opening at your company.

I am a recent college graduate, with a degree in business administration. While in school I worked as an intern for several major area corporations.

I know much about the products and services offered by Consolidated Intergalactic, and would like to begin my career working at such a dynamic and successful organization.

I am available for an interview at your convenience and can provide references from former employers and professors.

General inquiry about available jobs in department

From individual to Human Resources or Employment Office

I am presently employed as a sales representative for a small manufacturing company. I have a proven track record of success in sales and marketing.

At this time, I am looking to move to a larger organization and greater challenges.

I would appreciate it if you would review my resume and contact me about any appropriate job openings that fit my background and experience.

I would welcome the opportunity to interview with your organization and can be reached at my home telephone number on the resume.

Submitting resume to be kept on file in Human Resources

From individual to Human Resources or Employment Office

I am enclosing my resume. I would appreciate it if you would keep it on file for any appropriate job openings at Consolidated Intergalactic.

I am a recent college graduate and have a proven record as a dependable, conscientious worker at various part-time jobs while in school.

I have done extensive research about Consolidated Intergalactic, and I am very impressed with the broad range of products and services you offer. I am willing to accept an entry-level position and would hope to be able to work my way up to a senior position over time.

I am available to come in for an interview at your convenience, and can provide letters of reference from former employers and professors.

I look forward to hearing from you.

Responding to request for specific details or documents about prior employment

From individual to Human Resources or Employment Office

Thank you for your letter of March 30 in response to my inquiry about the available position in Human Resources.

You asked for more details about my previous job experience and for several current references.

I have been employed for the past five years as a benefits manager at a manufacturing company in Massachusetts. My job responsibilities have included oversight of the health insurance plan; I am responsible for tracking the applications and reimbursement requests for more than 500 employees and serving as the in-house contact for questions from the insurance provider.

I have recently moved to Ohio, and I am looking for a position with a solid, growing company. Consolidated Intergalactic is very highly regarded in the industry, and I would be honored to be considered for a position with the company.

Attached is a list of references, including my previous supervisors. Please let me know if you have any further questions; I would be happy to come in for an interview at your convenience.

Requesting further information about advertised job

From individual to Human Resources or Employment Office

I am writing to request additional information about the financial analyst job advertised in the County Chronicle on March 18.

I am very interested in the possibility of working for Consolidated Intergalactic. I want to make sure that the available position is appropriate for me.

Can you please tell me a bit more about the job opening? Are specific academic credentials or certification required? Is the position located at your headquarters in Lumbertown or at one of your branch offices?

I look forward to hearing from you.

Requesting update on hiring process

From individual to Human Resources or Employment Office

I am writing to request an update on the status of my application for the position of senior assistant to the director of information technology.

I submitted my resume for the position three weeks ago, on March 30. I received an acknowledgment letter a week later telling me that I would be contacted for an interview.

As of today, I have not heard further about this application.

I am writing to again state my strong interest in the position; I feel that my background and experience make me an excellent candidate for the job.

Would you please bring me up to date on where the process stands?

Thank you.

Offering thanks for opportunity to interview for job

From individual to Human Resources or Employment Office

Thank you for the opportunity to interview for the position of financial analyst.

I was very impressed with what I learned about Consolidated Intergalactic and about the current job opening. I am convinced that I could more than meet your expectations.

Please let me know if there is anything else you need to help you make a decision. I would be happy to return for a second interview if that would be helpful.

Request for update on hiring status

From individual to Human Resources or Employment Office

Can you please advise me of the status of my application for the position of night security guard?

I was interviewed by Human Resources four weeks ago, on March 30. At the time I was told that I would be contacted for a second interview with the director of security within two weeks.

I remain very interested in the job, and would welcome the opportunity to come in and meet with the director.

Asking consideration for future job openings

From individual to Human Resources or Employment Office

Thank you for your phone call about the financial analyst position. I was disappointed to learn that someone else has been hired.

I was impressed with Consolidated Intergalactic and remain very interested in the possibility of a job with the company.

Please keep my resume on file for any future openings that fit my qualifications.

Withdrawing application for a job

From individual to Human Resources or Employment Office

I am writing to request you remove my name from consideration for the current job opening as financial analyst.

I have accepted a position with another company.

Thank you for the opportunity to interview with Consolidated Intergalactic. I was very impressed with the company and everyone I met during my visit on March 30. I appreciate being considered for the job.

Accepting a job based on stated details

From individual to Human Resources or Employment Office

Thank you for your offer of employment as senior financial analyst in the Accounting Department of Consolidated Intergalactic.

As I told you on the phone this morning, I am pleased to accept the position.

As we discussed and as you indicated in your offer letter of March 30, the initial salary will be $52,000 per year and benefits include a family health plan, 401(k) pension plan, and an allowance of up to $10,000 for moving and other relocation expenses.

I will be available to start work on April 23, and will be in touch with Human Resources before then to fill out necessary paperwork and prepare to begin the job.

Again, thank you for this opportunity. I am very excited to be joining the team.

Making counterproposal on job offer

From individual to Human Resources or Employment Office

Thank you for your offer of employment as senior financial analyst in the Accounting Department of Consolidated Intergalactic.

As I told you on the phone this morning, I am very excited about the prospect of joining the team. However, because I would be moving with my family from a great distance, I would like to ask for a few adjustments in the terms of the offer.

As we discussed and as you indicated in your offer letter of May 1, the initial salary will be $52,000 per year and benefits include a family health plan, 401(k) pension plan, and an allowance of up to $10,000 for moving and other relocation expenses.

Based on an estimate from two moving companies in my area, I would ask that the moving and relocation allowance be increased from $10,000 to $17,500.

And, because of the school calendar for my children, I would ask that my full-time starting date be moved forward one week, to June 1.

I hope this is agreeable to you. I very much look forward to coming to work at Consolidated Intergalactic.

Qualified acceptance of job offer

From individual to Human Resources or Employment Office

Thank you for your phone call this morning offering me the position of night security guard at Consolidated Intergalactic. I am very excited about the job.

As we discussed, would you please send me a letter outlining the details of salary, starting date, and expected working hours? I would also appreciate a copy of the employee manual.

I look forward to hearing from you soon.

Confirming acceptance of job offer made by telephone

From individual to Human Resources or Employment Office

Thank you for your call this morning.

I am writing to confirm my acceptance of the job of senior financial analyst at Consolidated Intergalactic.

As you indicated in your phone call, the initial salary will be $52,000 per year and benefits include a family health plan, 401(k) pension plan, and tuition reimbursement for job-related accreditation courses.

Requesting information about job benefits and employee handbook

From individual to Human Resources or Employment Office

I am looking forward to joining the team at Consolidated Intergalactic on June 1.

I would appreciate it if you would arrange to have an employee handbook and benefits packages mailed to me. I would also be glad to fill out any necessary forms ahead of my starting date with the company.

Turning down a job offer, without explanation

From individual to Human Resources or Employment Office

Thank you for your offer of employment as senior financial analyst in the Accounting Department of Consolidated Intergalactic.

I am honored to have received the offer; I was very impressed with the company and everyone I dealt with during the interview process.

However, I regret to inform you that I have decided not to accept the job offer.

I wish you the best of luck in filling the position. Please pass along my thanks to the search committee.

Turning down a job offer, with details

From individual to Human Resources or Employment Office

Thank you for your offer of employment as junior financial analyst in the Accounting Department of Consolidated Intergalactic.

I am honored to have received the offer; I was very impressed with the company and everyone I dealt with during the interview process.

However, I regret to inform you that I have decided not to accept the job offer. I have instead decided to return to school to seek a graduate degree in business administration; I believe this will qualify me for a management position, which is my goal.

I wish you the best of luck in filling the current position. Please pass along my thanks to the search committee.

I hope Consolidated Intergalactic will once again consider me a top candidate for employment after I receive an M.B.A. two years from now.

Application for summer internship

From student to Employment Office

Enclosed is my resume, submitted in application for a summer internship in the Media Relations Department at Consolidated Intergalactic.

I am in my second year of studies at Lumbertown Community College, majoring in public relations. My professor, John Billings, and the college placement office both recommended I apply for the Media Relations assistant position.

I would be happy to come to CI for an interview at your convenience, and I can provide references and writing samples. I look forward to hearing from you.

Thanks to reference for employment

From individual to employment reference

John Youkilis, Academic Dean
Lumbertown Community College

Dear Dr. Youkilis,

I want to thank you again for serving as a reference for me in my job search. I am happy to report that I have been offered a position as a quality control trainee at Consolidated Intergalactic and will begin work there on June 1.

I am very proud of what I accomplished at LCC and I will always be an advocate for the school.

Thank you.

5 Human Resources: To All Employees

Holidays, Social Events, and Personal Interests

From Human Resources to Staff

45

Holidays, Social Events, and Personal Interests

Veterans Day observance

From Human Resources to employees

Once again, Consolidated Intergalactic celebrates the contributions of all veterans in our workplace. We'll have a number of special events during early November, and in keeping with an old tradition around here, all veterans will be offered free lunch at the CI Café.

Just give the cashier your best salute any time between November 4 and 11 and your meal is on us.

Invitation to retirement party

From Human Resources or Executive Office to employees

The Mailroom staff has planned an informal party for Eddie Brizzard, who will be retiring from Consolidated Intergalactic after nineteen years of service.

All employees are invited to stop by on June 30, beginning at the close of business hours at 5 P.M., to wish Eddie well (and share in a piece of chocolate cake shaped like an oversized box of office supplies, crafted by CI's food services).

Policy on office parties and other social events in the workplace

From Human Resources or Employment Office to employees

I am writing to clarify company policy regarding departmental parties and other social events including birthday celebrations, wedding and baby showers, and holiday observances.

As noted in the employee manual, all such parties and observances must be scheduled during lunch breaks or outside of normal working hours and ending no later than one hour after the ordinary close of business.

Please refer to the manual if you have any questions about the company's total ban on alcohol and drugs in the workplace.

Policy on holiday parties and other social events in the workplace

From Human Resources or Employment Office to employees

As the end of the year approaches and the holiday season is upon us, we want to remind all employees that it is the policy of Consolidated Intergalactic to show respect for the diversity of our workers. As such, we have instituted a set of rules regarding holiday observances and parties in the workplace.

Please do not decorate your workspace or common areas with religious symbols, slogans, or artwork of any kind except for those listed in this memo. We are drawing the distinction here between cultural symbols such as Santa Claus and a religious symbol such as a crèche.

We consider the following to be acceptable: small decorated Christmas trees (no taller than three feet), small wreaths, small Chanukkah menorahs (without candles or electric bulbs), and Kwanzaa decorations.

We consider the following to be unacceptable: Crosses, Stars of David, crèches, and religious figurines.

If you have any questions about this policy, please contact Human Resources.

Announcing annual company-wide holiday party

From Human Resources or Executive Office to employees

We are pleased to invite you and your spouse or guest to attend the annual Consolidated Intergalactic holiday party to be held on Saturday, December 20, at the Lumbertown Marriott Hotel.

The party will begin at 7 P.M. and conclude at 10 P.M. We will provide a gourmet buffet dinner; in keeping with company policy and for the safety of our workers, no alcohol will be served at the party.

At 8:30 P.M. we plan a special musical surprise.

Please RSVP to Human Resources, telling us if you plan to attend and if you will be bringing a guest. Send an e-mail before December 10 to *holidayparty@consolidatedintergalactic.com*.

On behalf of all of us here at CI, we wish you a joyous holiday season and a healthy and happy New Year.

Amendment to employee handbook regarding dress code

From Human Resources or Employment Office to employees

Effective immediately we are instituting a ban on the wearing of flip-flops and other backless sandals.

We have determined that such footwear is not appropriate office attire. Because flip-flops provide no ankle support and the toes and foot are exposed, they may allow injury to the wearer. They also create noise that is a distraction to others.

This notice will be made a part of the employee handbook. If you have any questions, please contact Human Resources.

Amendment to employee handbook regarding dress code and casual days

From Human Resources or Employment Office to employees

Effective May 1, and running through Labor Day, we will be instituting Casual Fridays in the workplace. This relaxation of the dress code permits "business casual" clothing.

On casual days, male employees are not required to wear neckties or sport coats.

Here are acceptable items of clothing for casual days: clean blue or black jeans without holes, cotton trousers including khakis, dress shirts without neckties, polo or tennis shirts, or unstructured jackets.

Unacceptable items include T-shirts, tank or halter tops, shorts, sweat suits, athletic wear, bathing attire, hiking boots, canvas sneakers, or hats.

Please refer to the employee manual to see a list of unacceptable items, which includes clothing with any advertising or slogans, flip-flops, or other backless shoes.

Any employee who is scheduled to travel to a customer or supplier is expected to dress in standard business attire at all times.

Company policy on display of political material

From Human Resources or Legal Office to employees

As we enter the election season, we want to remind all employees of the company policy regarding the display of political posters, stickers, buttons, and other materials.

The employee manual expressly bans the display of any political material in the workplace. We fully support the right for all staffers to make up their own minds on important national, state, and local political issues and to participate in campaigns on their own time.

It is against company policy to display any political materials in the workplace or on clothing. The use of company telephones, computers, copying machines, and other equipment for political purposes is also banned.

If you have any questions about this policy, please contact Human Resources.

Company policy on religious activities in the workplace

From Human Resources or Legal Office to employees

(NOTE: Review with your in-house or outside legal counsel)

It is the policy of Consolidated Intergalactic to show respect for the diversity of our workers. We ask all employees to make a good faith effort to keep their religious beliefs and practices separate from the performance of their work assignments.

The employment manual makes reference to federal law and court decisions that support the company's right to discipline or dismiss an employee or manager who discriminates against, harasses, or demeans another individual because of their religious beliefs. We also note that proselytizing for particular religions may be considered harassment by some employees and may be considered inappropriate by clients and suppliers.

If you have any questions about this policy, please contact Human Resources.

Company policy on solicitation for charities at the workplace

From Human Resources or Legal Office to employees

Consolidated Intergalactic does not permit solicitation in the workplace for contributions to charities and community organizations. We do this out of respect for the diversity of our employees and to avoid interruptions to the accomplishment of the goals of the organization.

We ask that employees not distribute flyers or brochures, request contributions, or use telephones, computers, copy machines, or other office equipment for the purpose of solicitation for charities.

However, Human Resources reminds all employees that the company does endorse a limited number of nondenominational charities each year as part of the CI Cares Matching Grant Program. In recent years, Consolidated Intergalactic has matched employee contributions to organizations including the United Way, the Lumberton Community Hospital Construction Fund, and the Clark County Parks and Recreation Committee.

Information about the matching grant program is distributed with paychecks or direct deposit pay stubs in March, July, and December. If you wish to suggest an appropriate charity to be included in the program, please contact Human Resources.

From Human Resources to Staff

Internal announcement of new executive

From Human Resources or Executive Office to employees

I am pleased to announce that David Ramirez will be joining Consolidated Intergalactic as vice president for investor relations, effective June 1.

We are very excited to welcome David to the CI team. He has worked most recently as a senior assistant to the chairman of the Board of a major Chicago plumbing fixture manufacturer and has a total of fifteen years of experience in shareholder relations and similar posts.

David will be moving to Lumbertown with his wife Joanne and their two children, fourteen-year-old Robert and sixteen-year-old Sarah.

Announcement of informal meet-and-greet for new executive

From Human Resources or Executive Office to employees

All staffers are invited to an informal reception to welcome David Ramirez, our new vice president for investor relations. The get-together is scheduled for 4 P.M. on June 1, in Conference Room A.

Announcement to affected staff of closing of sales office

From Executive Office or Human Resources to affected employees

Dear (Name of Staffer):

As you know, we have decided to close our sales office here in Phoenix on April 15. Operations in the southwest will be conducted out of our existing office in San Diego.

We do so with regret, especially since we know that this may disrupt the lives of some of our most valued employees. We have determined, however, that the savings to the organization will be substantial and should help us expand in other areas.

I am writing to confirm our commitment to helping all affected employees. By the end of today it is our expectation that Harry Jones, vice president for Human Resources, will be able to meet with each of you individually to discuss options.

We hope to be able to offer transfers to San Diego or headquarters for many current staffers in Phoenix. Where this is not possible, or where a staffer may choose not to accept reassignment, we will offer all possible assistance to employees in seeking other employment as well as all appropriate benefits.

If you have any questions not answered by Mr. Jones, please feel free to contact Human Resources here at headquarters.

Internal announcement of promotion

From Human Resources or Executive Office to employees

We are pleased to announce that Maria Elena has been promoted to senior financial analyst in the Accounts Receivable Department. Maria has been a valued employee of Consolidated Intergalactic for six years.

It is our policy to promote from within whenever possible. We encourage all employees to consult the list of available positions posted on the Human Resources Web site and to take advantage of available training and certification programs supported by the company.

Internal announcement of retirement

From Human Resources or Executive Office to employees

Eddie Brizzard will be retiring on July 1 after nineteen years of service to the company.

Eddie has been the smiling face at the mailroom receiving platform for all of his years here at Consolidated Intergalactic. He has been a shining example of commitment to his job and a ray of sunshine to all who have met him and worked with him.

Please join me in wishing him well in retirement.

Notification of company policy banning drug and alcohol use and possession

From Human Resources or Employment Office to employees

(NOTE: Review with your in-house or outside legal counsel)

It is the goal of Consolidated Intergalactic to maintain a safe environment, free of alcohol and illegal drugs, including narcotics and abused or misused prescription medications. For this reason, we have established a policy banning use and possession of these substances in the workplace and in other situations related to the organization.

Effective immediately, it is prohibited in the workplace or while away from the workplace on a company assignment to

- Use, possess, buy, or sell narcotics or other controlled substances.
- Use, possess, or buy prescription medication without a valid prescription, or sell such medication to others.
- Use, possess, buy, or sell alcohol.
- Be impaired in the performance of your job by legal or illegal drugs or medications.
- Be found in possession of, or to buy or sell alcohol, narcotics or other controlled substances, or misused prescription drugs in any situation on or off company property that adversely affects the organization's reputation or standing in the community.
- Refuse to submit to any substance abuse test conducted in the workplace or elsewhere while on company business.
- Be determined to have failed a substance abuse test conducted in the workplace or elsewhere while on company business.

All employees are subject to being randomly selected for drug testing by the company or its representatives at any time. A supervisor may also require an immediate drug test when an employee's behavior indicates the possibility of impairment. Further, all employees involved in any accident that causes injuries in the workplace or while on company business are subject to drug testing.

Please read the above carefully and sign the following statement to indicate acknowledgment that you understand the policy.

I hereby acknowledge that I understand and agree to the policy banning the use, possession, purchase, or sale of illegal drugs or alcohol in the workplace or while on assignment for Consolidated Intergalactic. I agree to submit to a drug or alcohol test at any time when required to do so by a manager of the company, and I understand that failure to take such a test may result in immediate termination.

I further authorize the company or its representative to send any collected specimens to a certified laboratory for testing, and for that laboratory to release the results of such test to the company.

_____   _____   _____
Employee Name   Signature   Date

Notification of company policy banning tobacco use in workplace

From Human Resources or Employment Office to employees

(NOTE: Review with your in-house or outside legal counsel)

It is the goal of Consolidated Intergalactic to maintain a safe and healthy workplace for all of its employees. For this reason, we have established a policy banning smoking of tobacco in cigarettes, cigars, or pipes anywhere within the workplace.

It is our judgment that tobacco is a danger to the smoker as well as to others who may breathe in secondhand smoke. The use of tobacco is a significant contributor to health care costs, a major expense for the company. And smoke can also damage office furniture and equipment.

Effective immediately, there is no smoking permitted within the workplace or at any entrance to the building. We have established outdoor shelters at least 100 feet from the rear (parking lot) exit from the building, and employees and visitors may smoke there during their designated lunch hour or permitted fifteen-minute breaks once in each three hours.

Smoking is also prohibited within any company-owned or operated vehicle and we also require all employees to follow any smoking regulations at any location of our clients or suppliers.

Notification of company policy completely banning tobacco use by employees

From Human Resources or Employment Office to employees

(NOTE: Review with your in-house or outside legal counsel)

It is the goal of Consolidated Intergalactic to maintain a safe and healthy workplace for all of its employees. For this reason, we have established a policy banning smoking of tobacco in cigarettes, cigars, or pipes anywhere within the workplace.

It is also our judgment that the use of tobacco is a significant contributor to health care costs, a major expense for the company.

Therefore, effective immediately, we are putting into effect the following policy:

- No smoking is permitted anywhere on company property or in company-owned or -operated vehicles.
- Applicants for employment with Consolidated Intergalactic must agree not to smoke tobacco at the workplace or at home, and agree to random testing for the presence of nicotine in their system. Refusal to submit to a test, or a test result positive for tobacco use will be grounds for immediate dismissal.
- Effective ninety days from today, all current employees of Consolidated Intergalactic must agree not to smoke tobacco at the workplace or at home, and agree to random testing for the presence of nicotine in their system. Refusal to submit to a test, or a test result positive for tobacco use will be grounds for immediate dismissal.

To assist our employees in meeting these new requirements, the company medical office will provide counseling on tobacco-cessation techniques and programs. And the company will offer a one-time subsidy of as much as $500 per employee for any program arranged through the medical office.

Notification to staff of new hire

From Human Resources or Employment Office to employees and departments

Please join me in welcoming Sandra Yearling, our new assistant to the director of public relations who begins work today.

Ms. Yearling comes to the company with a very impressive background in communications. Her primary assignment will be dealing with electronic media, including local television and radio stations and she will be assisting us in expanding our presence on the Internet.

Letter to managers involved in hiring about equal opportunity policy

From Human Resources or Employment Office to department managers

(NOTE: Review with your in-house or outside legal counsel)

Consolidated Intergalactic is dedicated to providing equal opportunity and respect in all phases of employment and maintaining diversity in the workplace.

It is our policy that the company will not discriminate in employment opportunity on the basis of race, creed, color, religion, national origin, age, disability, sex, sexual preference, or marital status. Further, we are dedicated to honoring all other persons with legally protected status as defined by applicable federal, state, and local laws.

Consolidated Intergalactic conducts regular training sessions on equal opportunity policies and managers and staffers who violate stated policies and goals are subject to discipline or dismissal.

Please read the attached full statement of our company's Equal Employment Opportunity policy and sign and return to Human Resources the acknowledgment form to indicate you understand its elements.

If you have any questions about hiring procedures, accommodation of individuals with disabilities or special needs, or any other company initiatives or policies in this area please contact Human Resources before taking any action or making any statements on behalf of the company.

Offering training on hiring and promotion

From Human Resources or Employment Office to managers

Human Resources will be conducting refresher courses on the company's Equal Opportunity Employment policy in the month of June.

Consolidated Intergalactic is dedicated to providing equal opportunity and respect in all phases of employment and maintaining diversity in the workplace.

All managers involved in the hiring process are required to attend one of the sessions.

Please select the session that is most convenient for your schedule and return this form to Human Resources no later than May 15. You will receive e-mail reminders of your session one week before the scheduled time and again on the day of the meeting.

Internal job posting, notification of job availability

From Human Resources or Employment Office to employees

The Accounting Department is seeking to hire a senior financial analyst. Duties for this position include review of departmental budgets and expenditures. Candidates must have a minimum of a bachelor's degree in accounting or business administration and three years of professional experience related to the job tasks.

It is the policy of Consolidated Intergalactic to seek to promote from within whenever possible. Any current full-time or part-time employee who has been employed by the company for at least one year is eligible to apply and the search committee will seek to make a promotion from within when it is in the company's best interests to do so.

Please review the full job description, necessary qualifications, and details of salary and bonus as posted on the Human Resources Web site; printed copies of the job description are also available at the HR Office.

The deadline for application for an internal job posting is fourteen days from today. After that date the job will be advertised and open to applicants outside the company.

Notification of policy on recommendations and verification of employment

From Human Resources or Employment Office to employees

It is the policy of Human Resources of Consolidated Intergalactic to offer a basic letter of verification of employment to any staffer who resigns or retires from the company in good standing. This would exclude any staffer who is dismissed for cause or is otherwise removed from the payroll for failure to meet expectations.

As a manager, if you receive a request for a letter of verification of employment please refer the matter to Human Resources.

As a company, Consolidated Intergalactic does not send letters of recommendation.

However, individual managers may offer a former employee a letter of recommendation under the following guidelines:

- The letter must make it clear that the recommendation is based on your personal knowledge of the employee and does not represent the opinion of the company itself, and
- The letter honestly states positive attributes and accomplishments of the individual.

Under no circumstance is a manager to issue a letter that includes negative comments about attributes or accomplishments of an employee. If you can't say anything positive, you must decline to offer a letter of recommendation.

If there are any questions about this policy, please contact Human Resources.

Sample letter of recommendation

From Human Resources or Employment Office to employees

To whom it may concern,

As vice president for sales at Consolidated Intergalactic, I worked with and supervised Harold Jones for more than eight years. I have found him to be a highly motivated and effective salesman and an excellent representative of the company.

Our clients have consistently complimented us on his work on their behalf. He has also been a very valuable member of committees within the company that have focused on improving coordination between Manufacturing, Sales, and Marketing Departments.

In keeping with company policy, the above opinions are based entirely on my personal observations and experience as a manager.

Company policy regarding confirmation of current employment

From Human Resources or Employment Office to employees

We have been asked to clarify company policy regarding requests from outside parties for confirmation of current employment.

All such requests are to be routed to Human Resources. No manager or member of staff is to discuss any element of employment details.

Human Resources will determine whether any such inquiry is for legitimate reasons (including requests for mortgages and personal loans, applications for employment, and legal or court matters).

In certain situations, the HR Department may contact a current employee to request permission to provide information to an outside agency, business, or individual. Some financial institutions may ask applicants for loans to sign an authorization form allowing Human Resources to confirm employment and salary or pay rate.

If there are any questions about this policy, please contact Human Resources.

Company policy regarding references and confirmation for prior employment

From Human Resources or Employment Office to employees

At Consolidated Intergalactic, we are committed to safeguarding the privacy of all employees, former and current.

If you receive a telephone, e-mail, or written request for any information regarding a former employee do not provide any confirmation or details of employment. Please pass along the inquiry to Human Resources.

Human Resources will determine whether any such inquiry is for legitimate reasons (including requests for mortgages and personal loans, applications for employment, and legal or court matters).

In certain situations, the HR Department may contact a former employee to request permission to provide information to an outside agency, business, or individual. Some financial institutions may ask applicants for loans to sign an authorization form allowing Human Resources to confirm employment and salary or pay rate.

If there are any questions about this policy, please contact Human Resources.

Policy on confidentiality of payroll information

From Human Resources or Employment Office to employees

All employees are reminded that it is company policy that payroll information, including salary or hourly rates, bonuses, and commissions is considered confidential information.

Details of your income, or that of any other employee, are not to be disclosed to any other person or organization except in the context of an application for a loan or other financial instrument or for tax or other government-related purposes.

If you have any questions about this policy, please contact the Human Resources help line at extension 9856.

Requirement of notification of personal relationships in workplace

From Human Resources or Employment Office to employees

(NOTE: Review with your in-house or outside legal counsel)

All employees are requested to read the revised and expanded section of the employee handbook that requires notification to a superior of any personal relationship between a manager and a staffer under his or her supervision.

This policy is in place to protect the rights of all employees, avoiding where possible any situation where a supervisory relationship could lead to harassment or special favors in the workplace.

At Consolidated Intergalactic, we consider the security and dignity of our employees to be paramount. If you have any questions about this policy, or have any concerns about possible or actual harassment or favoritism in the workplace, please immediately contact a Human Resources counselor at extension 2323.

Introduction of employee referral bonus program

From Human Resources or Employment Office to employees

Here at Consolidated Intergalactic, we highly value our dedicated workforce, and we also know how hard it is to recruit and hire new staffers who meet our high standards.

We are pleased to announce an Employee Referral Bonus Program. Here's how it works: Any eligible employee (all full-time and part-time regular employees) can earn a reward of $1,000 if they refer an applicant who is hired by the company.

Employees of Human Resources and exempt salaried executives at the vice president or higher level are not eligible, and you cannot earn an award for referring someone when you are a member of a search committee for a particular position or if you will directly supervise the new hire.

In order to receive the reward, an applicant must list your name as a referral at the time they first apply for a job. To help the process, you can obtain a copy of a referral form from the Human Resources Office and put your name on it; applicants can include the form in their application package.

A cash bonus of $1,000 will be paid once a referred employee has successfully completed six months of continuous employment.

Introduction of employee retention bonus program

From Human Resources or Employment Office to employees

Human Resources is pleased to introduce a Retention Bonus Program for certain nonexempt positions with the company. Your present job qualifies you for this program.

Our goal is to reward the loyalty of members of staff with special skills and experience.

After completion of two years of service, eligible staffers will receive a bonus of 5 percent of base annual salary. On each successive anniversary of employment, eligible staffers will receive a bonus 1 percent higher than the year before.

Policy regarding jury duty

From Human Resources or Benefits Office to employees

In keeping with a recent change in state law regarding compensation paid to jurors, we have made the following change to the employee manual for all full-time employees.

Consolidated Intergalactic will pay regular hourly or salaried workers for their entire period of jury service. Employees will continue to accrue vacation and personal time, but will not be eligible for overtime pay during jury service.

If the employee receives compensation from the court for jury duty, it is required that the Payroll department be notified of the amount received and such compensation will be deducted from salary.

Any employee who is summoned to report for jury duty is required to immediately notify his or her supervisor or department head so that essential job tasks can be maintained. In certain circumstances, the company may ask an employee to seek a postponement of jury duty because of extraordinary needs in the workplace.

Policy on military leave of absence

From Benefits Office or Human Resources to employees

(NOTE: Review with your in-house or outside legal counsel)

A number of Consolidated Intergalactic employees have recently been summoned to active duty through their National Guard units. We wish them well.

In response to questions from supervisors, Human Resources has developed a detailed guide to procedures and benefits available to any regular employee who seeks a military leave of absence. Please review the guide, which is attached to this memo and is also posted on the HR Web site.

In summary, CI fully complies with the terms of the Uniformed Services Employment and Reemployment Rights Act (USERRA) and other applicable state and federal laws that are intended to ensure that members of the military can retain their rights to civilian employment and benefits and also provides specific protection for disabled veterans, requiring employers to make reasonable efforts to make accommodations in the workplace for disabilities.

Any affected employee is asked to immediately contact their supervisor and Human Resources to schedule an appointment to discuss all of the terms of applicable laws as well as any additional benefits that are offered by the company.

Policy on bereavement leave

From Human Resources or Benefits Office to employees

In response to requests from supervisors and employees, we have decided to make changes to our bereavement leave policy to allow additional time off when necessary.

Our existing policy provides for the following:

- In the event of a death in an employee's immediate family (spouse, domestic partner, parents and stepparents, children and stepchildren, grandparents, grandchildren, father-in-law, mother-in-law, brother, brother-in-law, sister, sister-in-law, son-in-law, or daughter-in-law) the company will grant as many as three days off, with pay, to make funeral arrangements or to attend a funeral.

A request for a bereavement leave must be made in writing to Human Resources, and the company may require verification of the details of the request.

The new elements of the bereavement leave add the following:

- Any regular full-time employee may take one day off, with pay, to attend the funeral of a close friend or acquaintance who is not a family member. A request for a bereavement leave must be made in writing to Human Resources, and the company may require verification of the details of the request.

- Part-time employees are permitted to request as many as three days off, without pay, to make funeral arrangements or to attend a funeral for a member of immediate family; part-time employees may take one day off, without pay, to attend the funeral of a close friend or acquaintance who is not a family member. A request for a bereavement leave must be made in writing to Human Resources, and the company may require verification of the details of the request.

The company may, at its discretion, grant additional unpaid time off for employees with exceptional needs including the distance to be traveled and other family needs. Application for additional bereavement leave must be made in writing to Human Resources and must also be approved by the employee's supervisor.

Flextime offered to reduce traffic problems

From Human Resources to employees, availability of flextime

As part of our efforts to reduce traffic on area roadways, Consolidated Intergalactic is offering flextime working hours to eligible employees.

Under the plan, staffers could begin work sixty or ninety minutes before or after ordinary business hours, adjusting their scheduled departure time accordingly.

All requests for flextime must be submitted to departmental supervisors and will be approved if they do not conflict with the staffing needs of the company. In addition, flextime schedules will be reviewed every four months to assure that they do not adversely affect company goals.

Ban on personal music devices

From Human Resources, Security Office, or department head to employees

Employees may not use personal music devices of any sort in the workplace. We consider use of these devices to be a safety hazard because they do not allow our staff to be aware of other activities and are also a bar to communication with others.

Supervisors are asked to warn any employee using a music player. Second and later violations should be reported to Human Resources for possible disciplinary action.

Policy on accepting gifts

From Executive Office or Human Resources to employees

We have updated our employee manual in regard to the company's official policy about accepting gifts from suppliers, vendors, and customers.

Effective immediately, no employee is permitted to solicit or accept a gift of any value from anyone with whom we do business or a company or organization seeking to do business with Consolidated Intergalactic. Although we recognize that in nearly all cases such gifts are ordinary pleasantries of a business relationship, the purpose of this policy is to avoid the appearance of a conflict of interest in all of our operations.

We will be advising all of our suppliers and vendors of this policy as part of any purchase order or contract we sign.

If you receive a gift, or an offer of a gift, please politely refuse acceptance. If you have any questions about this policy, or seek advice on dealing with a particular customer or supplier, please contact the Human Resources help desk at extension 3044.

Policy on accepting meals and entertainment

From Executive Office or Human Resources to employees

Effective immediately, no employee is permitted to solicit or accept meals or entertainment of any value from anyone with whom we do business or a company or organization seeking to do business with Consolidated Intergalactic.

The purpose of this policy is to avoid the appearance of a conflict of interest in all of our operations.

An exception to this policy is as follows: Employees may accept invitations to receptions, group dinners, and other events sponsored by suppliers, vendors, or customers.

We will be advising all of our suppliers and vendors of this policy as part of any purchase order or contract we sign.

If you receive an offer of a meal or entertainment, please politely refuse acceptance. If you have any questions about this policy, or seek advice on dealing with a particular customer or supplier, please contact the Human Resources help desk at extension 3044.

Policy on accepting gifts within company

From Executive Office or Human Resources to employees

Effective immediately, no employee is permitted to solicit or accept gifts, meals, or entertainment of any value from any other employee.

The purpose of this policy is to avoid the appearance of a conflict of interest in all of our operations, especially in regard to relationships between supervisors and staff.

The only exception to this policy is as follows: Exchanges of gifts between personal friends that take place outside of the context of the workplace and involve neither an actual conflict of interest or the appearance of a conflict of interest.

Employees may accept invitations to receptions, group dinners, and other events sponsored by suppliers, vendors, or customers.

If you receive a gift or an offer of a gift, please politely refuse acceptance. If you have any questions about this policy, or seek advice on dealing with a particular situation, please contact the Human Resources help desk at extension 3044.

Commendation to departments for exceptional service to customer

From Human Resources, Executive Office, Customer Service, or department head to employee

I would like to congratulate the Shipping and Installation Departments on their exceptional service on behalf of one of our most valued customers.

The order from Hudson Tubing for fifteen Excello Impellers came in late on a Friday afternoon. It was past deadline for our regular freight company and the Installation Department was not scheduled to work that weekend.

But in keeping with our corporate commitment to Customer Service, we pulled out all the stops to meet the emergency needs of Hudson Tubing. I want to thank all of the staffers involved in arranging for expedited freight and the installers who performed a mechanical makeover of Hudson Tubing's assembly line over the weekend.

Our customer was very pleased with the service we provided, but not nearly as pleased as we are here at Consolidated Intergalactic with the dedication of our team members.

Requesting participation in employee survey

From Human Resources to employees

Here's your chance to tell us what you really think about Consolidated Intergalactic.

We hope every facet of your employment here meets and exceeds your expectations in every way, but we realize that even a company like ours always has room for improvement.

We'd like to invite you to fill out the attached employee survey. Your responses will be kept confidential; the forms do not include your name and processing of the information will be done by an outside consultant.

We want to hear your opinions of our benefits, work rules, management style, products, and marketing efforts.

Please fill out the form and deposit it in the collection box outside the Human Resources Office. You'll also find a separate numbered identification ticket in the package; please place that ticket in the "lottery" box at HR; we will choose five participants to receive a Lumbertown Night on the Town, including dinner for two at a fine restaurant and a pair of movie passes.

Requesting participation in employee focus group

From Human Resources to employees

We would like to invite you to join a select group of Consolidated Intergalactic employees in participating in a professionally guided focus group to assess benefits and work rules.

The session, scheduled for Monday, August 5, from noon to 2 P.M., will be held at the Lumbertown Marriott Hotel. We will provide lunch.

The focus group will ask opinions about the benefits and work rules here at CI and we will solicit constructive suggestions for change.

Please advise your department head by July 20 if you are willing to participate in this important session.

6 Human Resources: To Individual Employees

Letters to Individual Employees

Acknowledging letter of resignation

From Human Resources or Employment Office to employee

We have accepted your letter of resignation, effective June 1.

You have been a valued member of the Consolidated Intergalactic team, and we wish you the best of luck in your next endeavor.

You will continue to receive your salary through your last day of employment. Your final paycheck will also include the cash value of any accrued and unused vacation time, following the provisions of the employee manual.

If you have any questions about your final paycheck or the exit process, please contact Human Resources as soon as possible.

Acknowledging letter of resignation, without comment

From Human Resources or Employment Office to employee

We have accepted your letter of resignation, effective June 1.

If you have any questions about your final paycheck or the exit process, please contact Human Resources as soon as possible.

Accept resignation, offer praise and reference

From Human Resources to employee

It is with regret that we accept your resignation from employment with Consolidated Intergalactic.

On behalf of everyone at CI, we wish you well in your new job in Chicago. We are certain you will be as successful in your new position as you were here in Lumbertown; if you ever require a job or personal reference, please feel free to request one.

Notification of change in job status (part-time to full-time)

From Human Resources or Employment Office to employee

We are pleased to inform you that we are able to change your employment status from part-time to full-time, effective June 15.

Your job description as a nonexempt employee and hourly pay rate will not change. However, you are now eligible for various health, vacation, and retirement benefits as described in the attached memo.

Please make an appointment to visit Human Resources before June 15 to sign up for benefits and make other changes to employment records.

Welcome to new employee

From Human Resources or Employment Office to employee

On behalf of the management and staff of Consolidated Intergalactic, we wish to welcome you as a new employee. We are very proud of our company and especially our workforce. We wish you every personal and professional success as a member of the team.

Please feel free to call or visit Human Resources with any questions about your job, benefits, or the company.

Commendation on employment milestone

From Human Resources or Executive Office to employees

Please join me in congratulating John Stone on reaching his twenty-fifth anniversary of employment here at Consolidated Intergalactic. John joined the company as a filing clerk and, as most of you know, is currently executive assistant to the chief financial officer.

John is the longest-serving employee of the company and was honored as part of the celebration of the company's twenty-fifth anniversary in June.

We will have an informal reception honoring John this Friday at 4 P.M. in Conference Room B. If you have the chance, please come by to applaud his service.

Acknowledgment of referral of new hire

From Human Resources or Employment Office to employee

Thank you for your recent referral of a job applicant. We greatly appreciate your assistance in helping us find more of a very rare type of person: someone with the dedication and skills to work at Consolidated Intergalactic

As part of our Employee Referral Bonus Program, you are eligible to receive a $1,000 bonus once the new hire has successfully completed six months of continuous employment. A copy of the referral form and a reference number is attached for your files.

Acknowledgment of payment of retention bonus

From Human Resources or Employment Office to employee

Congratulations on reaching your sixth anniversary with Consolidated Intergalactic. As a quality control engineer you are eligible for an annual Retention Bonus.

After two years, the bonus begins at 5 percent and increases by 1 percent on each anniversary.

Your bonus, which will be included in your paycheck in the first week of June, is 9 percent of your base annual salary (before overtime). Please note that the bonus is considered ordinary income for income tax purposes.

Offer of promotion

From departmental head, Human Resources, or Employment Office to employee

I am pleased to offer you a promotion to the position of senior benefits analyst in Human Resources. The job description and details of the salary and other benefits are attached to this letter.

We have been very pleased with your work in the Benefits Department over the past two years, as reflected in your performance evaluations and recommendations from your supervisors.

We hope you will accept this job and continue to have success here at Consolidated Intergalactic. Please advise me by letter of your intentions by August 19.

Offer of transfer

From departmental head, Human Resources, or Employment Office to employee

As you know, it is the corporate policy of Consolidated Intergalactic to seek to promote from within whenever possible.

We would like to offer you a promotion to a new position as director of Customer Service in our Columbus office. The job description and details of salary and benefits (including assistance in relocation and associated expenses) are attached.

Your supervisors recommended you very highly for this opportunity. This would be a significant advancement in your career here at CI, and we hope you will accept the offer.

If you have any questions about the job or the transfer process, please give me a call.

Decline offer to transfer instead of termination

From Human Resources to employee

We regret to inform you that we are unable to offer you a job in Cincinnati, as you requested in your letter of May 4. There are no available and appropriate positions in our office there at this time.

Accordingly, we must accept your resignation effective May 30. We wish you well in your job search in Cincinnati.

If you require a job or personal reference, please feel free to request one.

Notice of layoff

From Human Resources or Employment Office to employee

It is with deep regret that we must formally notify you of your layoff effective July 15.

As you were informed by your supervisor earlier today, we had hoped to be able to retain all of our employees even as the company underwent financial reorganization. Unfortunately, additional downturns in orders in this difficult economic environment have made that impossible.

You will be contacted by Human Resources within the next three days to schedule an appointment to review your available benefits, eligibility for severance pay, accrued vacation time, and assistance offered by the company in seeking other employment.

We appreciate your efforts on behalf of Consolidated Intergalactic during your employment here; once again, we apologize for this unfortunate turn of events. Please accept our best wishes for your future.

Notice of termination

From Human Resources or Employment Office to employee

(NOTE: Review with your in-house or outside legal counsel)

This is to inform you that your employment with Consolidated Intergalactic has been terminated, effective immediately.

You are terminated, with cause, for violation of elements of the employee manual.

Please accompany Mr. Byron to Human Resources immediately. There you will receive information on any benefits for which you may be eligible. You will be expected to vacate your work station after the end of the appointment at Human Resources.

Request for resignation to avoid termination

From Human Resources to employee

(NOTE: Consult your human resources office or legal department to be sure you follow applicable labor laws including those regarding unemployment insurance)

As you know, we are not satisfied with your performance as a Customer Service representative at Consolidated Intergalactic and have warned you of the possibility that we will be forced to terminate your employment.

Unfortunately, we are now convinced that you are not going to be able to show the improvements we asked to see. At this time, we would like to offer you the option of resigning from your position with CI effective immediately; doing so would allow you to avoid having a termination in your job history.

If you choose to resign at this time, we will pay you for any accrued vacation and overtime hours and offer you one week of severance pay.

If you do not accept this offer, we will terminate your employment for cause effective immediately.

Please contact the Human Resources Office before noon today to advise them of your decision.

Requiring return of laptop computer from departing employee

From Human Resources to departing employee

According to our records, you are in possession of a laptop computer owned by the company.

Please arrange to return the laptop computer, along with all power cords, cables, software, carrying cases, and other accessories to the Office Services Department at least one business day before your last day of employment.

In keeping with company policy, we will not issue a final paycheck to departing employees until all such loaned equipment is returned.

Withholding final paycheck for employee until equipment is returned

From Human Resources to departing employee

Your final paycheck is ready to be issued by Payroll Services, but in accordance with company policy it is being withheld until all loaned equipment has been returned.

According to our records, you still have a company-issued cell phone and a set of precision power tools owned by the company. Service to the cell phone has been discontinued, but the device must be returned.

Please arrange to return the loaned equipment to the Office Services department as soon as possible.

Regarding request for change from full-time to part-time status

From Human Resources to employee

We have received your request to change your job as a Customer Service agent from permanent full-time to permanent part-time status effective August 1, with a work schedule of twenty hours per week. Your schedule, subject to approval by your department head, would be weekdays from 8:30 A.M. to 12:30 P.M.

Before this change is put into effect, we want to advise you of the following conditions that will apply:

- As a permanent part-time employee you are not eligible for fully subsidized health insurance coverage under our company policy. You will be given the option to purchase health coverage through the Benefits Office, or you may choose to obtain coverage through a policy offered to your spouse or domestic partner. Please consult with Terry Omson at extension 3253 to discuss available options.
- As a permanent part-time employee, you will accrue personal days, sick days, and vacation time at a rate proportional to the number of hours you work. Since you will be working twenty hours per week, half of the number of hours of a full-time employee, you will accrue time off at 50 percent of the full-time rate.
- Bonuses, company pension contributions, and other such benefits from the company will also be paid at a rate proportional to the number of hours you work.
- As a permanent part-time employee, you are not guaranteed the annual raises, promotions, and job transfers that are offered to permanent full-time employees.

Please consider this information carefully and contact me no later than July 15 to discuss your plans to return to the workforce on August 1.

Denying request for change from full-time to part-time status

From Human Resources to employee

(NOTE: Consult your human resources office or legal counsel if you have any doubts about the appropriateness of this letter in your state.)

We have received your request to change your job as a Customer Service agent from permanent full-time to permanent part-time status effective August 1, with a work schedule of twenty hours per week.

We regret to inform you that we will be unable to accommodate you in this manner. Our present staffing needs are for a permanent full-time Customer Service representative, and that job slot has been held open for you.

Please advise me, at extension 2442, of your plans at your earliest convenience.

Suggesting job-sharing for part-time employee

From Human Resources to employee

We have received your request to change your job as a Customer Service agent from permanent full-time to permanent part-time status effective August 1, with a work schedule of twenty hours per week. Your schedule, subject to approval by your department head, would be weekdays from 8:30 A.M. to 12:30 P.M.

As you know, part-time workers are not eligible for company-subsidized health insurance and certain other benefits including pension contributions and bonuses.

Before we make your requested change, we would like to suggest that you consider engaging in a formal job-sharing contract with another employee. We can help pair you with another staffer in your department or with a similar job description.

Under a job-sharing agreement, two employees agree to provide the company with forty hours per week of labor, with time divided in any reasonable manner. (For simplicity and to assist the company in planning, we encourage 50/50 time splits.)

As an incentive for engaging in a job-sharing agreement, Consolidated Intergalactic provides the following special benefits to permanent part-time employees:

- The company will provide a subsidy equal to 50 percent of the cost of the same health insurance plan each employee would receive as a permanent full-time employee.
- Personal days, sick days, and vacation days will accrue at a rate proportionate to the number of hours worked each week by each partner in the plan, plus an additional annual bonus equal to 25 percent of time that would have been earned by a permanent full-time employee.

If you are interested in engaging in a job-sharing agreement, please contact me no later than July 15 to discuss your plans to return to the workforce on August 1.

Offer of assistance to family of ill employee

From Human Resources or Benefits Office to employee

(NOTE: Review with your in-house or outside legal counsel)

On behalf of all of us at Consolidated Intergalactic, we want to wish you a speedy and full recovery from your illness.

As you already know, you are covered under the terms of the federal Family and Medical Leave Act which allows as much as twelve workweeks of unpaid leave during any twelve-month period when an employee is unable to work because of a serious health condition.

In addition, our corporate benefits package includes a short-term disability insurance plan that will replace lost income.

It is also our standard practice to offer any employee who misses more than six weeks of work for covered medical reasons the assistance of our Human Resources Department in handling medical claims and special services. Please contact John Kelby to learn about how we might assist you.

Offer of assistance to employee with ill family member

From Executive Office, Human Resources, or Benefits Office to employee

We have been informed that you have requested an unpaid leave from work so that you can assist an ill member of your family.

On behalf of Consolidated Intergalactic, please allow me to offer you and your family our best wishes in this difficult time.

We would like to inform you of some additional benefits that we offer to valued employees in this time of need. Please contact Human Resources to schedule an appointment to discuss extended services that may help you take care of your family or return to work earlier; these include subsidized or discounted home nursing care, assistance in coordination of health care benefits, and counseling offered by our health insurance provider.

Introductions, References, and Recommendations

Letter of introduction for former employee leaving company

From Human Resources, Executive Office, or department head to outside organization

Frank Benson was a valued employee of Consolidated Intergalactic for more than fifteen years, most recently as director of our Quality Control Department.

I would be happy to provide additional information about Mr. Benson's abilities and performance. Consolidated Intergalactic policy does not permit disclosure of salary, health, or other private matters.

General letter of recommendation for former employee

From Human Resources, Executive Office, or department head to outside organization

To Whom It May Concern,

Frank Benson was a valued employee of Consolidated Intergalactic for more than fifteen years. He was a skilled technician, heading up our Quality Control Department.

Under his leadership, our customer satisfaction ratings improved significantly and our costs for repair and replacement of failed products declined by an average of 10 percent per year.

We were sorry to lose him when family obligations forced him to move from our area. In my opinion, any company that hires him will be adding a great asset to their team.

Specific letter of recommendation for former employee

From Human Resources, Executive Office, or department head to outside organization

Regarding your inquiry about Frank Benson, I can tell you that Mr. Benson was a valued employee of Consolidated Intergalactic for more than fifteen years, most recently as director of our Quality Control Department.

Mr. Benson had an exemplary career here at CI, demonstrating a strong commitment to our company and customers.

You asked whether he would be an appropriate candidate to manage a department of thirty engineers. In my personal opinion, Mr. Benson has already shown such capabilities here at CI.

General letter of recommendation for employee applying to college

From Human Resources, Executive Office, or department head to educational institution

To Whom It May Concern,

I am writing to recommend Janet Gould for acceptance to college as a business major.

Janet has worked as my assistant here in the Marketing Department of Consolidated Intergalactic for the past two years and shown remarkable abilities and initiative. She has taken on assignments well beyond those of her entry-level job description and has twice been rewarded with promotions.

Although we will miss her very much here at the company, we hope she will consider returning to CI as a young executive after graduation. I am certain she will be a success in any business environment she chooses.

Sincerely,

Specific letter of recommendation for employee applying to college

From Human Resources, Executive Office, or department head to educational institution

I am writing to offer my full recommendation of Janet Gould as a candidate for the M.B.A. program at Lumbertown Community College.

Ms. Gould has already demonstrated exceptional skills in marketing and financial analysis as my assistant. She is a very quick learner, and has taken advantage of several in-house training seminars to improve her skills.

It is my opinion that Ms. Gould is destined to become a senior executive in business and will reflect well upon Consolidated Intergalactic and Lumbertown Community College in all that she does.

Decline to offer letter of recommendation for former employee, company policy

From Human Resources, Executive Office, or department head to outside organization

I have received your request for a letter of reference for Donald Jones, a former employee of Consolidated Intergalactic.

Company policy at Consolidated Intergalactic does not permit qualitative letters of reference for any former employee.

I can confirm that Mr. Jones worked for CI for twelve years, from 1993 to 2005. His job title at the time he departed was senior financial analyst.

Decline to offer letter of recommendation for former employee

From Human Resources, Executive Office, department head to outside organization

I have received your request for a letter of reference for Donald Jones, a former employee of Consolidated Intergalactic.

Unfortunately, I do not feel it would be appropriate for me to comment on Mr. Jones's employment record or his qualifications for a job with your company.

Commendation to file

From Human Resources or departmental head, memo to file

Ms. Preston has demonstrated exceptional commitment to company goals in performance of her duties in the Shipping Department.

During the holiday period just ended, in addition to accepting all requests for overtime, Ms. Preston helped develop a system to organize products in a way that allowed for more efficient matching of destination to shipping carrier. As a result, our customers received their orders faster and the company was able to reduce shipping costs by at least 6 percent.

Reprimand to file

From Human Resources or departmental head, memo to file

According to his supervisor, Mr. Silver has been late for his assigned shift on twelve of the past twenty work days, resulting in lost productivity and inconvenience to other staffers.

With this memo to file, he is advised that a continuation of such inattention to company rules may result in his termination from employment. His attendance record will be reviewed two weeks from today.

Commendation to employee for exceptional service to customer

From Human Resources, Executive Office, Customer Service, or department head to employee

I want to thank you for your exceptional service to Parsifal Products as a sales representative for Consolidated Intergalactic. We have received several calls and notes from different departments at that important customer praising your work, most recently for your extra effort in helping them quickly alter and improve their manufacturing line using CI products to meet a major new order.

I have said many times that Consolidated Intergalactic's most important product is our staff. They are the face of our company. They go into the offices and factories of our customers before our machines are shipped.

As chairman of CI, I want you to know that your work is appreciated and we look forward to your future successes as part of the team.

7 Human Resources: From Employees

Letter of resignation (simple)

From employee to Human Resources or Employment Office

I am writing to inform you that I am resigning my position as director of communications, effective at the end of business on Monday, April 30.

I am very grateful that I have had the opportunity to work for Consolidated Intergalactic for the past seven years. I will always think of the organization as a first-class company.

If I can be of any assistance in preparing for the hiring of my replacement or appointment of a temporary director, I would be glad to help.

Letter of resignation (to take a new job)

From employee to Human Resources or Employment Office

I am writing to inform you that I am resigning my position as director of communications, effective at the end of business on Monday, April 30.

I have been offered and have accepted an exceptional opportunity as a member of senior management with another company, in another industry.

I am very grateful that I have had the opportunity to work for Consolidated Intergalactic for the past seven years. I will always think of the organization as a first-class company.

If I can be of any assistance in preparing for the hiring of my replacement or appointment of a temporary director, I would be glad to help.

Notification of intent to retire

From employee to Human Resources or Employment Office

I am writing to inform you of my intention to retire from Consolidated Intergalactic, effective May 1.

I have greatly enjoyed my career here at CI and will treasure my friends and our accomplishments.

Recommending employee for promotion

From department head to Human Resources

I wholeheartedly recommend Jamison Kennedy for promotion to a supervisor's position, even though we will miss her very much as a Customer Service agent in our department.

Ms. Kennedy has demonstrated total dedication to her job and has pursued every available avenue to improve her skills and training while in our employ. I am certain she will be a success as a supervisor in the Shipping Department.

Objecting to proposed promotion for employee

From department head to Human Resources

CONFIDENTIAL

At this time, I am registering an objection to the proposed promotion of Jamison Kennedy from Customer Service to a supervisory position in the Shipping Department.

At this time I feel that such a promotion would hurt two departments. Ms. Kennedy is a capable agent in Customer Service, completing her first year in our employ; although I believe she will eventually warrant a promotion and additional responsibilities, she has only just recently mastered her assignment.

I would recommend we consider a promotion for Ms. Kennedy in six months or one year after we have had the full benefit of her work here in our department and after she has completed available training courses on management skills.

Acceptance of promotion

From employee to department head, Human Resources, or Employment Office

I am happy to accept a new position as senior benefits analyst in Human Resources, effective as soon as is convenient.

I have reviewed the job description and salary offer, and I am very excited about the new challenges the position will offer. I will do my best to exceed your expectations.

Thank you again.

Acceptance of transfer

From employee to Human Resources or Employment Office

I am pleased to accept your offer of a new position as director of Customer Service in our Columbus office.

I have reviewed the job description and salary offer, and I am very excited about the new challenges the position will offer. I will do my best to exceed your expectations.

I would appreciate a short period of time to consider the best schedule for moving to Columbus; my wife will be leaving her job here in Lumbertown, and we also need to consider the school calendar for our children. I will call you to set up a meeting to discuss a proposed schedule within the next business week.

Thank you again.

Declining promotion

From employee to department head, Human Resources, or Employment Office

Thank you for the offer of a promotion to senior benefits analyst in Human Resources. I appreciate the show of confidence by my supervisors and the company.

However, I have decided that the new position takes me in a direction different from my career goals. Therefore, I respectfully decline the offer.

Thank you again.

Request for transfer from one department to another

From employee to Human Resources or Executive Office

At the suggestion of my supervisor, I am writing to request a transfer from the Accounts Receivable Department to the employee Benefits Office.

I note that the employee Benefits Office has posted an open position as a financial analyst on the Human Resources internal Web site. Although this transfer is lateral in terms of job responsibilities and pay grade, I am making this request to broaden my background in financial management here at Consolidated Intergalactic.

I look forward to the opportunity to interview for this job. Thank you.

Declining promotion with transfer

From employee to Human Resources or Employment Office

It is with regret that I must decline your offer of a transfer to Columbus and a new position as director of Customer Service there.

Although I appreciate the offer of a promotion and the confidence my supervisors have shown in my abilities, at this time family considerations would make it very difficult for me to leave Lumbertown. My wife is currently employed here, and our young children attend school.

I hope you will consider me for other opportunities with the company here at headquarters, and with your permission I will advise you when my family situation is such that I could accept a transfer out of the area.

Thank you.

Request to be considered for internal job opening

From employee to Human Resources or Executive Office

Regarding the position of senior travel planner posted on the Human Resources Web site, I would like to submit my name for consideration.

I have worked for Consolidated Intergalactic for five years, currently as an executive assistant to the vice president for employee benefits. I have performed many of the components of the job description and have an extensive background in budget management. In expectation of such a staff opening, I have recently completed a college-level course on travel planning at Lumbertown Community College.

I look forward to the opportunity to interview for this job. Thank you.

Notification of legal name change

From employee to Human Resources

I am writing to ask that you update my employee records to reflect my new legal name as the result of my marriage on June 6.

Please change my records as follows:

FROM: Mary Louis Poster

TO: Mary Poster-Smythe

There are no changes at this time to my legal mailing address.

Notification of legal name change, reverting to maiden name

From employee to Human Resources

Please update my employee records with my new legal name. As the result of my parents' divorce, I have chosen to accept my mother's maiden name as my own last name; this information has been filed with the county clerk's office as required.

Please change my records as follows:

FROM: John Glavich

TO: John G. Kopeckne

Thank you.

Notification of change of address

From employee to Human Resources

Please update my employee records with my new permanent address, effective immediately.

OLD ADDRESS: 360 Small Road, Syracuse, NY 13221

NEW ADDRESS: 8525 Lancaster Avenue, Syracuse, NY 13221

Thank you.

Notification of change of marital status

From employee to Human Resources

Please update my employee records to change my personal status from married to single (divorced), effective immediately.

There are no changes at this time to my address or phone number.

Please also advise me about any other necessary changes that need to be made to tax or insurance forms.

Thank you.

Request for clarification of vacation policy

From employee to Human Resources or Benefits Office

I am writing to seek clarification of the company vacation policy. According to my records I have seven days of vacation available to me as of today, and I am planning to request vacation time off for a period six weeks from now.

1. Can you please confirm the number of days in my account?

2. According to my reading of the employee manual, I am accruing vacation days at the rate of one day for each completed month of service. Is that correct?

3. If I schedule my vacation for six weeks from now, which would be the third and fourth weeks of August, how many days will I have in my account? Will I accrue my August vacation day while I am out of the office on vacation at the end of the month, and can I use that day as part of my upcoming vacation?

Thanks for your assistance.

Request for clarification of holiday schedule

From employee to Human Resources or Benefits Office

I am writing to seek clarification of the company holiday schedule. I do not celebrate Christmas, and for the past few years I have volunteered to work the emergency desk on that day so that others can be with their families.

I will be making that offer to my supervisor once again. I would like to know if I could be compensated with two personal days instead of being paid double-time for working on the holiday.

Request for clarification of overtime policy

From employee to Human Resources or Benefits Office

I have been asked by my supervisor to work at least six hours of overtime during each of the last four weeks of the fiscal year, beginning June 15.

I am aware that the company has the right to require a reasonable amount of overtime from its employees, and I am very willing to help in any way that I can, but my religious beliefs do not permit me to perform labor on Friday nights and Saturdays. I would be happy to work late on other nights of the week, or on Sundays.

Can you please clarify the company policy on overtime, and assist me in working out an acceptable schedule with my manager?

Request for clarification of use of accrued vacation time

From employee to Human Resources or Benefits Office

At the end of this year I will have approximately nine days of unused vacation time to my credit.

Can you please advise me of the date by which I must use that accrued time? Will the time be automatically converted to a cash payment if I do not use it? And if so, when would I receive payment?

Request for clarification of vacation policy, half-day vacation

From employee to Human Resources or Benefits Office

I am writing to request to split one of my available vacation days into two half-days off in August. I would like to leave work at 1 P.M. on the first two Fridays of the month to get a head start on weekend trips to our summer home.

I have consulted with my supervisor, and he said he has no problem with my proposed schedule. Please advise.

Request for flextime

From employee to Human Resources or department head

I would like to request a change in my working hours, as permitted under Consolidated Intergalactic's flextime program.

I would like to adjust my schedule to begin my day at 8 A.M., one hour earlier than ordinary business hours, and leave the workplace one hour early at 4 P.M. This will allow me to better coordinate my commuting schedule with available childcare for my daughter.

Attached is the required memo of approval from my supervisor.

Request for bereavement leave

From employee to Human Resources or Benefits Office

I am writing to request a three-day bereavement leave, effective immediately, to attend the funeral of a family member. Tammy Carpenter, my sister-in-law, passed away yesterday at Yawkey Memorial Hospital in Lumbertown, and services are planned for Friday of this week.

I have advised my supervisor of my need to assist my brother and family.

Thank you for your consideration.

Waiver of confidentiality for employment details

From employee to Payroll Office or Human Resources

I hereby grant permission to Consolidated Intergalactic to disclose details of my employment to the Bank of Lumbertown in connection with my application for a mortgage.

Specifically, I give permission to inform the BofL of my job title, date of hiring, current status of employment, and monthly or annual salary.

This permission is effective immediately, and shall expire thirty days from the date of this letter.

Thank you.

(Signed) _____   (Date) _____

Requesting change from full-time to part-time status

From employee to Human Resources

As I prepare to return to my job after maternity leave, I would like to request that my job in the Customer Service Department be changed from full-time permanent status to part-time permanent status effective August 1. I am asking for a schedule of twenty hours per week, weekdays from 8:30 A.M. to 12:30 P.M.

I have the support of my department head in this request.

8 Employee Evaluations

For a more detailed discussion of employee evaluations or appraisals, we suggest you read *Employee Appraisals That Work* by Corey Sandler and Janice Keefe, published by Adams Media. Some of the basic letters in this chapter are adapted from that book.

Advisory about performance evaluation

From Human Resources or Employment Office to employee

Your semi-annual performance evaluation is scheduled for June. Please give me a call to discuss the best date and time that meets both of our schedules.

Attached is a copy of the Employee Self-Assessment Form, which we ask you to complete and submit at least one week before your scheduled appointment.

The evaluation process is intended to help employees improve their performance and open the pathways to advancement. For managers, it offers the chance to intervene and offer assistance in a situation where improvement is necessary.

The full details of the performance evaluation process can be found in the employee manual; please review that information before your interview. If you have any questions, please contact Human Resources.

Confirmation of performance evaluation meeting

From Human Resources or Employment Office to employee

This is to confirm your performance evaluation, scheduled for Monday, June 1 at 11 A.M. in Conference Room A.

If you have not already done so, please be sure to submit your Employee Self-Assessment Form to your supervisor at this time.

Full details of the performance evaluation process are in the employee manual. If you have any questions please contact Human Resources.

Notification of memo to personnel file

From Human Resources or Employment Office to employee

Attached please find a copy of a memo that has been placed in your personnel file as a result of your performance evaluation conducted on June 1.

The purpose of the memo is to put on the record your manager's directives for actions that need to be taken by you.

Please read the memo carefully. If you have any questions about the contents of the memo, you may discuss them with your supervisor or contact Human Resources.

Notification of special training schedule, result of performance evaluation

From Human Resources or Employment Office to employee

As a result of a recommendation by your supervisor following your performance evaluation of June 1, the Training Office has set up a six-week course of study to improve your communication skills.

Attendance and successful completion of this course of study is an important element of satisfying requirements noted in your performance evaluation.

Classes for a small group of employees—no more than six—will be conducted on Mondays and Fridays at 9 A.M. in Conference Room B. Each session will last approximately forty-five minutes, and there will be some assignments that must be completed prior to each session.

Your supervisor has been advised of the schedule and you will be excused from your ordinary assignments for each training session and a reasonable amount of time for preparation each week.

The first class will be held on July 12. You will receive an information packet and reminder one week before then.

Commendation for extra effort

From Human Resources or Executive Office to employee

We have been advised by your department manager of your extraordinary efforts in helping the Shipping Department deal with a rush order from a very important client last week.

Knowing your history here at the company, I'm sure you feel that you were "just doing your job." That is, at the same time, true and an understatement of your level of commitment to the goals of the company.

Thank you for your service.

cc: To Employee Personnel File

Employee evaluation: chronic tardiness

From supervisor or department head to employee

I am writing to confirm the elements of our discussion this morning about your failure to meet our expectations for working hours.

Your job description calls for you to be at work each day for eight hours, with a thirty-minute lunch break. By agreement with your department head, you are permitted to adjust your starting time to be between 8 A.M. and 9:15 A.M., if such adjustment is necessary because of commuting difficulties.

As we discussed in your performance evaluation, you have been unable to maintain a consistent arrival time and have on more than one occasion arrived late and departed early on the same day.

You were advised in our meeting, and I am reiterating the point in this letter, that we must insist you maintain a consistent work schedule. Your unreliable working hours have an impact on the productivity of others in your department and elsewhere in the company.

We will be closely monitoring your working hours. If we determine that you are unable to consistently meet our work schedule expectations we will be forced to terminate your employment.

We hope you are able to adjust your schedule and hope for your success as a member of the Consolidated Intergalactic team.

Employee evaluation: violation of lunch break rules

From supervisor or department head to employee

I am writing to confirm the elements of our discussion this morning about your failure to meet our expectations regarding the length of lunch breaks.

Your supervisor reports that you cannot be relied upon to keep within the allotted thirty-minute lunch break that is stipulated in your job description.

We have offered an extension to your work day to allow for a sixty-minute lunch break; this would require arrival by 9 A.M. each day with departure at 5:30 P.M.

Alternatively, you can keep your current schedule of 9 A.M. to 5 P.M. and take a thirty-minute lunch break.

You told me today that you do not want to extend your work day until 5:30 P.M.

Your department head will closely monitor your working schedule; we will expect that your lunch breaks will stay within the allotted thirty-minute time. If we determine that you are unable to consistently meet our expectations in this area, we will be forced to terminate your employment.

We hope you will be able to meet our needs and hope for your success as a member of the Consolidated Intergalactic team.

Employee evaluation: violation of sick day policy

From supervisor or department head to employee

I am writing to confirm the elements of our discussion this morning about your apparent failure to meet our expectations regarding the use of sick days.

As we discussed, Human Resources has noted a recurring pattern which seems to indicate misuse of sick days for personal purposes; in the past year we have noted four instances where you have called in as sick on the day before or day after a holiday or a holiday weekend.

The published policy of Consolidated Intergalactic states that sick days may only be used for actual medical problems or appointments and may not be used to extend vacation or holiday periods. As an employee, you have agreed to permit the company to require documentation of illness or medical treatment.

Your department head and Human Resources will closely monitor your attendance record. If we see any further questionable use of sick days, we will request such documentation from medical providers; if we determine that sick days have been improperly used we will seek your termination from employment.

We hope you will be able to meet our needs and hope for your success as a member of the Consolidated Intergalactic team.

Employee evaluation: lack of availability for overtime

From supervisor or department head to employee

I am writing to confirm the elements of our discussion this morning about your apparent failure to meet our expectations regarding availability for overtime when required to meet production needs.

Your job description as a full-time hourly employee states that the company has the right to require a reasonable amount of overtime to meet our needs. Although we recognize that our employees may face difficulties in this area because of family obligations and for other reasons, the company's ability to rely on our staff for overtime is an essential element of your job.

Where possible, our department heads have been asked to make special arrangements with employees to allow for childcare during overtime periods.

However, in the past three months, you have turned down all requests by your supervisor for overtime assignments. This is not acceptable.

With this letter, we are advising you that a continued inability to make yourself available for overtime hours will result in termination of your employment.

If you would like to seek assistance from Human Resources in obtaining childcare, special transportation, or other accommodations that would allow you to meet our needs, please contact Bob Waylings at extension 4782.

Employee evaluation: absence from meetings

From supervisor or department head to employee

I am writing to confirm the elements of our discussion this morning about your apparent failure to meet our expectations regarding attendance at departmental meetings.

As we discussed, attendance at weekly departmental meetings as well as any other scheduled gathering is a requirement of your job. You are expected to attend all such meetings; if you have a scheduling conflict, you are expected to inform your supervisor in advance and the supervisor may ask you to adjust your schedule to allow attendance at a meeting.

This is the second time you have been formally advised that you have violated an important element of your job description. I must advise you that continued problems of this sort, or other violations of the employee manual, may force us to terminate your employment from Consolidated Intergalactic.

Employee evaluation: failure to meet deadlines

From supervisor or department head to employee

I am writing to confirm the elements of our discussion this morning about your repeated failure to meet reasonable deadlines in the performance of your job.

This is the third time such issues have been noted in employee evaluations by your supervisor, and I am sorry to say that we have seen no improvement in your ability to meet deadlines since this was first discussed with you twelve months ago.

We are not in any way questioning your commitment to your job or to the company as a whole. We have appreciated your willingness to accept coaching and training offered by the company; for our part we have sought to adjust your work load and relax certain deadlines in hopes that you will be able to improve your productivity.

However, at this time we must inform you that we have determined that you are not, at this time, in the appropriate job at Consolidated Intergalactic. We have an opening as a shipping clerk in the Mailroom, at a reduction in pay grade; if you choose not to accept this job, we will seek immediate termination from employment. Please contact Wilson Neves in Human Resources at extension 2342 today to make an appointment to discuss your employment.

Employee evaluation: inability to stay within financial plan

From supervisor or department head to employee

As we discussed this morning in a special performance evaluation follow-up meeting, we continue to have concerns about your ability to keep spending within the financial plan.

In the past six months you have received weekly reports from an analyst in the Accounting Department as well as coaching from your department head. However, your most recent monthly reports shows a significant amount of overspending in all of the budget lines you manage.

We value your dedication to the company and would like to find a way to help you in your career here at Consolidated Intergalactic. At this time, though, we have decided to offer you a new nonmanagerial position as a product specialist in the Customer Service Department; we hope you will accept this reassignment.

Employee evaluation: inability to meet sales goals

From supervisor or department head to employee

Your monthly sales figures continue to fall well short of goals. As we discussed today, you have not met your quota for five of the past six months, and overall have booked sales 31 percent below expectations for the current fiscal year.

We have offered you training and coaching as well as special pricing for several of your most important clients but we have not seen progress in your sales numbers.

In our meeting I offered you a transfer to a noncommissioned sales support job in the Marketing Department. I have received your follow-up e-mail in which you decline that offer; I am sorry you have chosen not to accept a transfer within the company.

Therefore, we have decided to terminate your employment with Consolidated Intergalactic, effective immediately. Please report immediately to Howard Mussina in Human Resources to discuss the package of benefits and assistance we offer terminated employees.

Employee evaluation: failure to meet quality standards for service

From supervisor or department head to employee

As I informed you in our meeting yesterday, we are not satisfied with the cleanliness of the restrooms on the second and third floors of the west wing of our headquarters building; these six bathrooms are one of your primary responsibilities as a janitor. As we discussed, it is our expectation that each bathroom receive an inspection and cleaning before noon, and a full cleaning and restocking of supplies at the end of each work day.

This is the second time in the past three months we have notified you of a failure to meet our expectations in the performance of your job as a janitor.

We will be closely monitoring your performance, including daily inspections by a supervisor from the Office Services Department. We sincerely hope that you will demonstrate noticeable improvement of your attention to the details of your job description; if we determine that we cannot rely on the quality of your work, we will seek your immediate termination from employment.

Employee evaluation: violation of health and safety rules

From supervisor or department head to employee

As we discussed in a special employee evaluation session this morning, we have noted on at least six occasions in the past month that you have not been properly wearing and using required health and safety equipment in the Manufacturing Department.

Use of this equipment is a requirement of continued employment with the company, and is based on regulations of the state and federal government, our insurance carriers, and our employee manual. As stated in your job description, you must wear safety shoes and gloves, a particulate mask, and an eye shield at all times when on the factory floor.

According to our records, you have received training in the use of safety and health equipment four times in the past eighteen months, including a three-day seminar soon after you were hired and three regularly scheduled refresher courses. You have also received two verbal and one written reprimand by your supervisor in the past month.

At this time we are putting you on notice that for your protection and in keeping with our obligations no further lapses of this nature will be tolerated. If you are found on the manufacturing floor without all required safety and health equipment you will be terminated from employment with Consolidated Intergalactic.

Employee evaluation: violation of computer security rules

From supervisor or department head to employee

According to an analysis by the Information Technology Office, you have continued to use your company-issued personal data assistant to access Web sites that are not related to your job. These include a sports news site, an online gambling site, and several other sites that are included on the department's alert list.

Company regulations require that employees not use computers or personal digital assistants (PDAs) to access any site that could compromise the integrity of our data services or is inappropriate to the mission statement of the company or a staffer's job description.

If you have any questions about policies regarding use of the company's computer resources, please contact me at extension 2344.

At this time we are advising you that a continuation of inappropriate conduct will be cause for immediate termination.

Employee evaluation: violation of rules on use of computer for personal purposes

From supervisor or department head to employee

Information Technology has determined that you have been using your workstation to access online auction sites and other commercial sites unrelated to your job description.

This is the third time we have noted such activities on your part. On March 12 of this year you received a written reprimand and were reminded that the company has an automated system that monitors Web sites visited by employees.

In the past week you have spent more than six hours logged on to UPay.com. Based on an alert generated by our system, we have determined that you were logged in to the site and managing the auction of a personal collection of china dolls.

We regret to inform you that you have been terminated from employment, effective immediately. Your department head will escort you to Human Resources where we will advise you of your rights and benefits as a terminated employee.

Employee evaluation: improper personal conduct

From supervisor or department head to employee

(NOTE: Discuss this with your security, human resources, and legal departments.)

In accordance with our company code of conduct, I am writing to advise you that you have been terminated from employment effective immediately. A representative of Human Resources will meet you at the security station at the entrance to the headquarters building to discuss the termination process; you will not be permitted to proceed past the security station.

According to reports from our Security Office and the Lumbertown Police Department, you became engaged in a physical altercation with another employee in the parking lot at the end of your shift yesterday. Copies of the police report and our own investigation have been placed in your confidential personnel file.

This is the second time you have become involved in a dispute with the same employee; you were given a written warning about this matter six weeks ago.

At Consolidated Intergalactic we consider any acts of violence, harassment, or threats of violence to be unacceptable and grounds for immediate termination.

9 Benefits Office Announcements

Announcements from Benefits Office to Employees

Announcements from Benefits Office to Employees

Notice of annual bonus

From Executive Office or Benefits Office to employees

We are pleased to tell you that the December 21 paycheck or direct deposit notification will include this year's annual bonus.

We are proud of our accomplishments as a company this year, even in the face of a difficult economic environment. In keeping with our established policy that links annual bonuses to projected profits after taxes, we will award all full-time nonexempt salaried and hourly workers a bonus equivalent to 4 percent of gross annual salary (equal to about two weeks pay).

Bonuses are subject to withholding and other tax as ordinary income.

We look forward to the coming year and hope we can meet or exceed this year's profits. Thank you for all of your good efforts. We wish all employees a joyous holiday season and a healthy and happy new year.

Notification of holiday policy

From Benefits Office, Executive Office, or Human Resources to employees

The company will observe the following holidays in 2009. As always, we will seek volunteers to staff essential positions during holidays; if necessary, department supervisors may require some members of staff to come in to work on these days. (Nonexempt employees are paid double time on holidays.)

Thursday, January 1	New Year's Day
Monday, January 19	Martin Luther King Jr.'s Birthday Observance
Monday, February 16	Presidents' Day
Monday, May 25	Memorial Day
Monday, September 7	Labor Day
Monday, October 12	Columbus Day
Wednesday, November 11	Veterans Day
Thursday, November 26	Thanksgiving Day
Friday, December 25	Christmas Day

Each full-time regular employee with at least one year of service is also permitted four personal days each calendar year. These may be used for any purpose, including observance of religious holidays. Personal days do not carry over from year to year and cannot be cashed in for salary.

Please note that employees need special permission to include a holiday within a vacation period or to take personal days to extend a weekend. Such permission will only be granted if a supervisor determines this will not have an adverse impact on operations, and conflicting requests for such special schedules will be decided on the basis of seniority.

Notification of change to sick leave policy

From Benefits Office or Human Resources to employees

Effective January 1, all full-time regular employees will be permitted to carry over as many as four unused sick days from the previous year.

The policy in the past has been that unused sick days expire at the end of each calendar year.

We are making this change as an additional benefit to qualified employees; we continue to expect that sick days will be used only for legitimate medical reasons including illness and necessary medical appointments.

Full-time regular employees with more than one year of service are entitled to ten sick days per calendar year; new employees accrue sick days at the rate of .83 days for each fully completed month of service.

As always, Human Resources is available to assist employees with serious medical problems with a variety of services, including granting extended unpaid leaves of absence and family leave, and providing assistance in making claims under the company's short-term disability program.

This change in policy has been added to the online version of the employee manual, viewable at the Human Resources Web site.

Policy statement on benefits for domestic partners

From Benefits Office or Human Resources to employees

(NOTE: Consult with your in-house or outside legal counsel for advice regarding laws in your state and regulations put in place by providers of your benefit programs.)

Consolidated Intergalactic is committed to the welfare of all of our employees and the members of their families.

We fully support all applicable state and federal laws and regulations that extend benefits and legal privileges to spouses and children of CI employees as well as any domestic partners who reside in the same household as employees.

We note that certain benefits and legal privileges may be limited by the provider to persons who are married or otherwise have a relationship that is recognized by a civil authority.

If you have any questions about whether a particular benefit extends to domestic partners, please consult with the Benefits Office.

Optional training seminar on benefits

From Benefits Office or Human Resources to employees

All staffers are invited to attend a special presentation about the changes in the health plan benefit that are scheduled to go into effect July 1.

The one-hour seminar will be presented three times during the week of June 15 to allow employees to choose the presentation that is best for their schedule. Two of the sessions will be offered during the lunch hour, and one will be offered an hour before the standard start of business; Human Resources has arranged for sandwiches, breakfast items, and drinks.

In addition, a transcript of the presentation including PowerPoint slides will be available for download and viewing through the Human Resources Web site beginning June 17.

If you have any questions about the seminar, please contact Human Resources. In addition, a special telephone and e-mail hotline to answer questions about the health plan will begin operations on June 17.

A copy of the schedule of seminars and the hotline information are attached.

Announcement of seminar on new health insurance plan

From Benefits Office or Medical Office to employees

The Benefits Office will present seminars on the changes to the basic health plan and various new options for Consolidated Intergalactic employees during the week of May 5. Please see the attached schedule of seminars and choose one that does not conflict with essential assignments; some department heads may ask staff to spread their choices over the entire week to avoid disruption to operations.

In addition to the seminars, all employees will receive a full packet of information about the available plans, and the Benefits Office help desk will answer questions at extension 3456.

Notice of increase in health insurance costs

From Human Resources or Benefits Office to employees

Due to rapidly rising medical costs, our health insurance provider has raised prices for all policies. As we have in the past, Consolidated Intergalactic will be absorbing a large portion of the increased cost.

Effective July 1, the payroll deduction for company-supported health insurance will increase between 5 and 7 percent, depending on the plan you have selected.

We apologize for the inconvenience.

Employees are encouraged to contact the Benefits Office at extension 2313 to discuss alternative plans that may be less costly. Please note, though, that lower-cost plans may require higher co-pays or deductibles.

Amendment to employee handbook regarding health insurance

From Human Resources or Employment Office to employees

Enclosed please find a revision to the employee handbook to add new information about the changes to the company-provided health insurance plan.

Please review the changes and place them in your copy of the employee handbook. The version of the employee handbook that is posted on the Human Resources Web site has been fully updated to include this new material.

If you have any questions about the changes to the health insurance plan, a special telephone and e-mail hotline to answer questions about the health plan will begin operations on June 17. The phone number and e-mail address is posted on the Human Resources Web site.

Announcement of explanatory session on employee stock purchase plan

From Human Resources, Benefits Office, or Financial Department to employees

(NOTE: Review with your in-house or outside legal counsel)

All full-time regular employees are invited to attend a one-hour seminar on the new Consolidated Intergalactic Employee Stock Purchase Plan.

It is the policy of Consolidated Intergalactic to offer employees the opportunity to participate in the success of our company by purchasing shares of the company at a discounted price from the publicly traded price. Shares can be purchased by direct investment or through payroll deduction.

The session will be held at 4 P.M. on Thursday, June 15, in Conference Room C. After the conclusion of the session, a streaming video and transcript of the session will also be available on the corporate intranet.

Announcement of explanatory session on 401(k) and other retirement programs

From Human Resources, Benefits Office, or Financial Department to employees

(NOTE: Review with your in-house or outside legal counsel)

On Tuesday, March 27, at 1 P.M. and again on Tuesday, April 3, at 4 P.M. the Employee Benefits Department will be offering a one-hour informational meeting about the company-sponsored 401(k) retirement plan.

The Consolidated Intergalactic 401(k) plan is a participant-directed plan which allows employees to choose to deposit pre-tax income in one or more available investment vehicles including several mutual funds, money market funds, and bond funds. The investment can also be made in the form of shares of stock in Consolidated Intergalactic.

At the session, experts from the Employee Benefits Department and our investment advisors will explain how to enroll in the plan, the various options for investment, and how to make changes in the allocation of funds.

Beginning June 16, a streaming video and transcript of one of the sessions will be available on the corporate intranet.

Notice of policy change on vacation day accrual

From Benefits Office or Human Resources to employees

We are pleased to announce an improvement in the company vacation policy for full-time regular employees, effective January 1.

New employees who complete six months of satisfactory service will begin to accrue vacation time at the rate of .5 days per full month of service up to a maximum of three days.

In the second and third year, employees will continue to accrue vacation time at the rate of .5 days per full month of service up to a maximum of six days.

Beginning in the fourth year and continuing in the fifth year, vacation time accrual will be at the rate of .83 days per full month of service up to a maximum of ten days. In the sixth through eighth year of service, vacation time will accrue at the rate of one day per full month of service, up to a maximum of twelve days.

From the eight year onward, employees will receive a bonus of one additional day in the following year in addition to a base of one day per full month of employment. For example, an employee who is in the twelfth year of employment with Consolidated Intergalactic is entitled to twelve days of regular vacation time plus four days of bonus vacation.

The maximum number of vacation days an employee can accrue is twenty.

All vacation days accrued in a calendar year must be used before the end of the following calendar year. If vacation days are not used, they will be paid as bonus days at the hourly or prorated salary rate in effect at the time of payment.

Staffers who leave employment will be entitled to a payment based on unused accrued vacation time in their final paycheck.

If you have any questions, please contact Human Resources.

Announcement of new on-site gym benefit

From Benefits Office to employees

At the request of a number of employees, we have decided to add a small exercise room with treadmills, stairclimbers, and other equipment. The room will be located nearby the employee locker rooms which include changing facilities and showers.

We expect the exercise room to be open on or about June 1. Use of the facility will be limited to regular part-time and full-time employees, and will be open one hour before regular business hours, during lunch breaks, and one hour after the regular close of business.

We are excited about this new benefit and hope it will be used by many of our workers.

Announcement of new childcare benefit

From Benefits Office to employees

We are pleased to announce that Consolidated Intergalactic has contracted with Little Lumbertown to operate an on-site childcare program. The facility, which is scheduled to open on September 1, will be available to regular, full-time employees' children ages six months to five years.

For more details about the program, which will include a daily rate that is substantially subsidized by the company, please pick up a brochure and application form at the Human Resources Office.

We expect to have space for fifty children in the facility. And we will continue to offer a subsidy of an equivalent amount to employees who choose to make their own arrangements for childcare at a licensed childcare facility.

Announcement of new health club benefit

From Benefits Office to employees

In cooperation with our health insurance provider, we are pleased to offer all regular full-time employees a discount on annual membership at any of twelve selected health clubs in the greater Lumbertown area.

We encourage all of our employees to take advantage of this opportunity to have a healthier lifestyle.

Information on the program can be found in the attached brochure. If you have any questions, please contact the Employee Benefits Office.

Announcement of tuition reimbursement program

From Benefits Office to employees

We are pleased to announce the establishment of a tuition reimbursement program in cooperation with several area colleges, trade schools, and certification programs.

Effective August 15, all regular full-time employees with at least a year of service are eligible to receive reimbursement for the cost of courses at one of the approved institutions.

Upon completion of the course, we will reimburse the cost of credits and fees up to $5,250 per year, per employee. Employees who receive a grade of B or higher will receive full reimbursement up to the maximum amount; employees who receive a B- through C- will receive 50 percent of the cost up to the maximum amount. Employees who receive a D+ or lower or who do not complete the course will not be reimbursed.

All courses must be related to your current or proposed job description, and all applications must be approved by your supervisor prior to enrollment.

We expect that students will take night or weekend classes. If a particular program conflicts with regular working hours, employees may seek to arrange for a temporary flextime schedule to allow them to attend classes. Please contact your supervisor to discuss schedules and to seek approval.

Tuition reimbursement forms are available through Human Resources.

Recommended courses for tuition reimbursement program

From Benefits Office to employees

The Benefits Office has posted a list of prescreened courses available this fall at Lumbertown Community College.

Consolidated Intergalactic has worked with LCC to request curriculum elements that support the corporate mission. All of the courses on the list—which is posted on the Benefits Office Web site—are considered appropriate for reimbursement by the company.

Employees still require pre-approval from their departmental supervisor in order to apply for tuition reimbursement, and payment will be made on the basis of the grade received. In order to receive 100 percent reimbursement, students must receive a grade of B or higher.

Posting of car pool match list

From Benefits Office or Human Resources to employees

The Employee Benefits Office has posted a car pool match list online. It is our hope that this will assist staffers in finding ways to reduce the cost and save on use of energy in commuting to work.

To use the match list, go to the employee Benefits Office Web site and enter your employee number. The program will automatically fill in the form based on your home address as listed in company records; if you are commuting from a different location, please make adjustments to the form.

The software, developed in conjunction with the state Department of Transportation, displays a map that shows designated car pool parking lots and pick-up areas nearest the address you supply.

Bonus offered to car pool participants

Announcement of bonus to car pool participants:

Consolidated Intergalactic is pleased to announce its participation in a statewide program that encourages workers to use car pools for commuting. The goal is to reduce the amount of traffic on area roads by as much as 20 percent and help save the planet by cutting down on use of energy and the creation of emissions.

All employees who register with the CI car pool plan will receive the following benefits: fully subsidized "toll-free" cards that eliminate tolls on thruways and bridges and a $25 per week car-pool bonus in each paycheck. In addition, cars registered under the program will be permitted to park in the priority car pool spaces at the front of the company parking lot.

Availability of company-owned vehicles for car pools

From Benefits Office to employees

In a pilot program that will begin September 1, Consolidated Intergalactic will offer use of company-owned or company-leased vehicles for car pools of three or more employees.

The vehicles will come from the company's fleet of vehicles available to the Sales and Marketing Departments for customer calls. They will be available each day after 5 P.M. and will be expected to be back in the company parking lot by 9 A.M.

Consolidated Intergalactic will provide gasoline, insurance, and fully subsidized "toll-free" cards that eliminate tolls on thruways and bridges.

For information about the program or to register to participate, please contact the vehicle desk of the Office Services Department, at extension 3982.

Discounted mass transit passes offered

From Benefits Office to employees

Effective July 1, Consolidated Intergalactic will offer all employees the right to purchase L-RAT (Lumbertown Rapid Transit) monthly passes at a 50 percent discount. This is part of our commitment to assist in the reduction of traffic and help cut down on energy use and automotive emissions.

Monthly passes, valid on all L-RAT trains, trolleys, and buses will be available at the Benefits Office in the last week of each month.

Bus pass regulations

From Benefits Office to employees

Please be advised that effective November 1, the Lumbertown Rapid Transit System will require all users of monthly passes to show a company photo ID each time the pass is used.

According to L-RAT, the purpose of this new regulation is to prevent transfer or other unauthorized use of the transit passes.

Consolidated Intergalactic will continue to encourage the use of mass transit by offering employees the right to purchase L-RAT (Lumbertown Rapid Transit) monthly passes at a 50 percent discount.

Prepaid legal services offered

From Benefits Office or Human Resources to employees

We are pleased to offer a new benefit to all full-time permanent employees: prepaid legal services.

Lumbertown Legal Services, an independent law firm, offers a range of standard civil law services including drafting real estate documents, real estate closings, simple wills and power of attorney, and ten hours of telephone consulting on legal matters. Members can also purchase additional legal services at a discounted rate.

For information about the prepaid legal plan, please contact LLS at (727) 555-0143.

Consolidated Intergalactic is not affiliated in any way with Lumbertown Legal Services and does not benefit from referrals to the service.

Dry cleaning services for employees

From Benefits Office to employees

Save time, dress well, and save a bit of cash: The Benefits Office is pleased to offer a new service in cooperation with several Lumbertown area businesses.

Beginning June 1, representatives of three area dry cleaning, laundry, and tailoring companies will be allowed to park vans in a designated area to the right of the main entrance to our Lumbertown facility every morning between 8 and 9:30 A.M. and again from 4 to 5:30 P.M.

Employees may drop off clothing for cleaning or repairs, and depending on the service option chosen, pick up packages later the same day or several days later. For security reasons, employees will not be allowed to bring packages into the workplace.

Oil change and tune-up service for employees

From Benefits Office to employees

In cooperation with Speedy Grease, we are pleased to offer a new service for CI employees that will save time and money.

Beginning August 1, employees can make arrangements with Speedy Grease—located across the street from our main entrance—to leave their vehicles at the facility for an oil change, lube, filter change, tune-up, and other services. Speedy Grease promises to complete the work before 5 P.M. on any business day and will drive your car into the CI lot; the keys and paperwork will be left with the security guard.

The Benefits Office welcomes suggestions from employees for other services that may be offered during the work day; our goal is make it easier for staff to manage their personal affairs while allowing us to maintain our high level of productivity.

Announcement of new vision care benefit

From Benefits Office or Medical Office to employees

We are pleased to announce that we have added a new vision care benefit to our medical plan. Each employee and covered dependent is entitled to an eye exam from participating opticians and ophthalmologists once each year for a fee of $25; some providers may choose to waive the fee entirely with the purchase of eyeglasses or contact lenses.

A full list of participating providers can be found at the Benefits Office Web site; click on the "Vision Care" icon.

Announcement of hearing assessment benefit

From Benefits Office or Medical Office to employees

Our health care provider has added a new hearing assessment benefit. Employees and covered dependents can obtain one free examination every two years by a qualified audiologist or medical specialist. For further details on this enhancement please consult the attached amendment to your health care plan or call the Benefits Office help desk at extension 3456.

Free on-site hearing test

From Benefits Office or Medical Office to employees

Representatives of our health care provider will offer a free hearing assessment test to any employee on Monday and Tuesday, May 7 and 8.

Lumbertown Blue Star Health will park a specially equipped van in the south parking lot on both days; the vehicle includes a sound booth and equipment to produce an audiogram for analysis by an audiologist.

To register for a fifteen-minute appointment, please call the Medical Office at extension 3424 no later than 4 P.M. on May 4.

Announcement of new dental plan

From Benefits Office or Medical Office to employees

Consolidated Intergalactic is pleased to announce the availability of a dental plan for all of our full-time employees and dependents. Details of the plan, including covered procedures, deductibles, and monthly costs are described in the attached brochure. For further details on this enhancement please call the Benefits Office help desk at extension 3456.

Eligibility for on-campus childcare

From Benefits Office to employees

The success of our on-campus childcare facility has brought some questions about eligibility. It is our intention to be as inclusive as possible; however, the present facility is limited to no more than 120 children.

Therefore, registration for childcare will be made on the following basis:

Full-time employees will have first priority, followed by part-time workers who are employed at least twenty hours per week.

Request for childcare emergency contact information

From Benefits Office to employees

All employees who have registered children with the on-campus childcare program are requested to review and update their emergency contact form on a regular basis. The form includes your office number, personal cell phone number, and a contact number for your spouse or domestic partner. You may also include an authorized caregiver other than a family member.

We also ask that you include the name and phone number for your child's pediatrician.

Request for childcare medical information form

From Benefits Office to employees

Please review the medical information form for your child, who is currently enrolled in on-campus daycare. This form must be updated every ninety days; your child will not be permitted to continue in the program with an outdated medical form.

Be sure to indicate any allergies and all current medications on the form.

Policy on requirement for pick-up of childcare participants

From Benefits Office to employees

If your child is a participant in the on-campus daycare program, he or she must be picked up by an authorized guardian before 5:30 P.M. daily.

Authorized guardians include the employee, a spouse or domestic partner, or another person whose name, address, and personal identification (driver's license or other government-issued ID card) is on register with the company. All changes to the list of authorized guardians must be made at least twenty-four hours in advance.

Human Resources offers childcare discounts

From Benefits Office or Human Resources to employees

Consolidated Intergalactic has negotiated a discount for all full-time and part-time employees who make use of one of a group of prescreened daycare facilities in the greater Lumbertown area.

For information on the approved daycare facilities, please consult the Human Resources Web site and click on the "Childcare" icon.

Offer of special discounts on company products for employees

From Benefits Office, Human Resources, or Employment Office to employees

Any full-time employee of Consolidated Intergalactic is eligible to purchase any of the company's products at a 50 percent discount. All such purchases must be for personal use or gifts, and not for resale.

To obtain information on the program, please contact the Special Sales Department at extension 1592.

Company sponsored day at area museums, benefits

From Human Resources or Benefits Office to employees

As part of our commitment to supporting area cultural institutions, Consolidated Intergalactic is pleased to announce that we will be sponsoring Museum Month in Lumbertown in June.

Just show your CI identification card at any of the listed museums to receive free admission for you and as many as three guests. We've got a supply of bright red CI Cares lapel buttons available at the Benefits Office, and we'd love to see our area museums filled with employees wearing their badges with pride.

Discounted admission to local museum

Benefits Office to employees

Consolidated Intergalactic has become a Corporate Circle supporter of the Lumbertown Historical Association. We believe very strongly in the importance of collecting artifacts and researching the history of our hometown as a legacy for generations to come.

Our position in the Corporate Circle brings a benefit for all employees of Consolidated Intergalactic: Show your employee identification card to receive a 50 percent discount on admission for yourself and as many as three members of your family or friends.

Announcement of matching grant program

From Benefits Office to employees

During the week of May 21 through May 28, Lumbertown's award-winning public radio station KLUM-FM will be conducting its spring fundraising drive.

Here at Consolidated Intergalactic we are deeply appreciative of the contributions made by KLUM to the community, and we encourage our employees to join us in supporting this important cultural institution.

During the fundraising drive, if you call the radio station to make a pledge be sure to identify yourself as a CI employee; we will match all contributions by our staff dollar-for-dollar.

Offering energy-saving light bulbs to employees for home use

From Benefits Office to employees

As part of our commitment to reducing greenhouse emissions and protecting the environment, Consolidated Intergalactic is pleased to offer a new benefit to all employees. Throughout the month of July we will be selling energy-saving compact fluorescent light bulbs at deep discounts (below wholesale prices). Depending on the wattage, bulbs will sell for fifty to ninety cents each.

We encourage all employees to change all appropriate lamps in their homes to this new technology. According to industry estimates, you'll save about $30 or more in electricity costs over each bulb's lifetime. The compact fluorescents also produce about 75 percent less heat, so they're safer to operate and can cut energy costs associated with home cooling.

If every American home replaced just one light bulb with an Energy Star certified bulb of this design, it is estimated that we would save enough energy to light more than 3 million homes for a year, more than $600 million in annual energy costs, and prevent greenhouse gases equivalent to the emissions of more than 800,000 cars.

The bulbs, available at the Benefits Office or at Office Services, will fit into any standard screw-in light socket.

Correspondence from Benefits Office to Departments

Notice of meeting for department heads about benefits program

From Human Resources, Benefits Office, and Executive Office to department heads and employees

Human Resources invites all department heads, or their designated management-level representatives, to attend an open meeting on Tuesday, May 14, at 3 P.M. in the Chairman's Conference Room to discuss proposed changes to the company's bonus and incentive award programs.

Consolidated Intergalactic is committed to regularly reviewing all elements of our employee compensation programs to assure that all employees are treated fairly and equitably.

We currently have programs in place that award bonuses to employees in the Sales and Marketing Departments based on meeting certain revenue goals; similar programs give special recognition to staffers in production and shipping jobs for meeting specific performance levels. One of the goals of this meeting is to discuss how to offer incentives to nonsalaried workers whose performance cannot be analyzed quantitatively.

Minutes of meeting, bonus and incentive programs

From Human Resources, Benefits Office, and Executive Office to department heads and employees

Attached please find a copy of the minutes of the May 14 meeting held to discuss proposed changes to the company's bonus and incentive award programs.

Please review the minutes and submit any proposed corrections or explanations to Mary McPherson, the chairman's executive secretary, no later than May 21.

This document, which includes discussion of incentive plans that have not yet been accepted by the Board of Directors, is considered company confidential. It is intended only for the use of the person to whom it was sent, and is not to be shared with others without specific permission from the chairman of the Board.

Corrected minutes of meeting, bonus and incentive programs

From Human Resources, Benefits Office, and Executive Office to department heads and employees

Attached please find a copy of the corrected minutes of the May 14 meeting held to discuss proposed changes to the company's bonus and incentive award programs.

As several attendees noted, the original version of the minutes misstated the company's proposed guidelines for annual bonuses. Our intention is to provide a bonus in the range of 2 to 4 percent (the equivalent of one to two weeks of base pay) in any year in which the company meets its sales and profitability goals.

The previous minutes incorrectly stated that the bonus range would be 20 to 40 percent.

We apologize for any misunderstanding. Please delete any copies of the previous minutes for the May 14 meeting.

This document, which includes discussion of incentive plans that have not yet been accepted by the Board of Directors, is considered company confidential. It is intended only for the use of the person to whom it was sent, and is not to be shared with others without specific permission from the chairman of the Board.

10 Benefits Office Correspondence

Personal Correspondence from Benefits Office to Employee

Personal Correspondence from Employee to Benefits Office

Personal Correspondence from Benefits Office to Employee

Notification of vacation time accrued

From Benefits Office or Human Resources to employee

As of December 31, you will have ten days of accrued vacation time in your account, all earned this calendar year. Under company guidelines, you must use those ten days before the end of next year; otherwise, they will be converted to bonus pay days.

In the coming year, you will begin earning vacation days at the rate of one day per full month of service, up to a maximum of twelve days.

We remind all employees that requests for vacation time off must be submitted in writing to your supervisor at least two weeks in advance and approval will be granted based on the staffing needs of your department.

Notification of excess accrued vacation time

From Benefits Office or Human Resources to employee

With the end of the 2008 calendar year now two months away, we want to remind you that you have accrued ten unused vacation days that were earned in 2007.

As stated in the employee manual, you must use those ten days before the end of 2008; otherwise, they will be automatically converted into bonus pay. Vacation days earned in 2008 can be used any time from now through the end of 2009.

If you are unable to use the accrued vacation days between now and the end of the year or prefer to receive payment for their cash value, you will see a bonus in your second paycheck of January. Vacation days are converted to cash based on your hourly or base salary rate in effect at the time the check is issued.

Approval of request for vacation

From Executive Office, Benefits Office, or Human Resources to employee

Your request for the following vacation days is approved: Monday, June 2, through Friday, June 6.

With the deduction of these five days, your employee records show a current total of five remaining vacation days. You are currently accruing vacation time at the rate of .83 days per full month of service.

Please meet with your departmental supervisor no later than two days before your vacation leave begins to discuss any ongoing projects or special coverage that may be needed while you are out of the office.

Notification of vacation policy violation

From Benefits Office or Human Resources to employee

We are unable to approve your request for ten days of vacation time beginning August 1. According to your personnel records you have only four days of accrued vacation at this time and will add only one more day between now and the date of your request.

If you have any questions about your vacation accrual, please contact Human Resources.

Denial of vacation request

From Executive Office, Benefits Office, or Human Resources to employee

We regret to inform you that your request for a vacation which includes the July 4 holiday cannot be granted because of the staffing needs of your department. This is a particularly busy time for the company and also a very popular vacation period for many employees. In granting time off, we give first preference on the basis of seniority.

We apologize for any inconvenience and encourage you to look for another period of time for your vacation.

Granting personal leave of absence

From Executive Office, Benefits Office, or Human Resources to employee

We are pleased to agree to your request for a six-week unpaid leave of absence for personal reasons, a benefit that is offered to employees who have completed at least ten years of service with the company. Your job will be kept open during your absence, which will begin on September 1 and run through October 14.

During that period, your health and retirement benefits will continue under the same terms as exist at the present time. You will not accrue vacation days or personal days during your leave of absence.

Please meet with your departmental supervisor no later than one week before your leave begins to discuss any ongoing projects or special coverage that may be needed while you are out of the office.

Denying leave of absence because of lack of availability of replacement staff

From Executive Office, Benefits Office, or Human Resources to employee

We regret to inform you that we are unable to grant your requested leave of absence beginning September 1. At this time we do not have a properly trained replacement to cover your job responsibilities.

We request that you meet with your supervisor to discuss this situation and assist us in preparing for a future request for a leave of absence.

Notification of apparent violation of holiday policy

From Benefits Office or Human Resources to employee

CONFIDENTIAL

According to payroll records, you called in sick on Monday, July 16. This was scheduled to be your first day back at work after a two week–long vacation for which you were given permission.

We have noted that this is not the first time in recent years that you have shown the same pattern of extending a scheduled vacation period.

While we understand that you may indeed have had a legitimate medical reason to miss that day of work, we do want to bring to your attention Section VII of the employee manual, which asks supervisors to monitor attendance records of nonexempt employees to avoid abuse of personal and sick days. The employee manual states that the company may request verification of medical treatment.

We hope this pattern does not repeat, and may request such verification of medical treatment in the future.

Granting home and family leave

From Benefits Office to employee

We have received your request for a leave of absence to assist your wife in the care of a newborn child. Congratulations on your joyous event.

As a covered employer under the federal Family and Medical Leave Act, we are required to grant eligible full-time employees as much as twelve weeks of unpaid leave during any twelve-month period for any of these reasons:

Birth and care of a newborn child of the employee;

Arrangement for adoption or foster care for a child of an employee;

Care of an immediate family member (spouse, child, or parent) with a serious health condition; or Medical leave for an employee who is unable to work because of a serious health condition.

Please fill out the attached form and submit it to Human Resources. We also ask that you meet with your supervisor as soon as possible to discuss any ongoing projects that may need special coverage by other employees. We would also appreciate it if you would keep in touch with the HR Department at least once every two weeks to keep us up to date on your plans.

Request for unpaid time off for permissible family needs (leave of absence)

From employee to Human Resources or Benefits Office

I am writing to request an unpaid leave of two weeks to allow me to attend to an important personal matter. As stated in the employee manual, the company may grant such a leave at its discretion if a supervisor or departmental manager gives permission.

Attached is a memo from my supervisor stating that my absence for two weeks in June will not adversely affect our operations. I have assured him that I will be available for overtime if requested.

I appreciate your consideration.

Thank you.

Response to request for new benefit

From Benefits Office to employee

Thank you for your suggestion of a new benefit for our employees. We were not aware of the "affiliate" program of the Lumbertown Historical Association, and upon investigation we have determined that a corporate donation by Consolidated Intergalactic to this worthy institution will allow all of our employees to visit the museum at a deeply discounted ticket rate.

Your idea will benefit both the LHA and our employees, and we are happy to do so.

Request for details of course for tuition reimbursement

From Benefits Office to employee

We have received your application for participation in the Tuition Reimbursement Program.

Before we can approve the request, we would like to see a full course description as published by the college or trade school. Please also attach a memo in which you explain how this course relates to your current or proposed job description.

We look forward to hearing from you soon.

Request for grade report for reimbursement

From Benefits Office to employee

We have received your request for payment under our Tuition Reimbursement Program. In order to process this request, please submit an official copy of your grade report.

Under terms of the plan, we will reimburse the cost of credits and fees up to $5,250 per year, per employee. Employees who receive a grade of B or higher will receive full reimbursement up to the maximum amount; employees who receive a B- through C- will receive 50 percent of the cost up to the maximum amount. Employees who receive a D+ or lower or who do not complete the course will not be reimbursed.

Personal Correspondence from Employee to Benefits Office

Request for clarification of health benefits

From employee to Benefits Office or Human Resources

My daughter will be enrolling in college this fall. Will the company-supported health plan continue to cover her through her four years at school?

Are there any special forms I need to prepare or proof of enrollment I need to provide?

Thank you for your assistance.

Request for health benefit forms

From employee to Benefits Office or Human Resources

I would like to make a change in the health insurance plan we are enrolled in through the company. Can you please provide full descriptions of the various PPO and HMO plans, and enrollment forms for each?

Thank you.

Request to add family member to insurance

From employee to Benefits Office or Human Resources

My husband and I completed the adoption of a child on May 1. Can you please advise me what forms I need to file in order to include her under our health insurance coverage?

Notification of intention to use family and medical leave time

From employee to Human Resources or Benefits Office

I am writing to request an unpaid leave from my post as senior financial analyst under terms of the federal Family and Medical Leave Act.

I need to travel to Florida to assist with the health care for my father, who is scheduled to undergo surgery on May 10. Under terms of the law, I am allowed a leave of as much as 12 weeks; I hope that my stay in Florida will be much shorter, perhaps three or four weeks. I will keep my supervisor and the Human Resources Office advised of my plans as soon as they are set.

I regret any inconvenience this causes the company and my department.

Advising change in personal information, dependents

From employee to Human Resources or Benefits Office

Please adjust my personnel records to reflect the fact that my daughter is now married and living outside of the home. She is also covered under her husband's health plan, and according to the employee manual she is no longer covered under the Consolidated Intergalactic plan.

Thank you.

11 Business Invitations

Invitations to Employees

Invitations to Customers, Partners, and Organizations

Invitations to Employees

Announcement of open house

From Executive Office to employees, family, and friends

All members of the Consolidated Intergalactic team (and their families and friends) are invited to attend an open house at our new regional warehouse and shipping facility in Eumonia.

The building, at 4528 East West Street (just off Northern Boulevard), will be open for visitors on Sunday, August 5, from 11 A.M. to 2 P.M.

We'll be offering tours of the facility, which includes a state-of-the-art robotic parts retrieval system, and we'll be offering a down-home country barbecue in the parking lot and carnival games for the children.

We hope to see you there.

Formal invitation to employee recognition dinner

From Executive Office to employees

On behalf of the Board of Directors of Consolidated Intergalactic, I am honored to invite you and a guest to attend our annual Honors Banquet for Employees of Distinction.

Each year we make note of those members of staff who demonstrate exceptional skills and dedication in performance of their jobs. We invite winners of Employee of the Month, sales champions, and other employees nominated for their special accomplishments.

The dinner is held in the ballroom of the Lumbertown Kiwi Club, at 50 West Main Street. This year's event is scheduled for Thursday, May 31, at 7:30 P.M.

We hope you will attend. For more than thirty years, it has been our tradition to individually recognize all nominees and for the chairman of the Board to make special awards.

Please RSVP by May 15.

Announcement of Family Day

From Executive Office to employees and family

Do you miss your wife and kids? Does your husband have no idea what you do at work? Want to show off your workspace to mom and dad?

On Friday, May 18, beginning at 4 P.M., we're opening the doors to Consolidated Intergalactic for our annual Family Day. You're welcome to invite your spouse, domestic partner, children, and other members of your immediate family to come to our Lumbertown headquarters.

We'll be offering escorted tours of the manufacturing line and you're welcome to show your family around your own department. At 5 P.M. we'll gather in the south parking lot for a catered barbecue, with a surprise entertainment act.

Please submit a list of all guests you expect to attend Family Day to your departmental supervisor no later than noon on May 16; you will receive preprinted guest passes to bring home on May 17. All attendees over the age of sixteen must bring a government-issued photo ID; children sixteen or younger must be accompanied by an adult.

Announcement of Take Our Daughters and Sons to Work Day

From Executive Office to employees and family

We invite all fathers and mothers in the Consolidated Intergalactic family to bring their daughters and sons (and any other children in their immediate household) to work on Thursday, April 26.

Our purpose, shared with many other companies and organizations around the country, is to give youngsters the chance to learn about the workplace from their most important role models: you.

Children are welcome to spend the entire day with you; most area school districts permit students to take the day as a learning experience—check with the administrative office of your child's school for details.

Here at CI, we'll be offering special programs throughout the day, including demonstrations in our factory, special presentations by Human Resources about the wide range of job opportunities at companies like ours, and special entertainment running all afternoon in a tent in the south parking lot.

Please submit a list of all guests you expect to attend Take Our Daughters and Sons to Work Day to your departmental supervisor no later than noon on April 24; you will receive preprinted guest passes to bring home on April 25.

Invitation to reception for retired employees

From Executive Office to retired employees and family

Come back . . . for the day.

On Friday, September 18, we're inviting former employees of Consolidated Intergalactic to our annual Homecoming Day luncheon.

We'll include tours of the offices and manufacturing plant, a demonstration of our current products, and lunch with senior executives. And we promise a few special surprises, too.

You're welcome to invite your spouse, domestic partner, or other members of your immediate family to come to our Lumbertown headquarters.

Tours will depart at 11 A.M., and lunch will be served at 12:30 P.M. in a tent set up in the south parking lot.

We hope you'll be able to attend. Please call the Executive Office at extension 2321 to register.

Invitation to business-related social event

From Executive Office, Manufacturing Department, or department head to employee

We would like to invite you to attend an upcoming meeting of the Bright Idea of the Month awards.

The session, held to honor all employees who have made valuable suggestions for improvements to our products and services, will include a special presentation by the chairman of the Board.

The meeting will be held Monday, March 1, at 12:30 P.M. in the Directors' Dining Room on the fourth floor. Lunch will be served.

Please confirm your attendance by calling Marjorie Atled in the Chairman's Office, at extension 675.

Invitations to Customers, Partners, and Organizations

Invitation to open house

From Executive Office to honored guest

The Honorable George Thatcher
Mayor of the City of Eumonia

Dear Mayor,

On behalf of the Board of Directors of Consolidated Intergalactic, I would like to invite you to be an honored guest at an open house to mark the opening of our new regional warehouse and shipping facility in Eumonia.

At noon on Sunday, August 5, we will have a ribbon-cutting ceremony, and we would be honored to have you share in the event with company officials.

We are very pleased to be opening this building in your town, adding about fifty new jobs. We very much hope you can join us at this event. I look forward to hearing from you.

Formal invitation to elected official to meet with Board

From Executive Office to elected official

The Honorable Argent Larron
United States House of Representatives
Rayburn House Office Building
Washington, DC

Dear Congressman,

We would be honored if you would accept our invitation to meet with the Board of Directors of Consolidated Intergalactic on your next visit to Lumbertown.

The Board would like to learn more about how we can work with you to support your legislative initiative to eliminate tariffs on processed organic oils. And we would also like to tell local media about how your efforts to establish tax incentives have allowed our company to expand its local operations including our new warehouse and shipping facility in Eumonia.

Formal invitation to reception for distributors or sales partners

From Executive Office to sales partner

On behalf of all of us here at Consolidated Intergalactic, I would like to invite you and a guest to attend a special event honoring our most valuable partners: our leading distributors and sales partners.

The event will be held on Saturday, May 12, at 7:30 P.M. at the Lumbertown Marriott and will include a reception, dinner, and a surprise celebrity entertainer.

Please RSVP before May 1 by calling Mary Papelbon at extension 1007.

Formal invitation to reception for customers

From Executive Office to customers

Every year Consolidated Intergalactic turns the tables and treats its best customers to a party that we hope makes obvious our appreciation and thanks for your business.

You and a guest are invited to attend a reception and buffet dinner at the Lumbertown Lumberjack Restaurant on Friday, May 4, at 7 P.M. We'll be offering entertainment and a giveaway of gifts including a grand prize of an all-expenses-paid trip to Acapulco. (Customers whose companies do not allow them to accept gifts can arrange to request a donation to the charity of their choice.)

Please RSVP before April 15 by calling Harry Okajima at extension 7007.

Invitation to annual Career Day

From Executive Office to educational institutions

On Monday, September 21, Consolidated Intergalactic will host graduating seniors interested in a career in manufacturing.

Our annual Career Day includes tours of the offices and manufacturing plant, a demonstration of our current products, and lunch with senior executives. A special presentation by the Employment Office will discuss available career paths with Consolidated Intergalactic and tips on how to prepare for a job.

We would welcome nominations for as many as twenty-five students. As always, we're counting on academic advisors to help select the best candidates for the event; we're looking for young men and women with an interest in working in sales, marketing, engineering, and administrative jobs. Some of the jobs are available to high school graduates while others require advanced studies in a two- or four-year college.

Please contact the Employment Office at extension 3246 to discuss candidates for Career Day. The deadline for submission of names is September 5; we will issue invitations on September 12.

Invitation to participate in seminar on environmental campaign

From Executive Office to area companies

Consolidated Intergalactic will host the 2009 Lumbertown Environmental Action Seminar at its facility on Earth Day, April 22.

Representatives of all area manufacturing, service providers, transportation companies, and other commercial enterprises are invited to attend this free event. LEAS will host presentations from manufacturers of earth-friendly chemicals, solvents, processes, and heating and cooling equipment.

To register to attend, please call LEAS at (727) 555-0003 before April 19.

12 Government Affairs

To Elected Representative or Government Agency

Advocating enactment of legislation

From Executive Office to elected representative

Dear Congressman Wormsley,

I am writing to ask your support for H.R. 731, the National Small Business Regulatory Assistance Act.

As you know, our company employs more than 200 people in your district and we have plans for future expansion. However, we join with the National Association of Plumbing Fixture in asking Members of Congress to move quickly to enact this important bill that will reduce the regulatory load on small businesses.

We have made tremendous advances in our manufacturing efficiencies, and we believe we have the most dedicated and best-trained workforce. But we are constantly battling against foreign companies that do not bear the same expensive burden of regulation and taxation that we do.

I am sure that you will want to cast your vote to support jobs here in your home district.

Please feel free to contact me anytime to discuss this bill or any other matter related to our operations.

Opposing enactment of legislation

From Executive Office to elected representative

Dear Senator Siracusa,

On behalf of Consolidated Intergalactic, I am writing to express our hope that you will help defeat the proposed ad valorem tax increase on imported dyestuffs that is included in Senate Bill 103, which is scheduled for a committee hearing next week.

As you know, we have 250 employees here in Lumbertown and they are our principal asset. Although our company is nearly ninety years old, it has been many decades since we were able to use local raw materials in our manufacture.

The long-term implication of increased taxes for our company and many others like us is increased pressure to move our business out of state or even out of the country.

It is my intention to attend the hearing at the statehouse. I would be happy to testify or make my staff available to you in preparing information for the committee.

I look forward to hearing from you.

Asking for assistance in obtaining government grants

From Executive Office to elected representative

Dear Congressman Wormsley,

As always, we appreciate your legislative accomplishments on behalf of manufacturers. Much of the recent successes of Consolidated Intergalactic have been made possible by your good work.

I am writing to ask your assistance in locating federal research and development grants to support our efforts to protect the environment and save natural resources. Our manufacturing and research departments are working on a plan that would allow recycling of many of the rare oils and coatings that are applied to our nonmetallic geegaws. It would be our intent to work with our customers and the federal government to come up with an economically feasible program that would allow recapturing these materials.

I would appreciate it if you could direct us to an appropriate agency or department of the federal government where we might obtain research grants and technical assistance.

Asking for assistance in obtaining minority employment grants

From Executive Office to elected representative

Dear Congressman Wormsley,

We appreciate your support of H.R. 129, the Inner-City Job Training Corps, and are pleased to see that it has passed and been signed into law.

Here at Consolidated Intergalactic, we would be happy to be one of the first participants in the new program. Each year we have several dozen entry-level jobs that would be appropriate for inner-city youths, but we have not had great success in hiring because of gaps in education, job skills, and language barriers.

The Inner-City Job Training Corps seeks to address these problems by allowing employers and nonprofit community organizations to work together—with the assistance of federal funding—on the design of individualized job training courses that are directly aimed at available jobs.

We would appreciate any assistance you or your staff can provide in helping us get a training corps underway here in Lumbertown.

Requesting assistance in dealings with government agency

From Executive Office to elected representative

Dear Representative Espon,

I am writing to ask your assistance in resolving a problem we have encountered with the State Department of Transportation.

I have enclosed copies of recent correspondence we have received from the department in which they have denied our request for relief from an administrative ruling that upheld a decision to place a traffic barrier on State Route 52 in front of our factory.

The purpose of the barrier, according to the agency, is to prevent traffic jams caused by cars and trucks waiting to make left turns from the northbound lane of the road. Instead, the State DOT plans to require vehicles to travel an additional mile farther north to an intersection where traffic will be routed onto a tight cloverleaf to reverse directions and head south.

Under this plan, nearly all of our heavy commercial trucks and most of the vehicles of our employees will be traveling through a residential district. And over time, the extra mileage will amount to a significant waste of fuel at a time when we are all seeking ways to reduce energy consumption and pollution.

Our company has offered to donate to the state a strip of land we already own on the northbound side of the road to allow the creation of a turning lane and a through-lane on the road. We have also offered to pay the cost for a traffic officer during morning and evening rush hour.

I hope you will support us by contacting the State DOT and convincing them to accept our offer. Please feel free to call me anytime to discuss this matter.

Requesting change to traffic engineering

From Executive Office to city transportation department

We would like your assistance in improving the flow of traffic at the parking lot for our headquarters in Lumbertown.

At present, there is a standard two-way traffic light on SR50 in front of our lot. During the morning rush hour there is often a considerable backup of cars heading north and waiting for their chance to make a left turn into the lot; at the end of the day, there is a similar traffic jam of vehicles seeking to exit our lot and make a left turn to go south.

We have at times obtained assistance from the Lumbertown Police Department, employing an off-duty patrolman to direct traffic. It would seem that a better solution would be to install a computerized controller and a set of left turn arrows on the south and west faces of the traffic signal.

We would be happy to assist your department in planning for such a change, and would be willing to contribute company funds toward the cost of purchase and installation of new equipment.

Requesting legislative input on traffic engineering

From Executive Office to mayor or city council

We would like your assistance in improving the flow of traffic at the parking lot for our headquarters in Lumbertown. We have previously made a direct request to the Lumbertown City Transportation Department, but we did not receive a satisfactory response.

At present, there is a standard two-way traffic light on SR50 in front of our lot. During the morning rush hour, there is often a considerable backup of cars heading north and waiting for their chance to make a left turn into the lot; at the end of the day, there is a similar traffic jam of vehicles seeking to exit our lot and make a left turn to go south.

We would suggest that it would help traffic throughout downtown Lumbertown to install a computerized controller and a set of left turn arrows on the south and west faces of the traffic signal.

We would be happy to assist the city in planning for such a change, and would be willing to contribute company funds toward the cost of purchase and installation of new equipment.

Complaining about policies of governmental agency

From Executive Office to elected representative

The Honorable Patricia Kramden
United States House of Representatives
Washington, DC 20515

Dear Ms. Kramden,

On behalf of the Board of Directors and the 2,487 employees of Consolidated Intergalactic, I am writing to seek your help in resolving a significant problem that is threatening our ability to do business here in the Sixth Congressional District.

The Investigations Unit of U.S. Customs and Border Protection has blocked import of Organic Cold-Pressed Extra Virgin Brazil Nut Oil because of an isolated instance of drug smuggling by one supplier of this commodity.

As you may know, high-quality Brazil Nut Oil is an essential manufacturing component for many of the geegaw and doodad products of Consolidated Intergalactic.

We anticipate having to shut down two assembly lines, employing 248 of your constituents, if we do not receive fresh supplies of this oil within the next thirty days.

Our competitors in China and Guatemala face no difficulties in obtaining sufficient supplies of Brazil Nut Oil, and Customs and Border Protection does not block the importation of finished products that use the oil in their manufacture.

We ask for your immediate help in resolving this problem and saving jobs and protecting families here in Lumbertown.

We stand ready to assist you in any way. I look forward to hearing from you soon.

Congratulating official on re-election

From Executive Office to elected representative

Dear Congressman Keefe,

I was very pleased to see that the voters of our district have once again shown their good judgment and returned you to office.

We have appreciated your assistance in Washington and look forward to working with you in coming years.

Again, congratulations.

Congratulating newly elected official

From Executive Office to elected representative

Dear Senator-elect Beecher,

Congratulations on your election to the Senate.

As you know, we are one of the largest employers in Lumbertown and we hope to grow and prosper here. Please feel free to call me anytime to discuss our legislative concerns and other matters.

We look forward to working with you in coming years.

Invitation to elected official to attend press event

From Executive Office to elected official or honored guest

Councilman David Miller
Lumbertown Town Council

Dear Councilman,

We would like to invite you to join executives of Consolidated Intergalactic in hosting an appearance by Congressman Argent Larron on September 15 at 2 P.M.

Congressman Larron will be meeting with the press to discuss his legislative efforts to eliminate tariffs on processed imported organic oils and new laws offering tax incentives to manufacturers in this vital industry. As chairman of the Lumbertown Town Council's Committee on Industrial Development, we would be honored if you would introduce the congressman at the press conference.

Government Relations Planning

Distribution of proposed government submission for review

From Executive Office, Legal Office, or Compliance Office to executives, department heads, and affected staff

COMPANY CONFIDENTIAL

Enclosed please find a draft copy of the Environmental Impact Statement for the proposed expansion of the wastewater treatment facility at our Atherson location.

Please review the document for any legal, environmental, and other issues. I need your comments no later than Thursday, March 30, so that we can make final adjustments before the document is submitted the first week of April.

Until this document is formally submitted to the governmental agencies, the contents of this file is considered confidential. It must not be removed from office premises or shared with other persons not specifically listed on the distribution list on the front page of the document.

Response to request for comments on document prior to submission

From executives, department heads, and affected staff to Executive Office, Legal Office, or Compliance Office

COMPANY CONFIDENTIAL

Enclosed please find my comments on the proposed Environmental Impact Statement for the proposed expansion of the wastewater treatment facility at the Atherson location.

In general, I found the document to be without problems. I have noted several sections that need minor clarification.

However, I have marked one section that I feel should be substantially revised or removed. On page 8, in paragraphs 3 and 4, we make mention of the possibility of future expansions of the water treatment plant in decades to come.

Although this may be necessary in coming years, I feel that including it in this submission will likely result in a possibly unnecessary expansion of the agency's review of the document, which would delay the process.

Distribution of proposed government submission for final review

From Executive Office, Legal Office, or Compliance Office to executives and affected staff

COMPANY CONFIDENTIAL

Attached please find a draft copy of the Environmental Impact Statement for the proposed expansion of the wastewater treatment facility at our Atherson location.

Please review the document for any legal, environmental, and other issues. I need your comments no later than Thursday, March 30, so that we can make final adjustments before the document is submitted the first week of April.

Until this document is formally submitted to the governmental agencies, the content of this file is considered confidential. It must not be removed from office premises or shared with other persons not specifically listed on the distribution list on the front page of the document.

This message (including any attachments) is a confidential and privileged communication to the intended addressee.

If you are not the intended addressee, you have received this message in error. In that case, please permanently delete this message and call us at 999-555-0198 so that we can correct this error and avoid inconvenience in the future.

Thank you.

Response to document submitted for review

From executives and affected staff to Executive Office, Legal Office, or Compliance Office

Attached please find my comments on the proposed Environmental Impact Statement for the proposed expansion of the wastewater treatment facility at the Atherson location.

I have used the Track Changes function of Microperfect Word to indicate my proposed changes.

In general, I found the document to be without problems. I have noted several sections that need minor clarification.

However, I have marked one section that I feel should be substantially revised or removed. On page 8, in paragraphs 3 and 4, we make mention of the possibility of future expansions of the water treatment plant in decades to come.

Although this may be necessary in coming years, I feel that including it in this submission will likely result in a possibly unnecessary expansion of the agency's review of the document which would delay the process.

This message (including any attachments) is a confidential and privileged communication to the intended addressee.

If you are not the intended addressee, you have received this message in error. In that case, please permanently delete this message and call us at 999-555-0198 so that we can correct this error and avoid inconvenience in the future.

Thank you.

13 Media Relations: To Media Outlets

Announcement of press conference

From Publicity and Media Relations Department to media outlets

Consolidated Intergalactic invites all members of the print and electronic media to a press conference on Wednesday, April 19, at 2 P.M.

The session at the company's Lumbertown headquarters will feature a major announcement by Lauren Jamison, president of the company, about plans for expansion in Broome County.

Members of the media wishing to attend the conference should arrive no later than 1:45 P.M. at the main entrance lobby of the company. Escorts from the Public Relations Office will be available to bring reporters and equipment to Conference Room A.

Copies of the announcement itself, with an embargoed release time of 2 P.M., will be available through the Public Relations Office at noon on April 19.

If you have any questions about the press conference, or questions about the details of the announcement, please contact the Public Relations Office at extension 5555.

Announcement of Webcast for media

From Publicity and Media Relations Department to media outlets

Consolidated Intergalactic will "Webcast" its entire annual meeting this year. The meeting will stream live onto the Internet beginning at 9 A.M. on Monday, September 30; to view the session at that time, go to *www.webcast.consolidatedintergalactic.com*. There is no need to register to view the session.

Within an hour after the end of the annual meeting, the full video and audio of the meeting will be available on demand at the same Web address.

We encourage all stockholders, employees, customers, and other interested persons to view the Webcast. We're proud of our company and all of our people, and we use the annual meeting to salute our accomplishments, along with our sales and profit.

Announcement of video news release for media

From Publicity and Media Relations Department to media outlets

Consolidated Intergalactic's upcoming announcement of its expansion plans in Eumonia will be available in a video news release by satellite and on tape for all interested electronic news media.

The VNR will include the official announcement of the expansion as well as interviews with company executives and the architect for the new building. We will also provide B-Roll images for use as backdrops for studio reporters.

To obtain a login and password for the satellite VNR or to arrange to pick up a videotape of the same material, please contact the Media Relations Office at extension 3898.

Issuing a press release in advance of press conference

From Publicity and Media Relations Department or Executive Office to media outlets

Consolidated Intergalactic will announce a major new expansion in Lumbertown at a press conference today, April 30, at 2 P.M. in Conference Room A of our headquarters building.

Please find attached a copy of a press release with full details of the expansion.

We ask that you respect the embargo on publication or broadcast of the information in the release until 2 P.M. on April 30.

Representatives of the CI Public Affairs Office will be available at the press conference to assist reporters. In addition, a news hotline will be in operation on April 30 from 10 A.M. until 5 P.M. to answer telephone inquiries from reporters; the number is (727) 555-1001. Please note that this telephone number is not to be published or broadcast.

Announcing exhibition opening

From Media Relations to media outlets

A special exhibit celebrating the twenty-fifth anniversary of the founding of Consolidated Intergalactic will open to the public on Monday, May 5.

The show, mounted in the main lobby of the company, includes some of the earliest prototypes of geegaws, doodads, and thingamabobs made by CI, as well as old photographs, advertisements, and other memorabilia.

Members of the public can view the exhibit any weekday during the month of May between the hours of 9 A.M. and 4:30 P.M. Nonemployees are asked to park in the satellite lot on West Main Street.

Press advisory on exhibition

From Media Relations to media outlets

The geegaw that launched a company—and an entire industry—will be the centerpiece of an extraordinary exhibit that will be open to the public throughout the month of May at the worldwide headquarters of Consolidated Intergalactic in Lumbertown.

The Model 1 Involuted Reverser, handcrafted out of original growth betel nut wood by Consolidated Intergalactic founder Harry Simplon Jones in 1983, has been brought out of the vaults for the twenty-fifth anniversary celebration. Model 1, still functional, will be displayed in a temperature and humidity-controlled case in the main lobby along with more than 150 other artifacts.

Members of the media are invited to preview the show before it is unveiled at a special company gathering. The display will be available, by appointment, on Friday, May 2, from 9:30 A.M. to 2 P.M.

To arrange an appointment and discuss company executives available for interview, please contact the Media Relations Department at extension 3322.

Notice to media of availability of spokesperson

From Publicity and Media Relations Department to media outlets

Consolidated Intergalactic has designated Addie Chase as official spokesperson for the company. Please call her directly with any questions about the company or its operations; her office and cell phone number are listed on the attached business card.

As a reminder, we ask that members of the media do not call individual employees of Consolidated Intergalactic seeking information or quotes.

If you have need to speak with a particular executive or other employee of the company, please make any such arrangements through Ms. Chase.

Inviting press to demonstration

From Media Relations to media outlets

David Papi, head of Office Services at Consolidated Intergalactic, will be available for interviews and demonstrations of the first of the company's new hybrid vehicles on Thursday, August 31, from 9 A.M. to 4 P.M.

Beginning September 1, Consolidated Intergalactic will begin phasing in a fleet of hybrid vehicles for use by all sales representatives. The cars will use the latest technologies to permit use of electric batteries for low-speed travel; a small, efficient gasoline engine automatically turns on at highway speeds and when necessary to recharge the batteries.

Please call the Media Relations Department at extension 3434 to make an appointment. We will provide camera mounts to allow in-car videotaping for interviews. In addition, the south parking lot will be available for live standups from 9 A.M. to 7 P.M.

Compliment to member of media for coverage

From Publicity and Media Relations Department to media outlet

I wanted to thank you for your coverage of our recent announcement of expansion of our facilities here in Lumbertown. I thought you and your station did an excellent job of reporting the news and placing it in the context of its significant impact on the local economy.

If you have any further questions or would like to schedule a follow-up interview with Lauren Jamison or other executives of the company, please give me a call.

Letter to editor correcting error in story

From Publicity and Media Relations Department to media outlets

To the editor:

We appreciate the publication in the Lumbertown Times of the article about Consolidated Intergalactic's major expansion of its local headquarters. ("CI Plans New Automated Factory," April 20.)

However, it is important that we correct a significant misstatement in the article. While it is correct that the new assembly line will use highly sophisticated robotic assembly devices that will perform many duties formerly done by humans, we have no intention of reducing our Lumbertown workforce as a result of the new factory.

We expect that the new equipment will allow us to increase our overall production by about 20 percent without any associated reduction in staff; in fact, there will be a number of new, more skilled positions created to support the new factory. Some of those jobs will likely be filled from within Consolidated Intergalactic, while others will likely require additional employees.

Demanding retraction or correction of coverage

From Publicity and Media Relations Department to media outlets

On behalf of Consolidated Intergalactic, I am writing to ask for an immediate retraction or correction to your coverage of our April 19 announcement of expansion plans here in Lumbertown.

Your broadcast report, which aired on the 6 P.M. and 11 P.M. news on April 19, indicated that the new factory will employ 20 percent fewer workers than the existing facility. This is incorrect.

As we announced, "We expect that the new equipment will allow us to increase our overall production by about 20 percent without any associated reduction in staff; in fact, there will be a number of new, more skilled positions created to support the new factory. Some of those jobs will likely be filled from within Consolidated Intergalactic while others will likely require additional employees."

If you have any further questions about the announcement, please contact me at (727) 555-1000 extension 5555.

Submitting an article for publication

From individual to publication

Have you ever wondered how a barrel of damiana extract makes its way from a field of flowers in the jungles of Central America to an assembly line for nickel-plated geegaw detanglers in Lumbertown, Ohio?

It's a fascinating story that begins with hand-planted fields, canoe freighters, and mule trains and progresses to container ships that cross the equator to meet up with fleets of refrigerated trucks that bring the flowers from California to Ohio and into the high-technology processing plant of Consolidated Intergalactic.

I'm a quality control engineer for Consolidated Intergalactic, and I'd like to tell this story to your readers. I can provide a 1,000-word article, along with digital photos.

I look forward to hearing from you.

Offering to write an advice column

From individual to publication

I've been a loyal reader of *Geegaw and Doodad Monthly* for more than a decade. I've also been a design engineer at one of this nation's largest manufacturers of nonpareils and thingamabobs for all of that time.

I'd like to offer my expertise to your readers in a question-and-answer column that would deal with all manner of issues ranging from procurement to quality control to manufacturing.

I've enclosed some writing samples for articles I have written for the Consolidated Intergalactic Newsletter and a copy of my resume that includes my academic credentials and work experience.

I look forward to hearing from you.

14 Media Relations: To Employees and Departments

Announcements to Media Outlets

Announcement of new executives

From Publicity and Media Relations Department to media outlets

Lauren Jamison has been appointed as the new president and chief executive officer of Consolidated Intergalactic. She will take office on May 1.

"Ms. Jamison has a proven record of innovation and experience in the nonmetallic widget industry," said David Hansen, chairman of the Board of Directors of CI. "We are thrilled to add her vision and experience to our talented team."

Lauren Jamison brings more than twenty years of experience in product design, manufacturing, sales, and management. She is currently executive vice president of Associated International, an Atlanta-based dowel and ferrule manufacturer.

"I look forward to joining such a dynamic company as Consolidated Intergalactic," Ms. Jamison said. "I have much to learn, and I hope a great deal to teach."

Ms. Jamison will move to Lumbertown with her husband Jerry, a software engineer, and their two children, Marjorie and Sarah, who will enroll in Lumbertown High School in the fall.

Consolidated Intergalactic is the world's largest manufacturer and distributor of nonmetallic widgets, gadgets, and geegaws. The privately held company, headquartered in Lumbertown, employs more than 12,000 at factories and warehouses across the United States and in Canada, Japan, Luxembourg, and New Guinea.

Announcement of promotion

From Publicity and Media Relations Department to media outlets

Hendrick Cook has been appointed to the position of executive vice president for sales for the southern hemisphere. Mr. Cook, an eighteen-year-veteran in various sales and marketing positions for Consolidated Intergalactic, had previously been senior account executive for New Guinea operations for the company.

"We are very pleased to be able to promote from within," said Lauren Jamison, president of CI. "Mr. Cook is one of our most successful and creative salespeople and we look forward to continued strengthening of our position in New Guinea and Indonesia."

Consolidated Intergalactic is the world's largest manufacturer and distributor of nonmetallic widgets, gadgets, and geegaws. The privately held company, headquartered in Lumbertown, employs more than 12,000 at factories and warehouses across the United States and in Canada, Japan, Luxembourg, and New Guinea. Some 40 percent of the company's raw materials are imported from New Guinea and Indonesia, and sales of finished products to the same region represent about 20 percent of company revenues.

Announcement of retirement

From Publicity and Media Relations Department to media outlets

Jarrod Bean will be retiring from Consolidated Intergalactic on October 31. Mr. Bean has been with the company for twenty-six years, currently serving as manager of the Quality Control Unit in the Manufacturing Department.

"It is with regret, and appreciation, that we salute Mr. Bean's long years of service to the company," said Lauren Jamison, president of CI. "He is one of the pillars upon which Consolidated Intergalactic was built, and he will not easily be replaced."

Mr. Jamison is a former president of the Continental Geegaw Association, the national trade group for the industry. He has also served on the Board of Trustees of the Lumbertown Boys and Girls Club and is an active participant in a number of other community organizations.

Consolidated Intergalactic is the world's largest manufacturer and distributor of nonmetallic widgets, gadgets, and geegaws. The privately held company, headquartered in Lumbertown, employs more than 12,000 at factories and warehouses across the United States and in Canada, Japan, Luxembourg, and New Guinea.

Announcement of contribution

From Publicity and Media Relations Department to media outlets

Consolidated Intergalactic today announced a $50,000 contribution to the building fund of the Lumbertown Boys and Girls Club.

"We are deeply committed to our community," said Lauren Jamison, president of CI. "We look forward to the expansion of the club as a benefit for all of the citizens of Lumbertown, including the families of our 6,000 employees here."

Consolidated Intergalactic is the world's largest manufacturer and distributor of nonmetallic widgets, gadgets, and geegaws. The privately held company, headquartered in Lumbertown, employs more than 12,000 at factories and warehouses across the United States and in Canada, Japan, Luxembourg, and New Guinea.

Announcing new company vehicles to be hybrids

From Media Relations to media outlets

Consolidated Intergalactic, already one of Lumbertown's "greenest" companies, is extending its environmental action to the place where the rubber meets the road.

Beginning September 1, Consolidated Intergalactic will begin phasing in a fleet of hybrid vehicles for use by all sales representatives. The cars will use the latest technologies to permit use of electric batteries for low-speed travel; a small, efficient gasoline engine automatically turns on at highway speeds and when necessary to recharge the batteries.

CI expects to use at least 20 percent less gasoline per year for the vehicles, saving money and reducing pollution.

Introducing use of environment-friendly packing material

From Media Relations to media outlets

Consolidated Intergalactic's Shipping Department has gone green.

"We're happy to be able to help the environment while improving the service we provide to our customers," said Rachel Wang, director of environmental planning for the company.

Effective immediately, all packages shipped by CI will use recycled cardboard boxes and biodegradeable packing "peanuts."

"We've been looking for an alternative to Styrofoam for many years," Ms. Wang said. "Our new peanuts are made from cornstarch and quickly dissolve when exposed to water. They protect our environment and our products."

Consolidated Intergalactic is the world's largest manufacturer and distributor of nonmetallic widgets, gadgets, and geegaws. The privately held company, headquartered in Lumbertown, employs more than 12,000 at factories and warehouses across the United States and in Canada, Japan, Luxembourg, and New Guinea.

From Media Relations to Employees

Guidelines for handling of press inquiries

From Publicity and Media Relations Department to employees

All employees are reminded that it is company policy for all inquiries by a print or electronic media reporter or editor to be forwarded to the Publicity and Media Relations Department for handling.

Please do not answer any questions about the company, its products, or its staff. Do not engage in an argument with a reporter, answer a question "off the record," or respond "no comment."

Instead, obtain the name, phone number, and media affiliation of the caller and transfer the call to extension 3333.

Follow-up on press inquiry to employee

From Publicity and Media Relations Department to employees

Thank you for your professional handling of this morning's inquiry from a reporter for the Lumbertown Times. We have spoken with the reporter and given him the information he sought, along with an official response from the company.

Inviting employees to contribute artifacts to exhibition

From Media Relations to employees

As we prepare for the gala celebration of Consolidated Intergalactic's twenty-fifth anniversary in May, we would like to hear from any employees who have old photographs, sales and marketing materials, and other memorabilia dating to the founding of the company. We have our own vast collection of test models and original products from the company, but we would be thrilled to be surprised by antique geegaws, doodads, or thingamabobs that may have escaped our notice.

If you have any of this sort of material, please contact Constance Moquito at extension 2453. She will arrange pick-up of the items for scanning or other duplication and will be overseeing the development of an exhibit to celebrate the anniversary.

Any employee (or family member) who loans artifacts will be credited in the exhibit and invited to a special reception to mark its opening.

Inviting employees and family to preview of anniversary exhibit

From Media Relations to employees

All employees (and their families and friends) are invited to a special preview of the lobby exhibit that celebrates the twenty-fifth anniversary of the founding of Consolidated Intergalactic.

The Model 1 Involuted Reverser, handcrafted out of original growth betel nut wood by Consolidated Intergalactic founder Harry Simplon Jones in 1983, has been brought out of the vaults for the twenty-fifth anniversary celebration. Model 1, still functional, will be displayed in a temperature and humidity-controlled case in the main lobby along with more than 150 other artifacts.

The preview reception, including hors d'oeuvres and nonalcoholic drinks, will be held Friday, May 2, from 4:30 to 6 P.M. Special guests will include ninety-five-year-old Harry Simplon Jones, who founded the company in 1983.

Nonemployees will be asked to park in the satellite lot on West Main Street. Free shuttle bus service will run from 4:15 to 6:15 P.M. from the lot to the main offices and back.

Seeking articles for company newspaper

From Media Relations to employees

The Media Relations Department is pleased to announce the launch of CI News, a monthly newsletter for and about our employees.

The newsletter will arrive in your e-mail inbox on the first Monday of each month. (Our electronic publication will save a few trees, and there's no ink to come off on your fingers.)

The newsletter will include recaps of company announcements and press releases and will also include news about accomplishments and personal notes about our employees. To submit information for inclusion in the publication, please send it as a text document to *newsletter@consolidatedintergalactic.com*.

Please note that it is company policy not to become involved with political or religious issues.

Seeking articles from regional offices and manufacturing sites for company newsletter

From Media Relations to employees

Our monthly newsletter, *CI News,* is now in regular publication. We've heard from a number of employees in regional sales and manufacturing offices about how much they appreciate learning more about events here in Lumbertown.

We'd like to turn the tables: We are especially interested in receiving news about company and personal achievements from our staffers who are located so far away from headquarters. Please tell us about life in New Guinea, New York, and all points in between.

To submit information for inclusion in the publication, please send it as a text document to *newsletter@consolidatedintergalactic.com.*

Rejecting an article submitted for publication

From publication to individual

Thank you for your very well thought-out proposal for an article about the secret story of damiana extract in the geegaw and doodad industry.

Although your proposed article brings together the entire, fascinating story in one piece we feel that our readers already know more than enough about this subject at this time.

I would like to encourage you to look for other topics you might write about for our magazine. Please send any other ideas for stories directly to me; I will keep your name in my desktop organizer and will give any proposals you send my personal attention.

Rejecting an article submitted for publication because of conflict of interest

From publication to individual

Thank you for your proposal for an article about the geegaws and whirligigs.

It is our policy not to accept or publish articles written by persons employed in the industry. In order to offer the highest level of independent journalism, we employ our own staff of writers.

Rejecting an article submitted for publication because of political views

From publication to individual

Thank you for your proposal for an article for the *CI News*. We are always happy to publish contributions from members of staff.

However, it is against company policy to publish any articles that advocate a particular political or religious point of view.

We would welcome articles about nonpartisan community organizations as well as training or educational issues that relate to the activities of Consolidated Intergalactic.

Advisory about photographer in offices

From Media Relations to employees

A photographer will be roaming through the Executive Offices, Manufacturing Department, Shipping Department, and other departments tomorrow all day taking pictures for use in the annual report.

We're proud of all of our employees and the work we perform, but we also recognize that some people are camera-shy. If you would prefer not to be in the foreground of any photos, please alert one of the representatives of the Media Relations staff escorting the photographer.

15 Legal and Compliance Offices

Policies and Statements to Employees

Availability of legal consultation to managers

From Legal Office to employees

The Legal Office has added a twenty-four-hour hotline, available to all managers and supervisors, for consultation on any matter related to the operations of Consolidated Intergalactic.

It is the policy of the company that we address any actual or potential legal question of issue immediately. If you have any questions about the propriety of any action, any employment issue, an element of any contract or agreement, or any other element of our business you are instructed to consult with the Legal Office without delay.

The Legal Office hotline is at extension 3030. After regular business hours the phone will automatically roll over to an in-house or outside counsel on call.

Statement of policy on compliance with Sarbanes-Oxley Act

From Legal Office or Compliance Office to employees

We are committed to full compliance with all of the provisions of the Public Company Accounting Reform and Investor Protection Act of 2002, also known as the Sarbanes-Oxley Act.

At the heart of our responsibilities under the law is the requirement that we evaluate the effectiveness of all internal controls and policies related to financial reporting, and disclose the results of all assessments. Further, we must work with independent auditors who are charged with attesting to the accuracy of all such disclosures.

All department heads and any employee involved in accounting, investor relations, media relations, and government relations must receive training on their responsibilities under the Sarbanes-Oxley Act.

If you have any questions regarding this mission-critical element of our operations, please contact the Compliance Office at extension 2314.

Confirmation of training on compliance with Sarbanes-Oxley Act

From Legal Office or Compliance Office to employees

Congratulations on your successful initial training on your responsibilities under the Sarbanes-Oxley Act.

Please sign and return to the Compliance Office the attached form attesting to the completion of training. This is a required step in our compliance with the elements of the law.

Statement on compliance with antidiscrimination policy in hiring and promotion

From Legal Office, Human Resources, or Compliance Office to employees

Consolidated Intergalactic is committed to eliminating discrimination of any sort—including improper actions based on a person's race, creed, religion, sex, sexual orientation, disability, or other protected status or class—in hiring and promotion.

All employees are required to attend training classes on these matters at the time of hiring and review refresher materials or additional training at least once a year.

If you have any questions about our policies, or if you have any questions related to a current or past hiring process, please contact the Legal Office help desk at extension 3823.

Confirmation of training on compliance, antidiscrimination in hiring and promotion

From Legal Office or Compliance Office to employees

Congratulations on your successful initial training on your responsibilities as part of Consolidated Intergalactic's commitment to eliminating discrimination of any sort in the hiring and promotion processes.

Please sign and return to the Compliance Office the attached form attesting to the completion of training. This is a required step in our compliance with the elements of the law.

Policy on claims of discrimination

From Legal Office or Compliance Office to employees

Consolidated Intergalactic is committed to eliminating discrimination of any sort—including improper actions based on a person's race, creed, religion, sex, sexual orientation, disability, or other protected status or class—in hiring and promotion.

If you believe you have been improperly treated in a hiring or promotion action, please contact the Legal Office hotline at extension 6666.

Statement on commitment to statutes barring sexual harassment

From Legal Office or Compliance Office to employees

(NOTE: Discuss this letter with your legal department or outside counsel.)

Consolidated Intergalactic has a no-tolerance policy for any substantiated claim of sexual harassment in the workplace or for incidents outside of the workplace that are related to employment status.

A copy of our official policy is included in the employee handbook. All employees and supervisors are expected to understand and comply with its provisions.

If you have any questions about our policy in this regard, or if you have any concerns about the way you or another employee has been treated, please immediately contact the Legal Office hotline at extension 6666.

Confirmation of training on sexual harassment policies

From Legal Office or Compliance Office to employees

As part of our commitment to full compliance with all federal and state laws barring sexual harassment in the workplace, please sign the attached acknowledgment form and return it to the Legal Office to be kept on file.

The form acknowledges that you have read and understand our policies in this regard and that you have been informed of the proper procedures to follow in hiring, promotion, and supervision of employees.

Policy on claims of sexual harassment

From Legal Office or Compliance Office to employees

Consolidated Intergalactic is committed to a zero-tolerance policy regarding sexual harassment in the workplace or improper actions away from our place of business but related to the employment status of a member of staff.

If you have any concerns about the way you or another employee has been treated, please immediately contact the Legal Office hotline at extension 6666.

Policy on retention of records

From Legal Office, Compliance Office, or Office Services to employees

As part of the company's commitment to full compliance with federal and state laws regarding financial disclosure, prevention of discrimination in hiring, promotion, or supervision, and prevention of sexual harassment, all employees and supervisors are advised that they should immediately notify the Legal Office hotline, at extension 6666, of any actual or potential problem in these areas.

In addition, do not destroy any documents or other evidence, including electronic files and e-mails. Anything you do to remove evidence has the appearance of covering up guilt.

Policy on retention required notification before disposal of records

From Legal Office, Compliance Office, or Office Services to employees

It is company policy that all records regarding job applications, the hiring process, human resources issues, and employee evaluations be maintained and archived.

In no instance are such records to be edited or altered in any way. Paper records must be kept on file for at least two years, and after that date Human Resources must be given sixty days notice before any are destroyed.

Electronic files related to employment are not to be deleted until at least eighteen months after first created; this allows for automatic monthly backups and an annual archive of all files that will preserve information.

We do this as part of our commitment to eliminating discrimination or harassment in the hiring or supervision of any employee.

If you have any question about this policy, please contact the Legal Office at extension 6666.

Policy on backup of electronic files

From Legal Office, Compliance Office, Information Technology, or Office Services to employees

Electronic files related to employment are not to be deleted until at least eighteen months after first created; this allows for automatic monthly backups and an annual archive of all files that will preserve information.

We do this as part of our commitment to eliminating discrimination or harassment in the hiring or supervision of any employee.

The Information Technology Department automatically makes backups of all new files as they are created, and these backups are archived to offsite storage including tape, DVD, and cartridges once a week. In addition, a complete archive of all activity is recorded to an off-site storage medium once a month.

Letters to Employees

Request to meet with government agency

From Legal Office or Compliance Office to employee

Representatives of the Occupational Safety and Health Administration will be in our offices on Monday, September 12, to audit our procedures and compliance with federal regulations.

The Legal Office asks that you attend a meeting with the OSHA inspectors on September 12 at 2 P.M. to answer any questions they may have. Please call James Earl in the Legal Office, at extension 8934 to set up an appointment to discuss the procedure for the meeting and to identify any documents or files you may be asked to produce.

Requesting employee meet with in-house lawyer or outside counsel for briefing

From Legal Office or Compliance Office to employee

To assist the Legal Office and our outside counsel in preparation of the company's response to a workers compensation case, you are requested to attend a meeting on Tuesday, October 5, at 10 A.M.

The session, to be held in the Legal Office, will discuss the work performance and other issues related to the employment of Robert Bruney who worked under your supervision. Please bring with you any paper files and notes you have that relate to this matter; we will also review all electronic files on record with the Employment Office, Human Resources, the Health Office, and any other relevant documents.

This meeting is considered company confidential, conducted under attorney-client privilege. Please do not discuss this case with anyone other than the attorneys without specific permission from the Legal Office.

Please call James Earl in the Legal Office, at extension 8934, if you have any questions prior to the meeting.

Requesting employee meet with in-house lawyer or outside counsel for briefing on legal procedure

From Legal Office or Compliance Office to employee

As you are aware, you are scheduled to give sworn testimony on June 1 to an administrative officer investigating a workers compensation claim.

We ask that you meet with James Earl in the Legal Office on May 29 at 9 A.M. to review the procedures for the testimony and discuss the facts of the case.

It is the policy of Consolidated Intergalactic that all employees provide all legally requested documents and testimony and cooperate with government authorities in a proper manner; the purpose of this meeting is to answer any questions you may have about the process and to assist you in gathering information in anticipation of the hearing.

Notification of scheduled deposition

From Legal Office or Compliance Office to employee

As you are aware, you are scheduled to answer questions from opposing counsel on August 2 in a deposition regarding a product liability case.

We ask that you meet with James Earl in the Legal Office on May 29 at 9 A.M. to review the process involved in giving a deposition and to review the facts of the case. Mr. Earl will be present with you during the deposition and will be able to raise objections and otherwise represent the company's interests in this matter.

It is important that you do not discuss the facts of this case or any opinions you have about the matter that is in contention with any other employee or with any outsider. Please refer any questions about the case to Mr. Earl, at extension 3242.

Legal Forms

Legal release for submitted product suggestion

From Legal Office or Compliance Office to individual

(NOTE: Check with your legal department or outside legal counsel if you have any concerns about proper use of this release form.)

Thank you for submitting an idea for a possible product or service.

Here at Consolidated Intergalactic our own research and development laboratory is constantly working on projects generated within the company, and we also enter into licensing agreements with individuals and other companies for the use of patented ideas.

It is possible that your idea is one that we are already working on, or one that another person or company may have already developed.

For that reason, we must ask that you read and agree to the terms of this letter before we review your idea.

By signing this release, you acknowledge that

- Consolidated Intergalactic or another company or individual may have independently developed its own product or service which may be similar to your idea;
- Consolidated Intergalactic accepts no obligation to hold the details of your idea for a product or service in confidence;
- Consolidated Intergalactic accepts no responsibility for damage or loss to any samples or other materials you may have submitted, and will only return them to you if return shipping costs are prepaid; and
- Consolidated Intergalactic will only pay such compensation, licensing fee, or royalties as are agreed to if we accept the idea from you and sign a contract with you for its use.

If you agree to these terms and conditions, please sign below and return this form to the Legal Office of Consolidated Intergalactic at the address listed on this letter.

Photo release form, simple

From Legal Office or Compliance Office to individual

(NOTE: Check with your legal department or outside legal counsel if you have any concerns about proper use of this release form.)

Your name:
Your address:
Your phone:

    With my signature below, I hereby grant Consolidated Intergalactic permission to use my picture in publicity and advertising campaigns related to the products and operations of the company. I will not receive payment for the use of my image and release Consolidated Intergalactic from any liability related to such use.

Signature:
Date:

Photo release form, detailed

From Legal Office or Compliance Office to individual

(NOTE: Check with your legal department or outside legal counsel if you have any concerns about proper use of this release form.)

Photographic Release and Consent Agreement

    I hereby grant to Consolidated Intergalactic the irrevocable right and permission to use photographs of me (or group photographs in which I am included) for illustration, promotion, art, advertising, or commercial trade, or for any other purpose whatsoever.

    Further, unless this sentence is stricken from this release, I grant Consolidated Intergalactic to use my name in connection use of the photograph or photographs.

    I grant permission to Consolidated Intergalactic to copyright any use of my image in its own name or to license or assign the rights to others throughout the world. I also permit Consolidated Intergalactic to use or reuse, publish, republish, modify, or edit the image, and combine my image with any other copyrighted matter, in any media now available or developed at a later time. Consolidated Intergalactic may sell, trade, assign, license, or transfer any rights granted to it under this release and this authorization shall transfer to the new owner or licensee without limitation.

    I hereby release and discharge Consolidated Intergalactic from any and all claims related to the use of my image including claims for libel or invasion of privacy.

    This release shall be binding upon me and my heirs, legal representatives, and assigns. I certify that I am age eighteen or older and have the right to sign this release in my own name. If I am younger than eighteen years of age, this release shall be valid only if signed by a parent or legal guardian.

This consent applies to all images taken or obtained in the time period beginning (DATE) and ending on (DATE) or at the end of my last day of employment by Consolidated Intergalactic.

(Name of Grantor of Permission)
(Signature of Grantor of Permission)
(Date signed)
(Address)
(City, State, Zip)

Addendum to photo release form granting permission by parent or guardian

From Legal Office or Compliance Office to individual

(NOTE: Check with your legal department or outside legal counsel if you have any concerns about proper use of this release form.)

As the parent or guardian of the above-named minor, I hereby consent to the terms of the above release on behalf of a minor child.

(Name of parent or legal guardian)
(Signature of parent or legal guardian)
(Address)
(Date signed)

Video release form for minor

From Legal Office or Compliance Office to individual

(NOTE: Check with your legal department or outside legal counsel if you have any concerns about proper use of this release form.)

(Name of minor)
(Date of birth of minor)
(Name of parent/guardian)
(Address)
(City, State, Zip)
(Daytime telephone)

I am the parent or legal guardian of the above-named minor child. I hereby grant consent to Consolidated Intergalactic to take film or digital images, motion pictures, or video and use the images for any legal purpose including advertising, promotion, and sales.

I release Consolidated Intergalactic from any liability for any claim related to the use of such images, film, or video recordings.

(Name of parent or guardian)
(Signature of parent or guardian)
(Date)

Request for use of copyrighted material

From employee or Legal Office to individual or other company

(NOTE: Check with your legal department or outside legal counsel if you have any concerns about proper use of this release form.)

I am writing to request permission to make use of copyrighted material in a project, as described below.

Material requested: (Name of book, publication, electronic media, film, or other)

We seek to use this material in the following manner: (DESCRIBE TYPE OF USE).

We request nonexclusive worldwide rights in all languages in any and all printed, filmed, or digital media now existing or developed at a later time. We seek the right to publish, sell, distribute, or transmit the material in any fashion.

We will be happy to include such acknowledgment of the author and copyright information as you would request.

We appreciate your assistance and look forward to receiving permission for this use of copyrighted material.

(Name of requestor of permission)

(Signature of requestor of permission)

(Date of request)

Grant of Permission

Regarding the above request for authorization to make use of copyrighted material, we grant permission for the stated use. I certify that I am an authorized representative of, or the actual copyright holder, and have permission to give such authorization.

Name of person granting permission:

Signature of person granting permission:

Title of person granting permission:

Requested copyright credit to be published:

Date of permission:

Noncompete agreement

From Legal Office or Compliance Office to employee

(NOTE: Check with your legal department or outside legal counsel if you have any concerns about proper use of this release form.)

The following contract between Consolidated Intergalactic (the Company) and the undersigned employee (Employee) summarizes the terms of a noncompete agreement.

For good consideration and as an inducement for the Company to offer employment, the Employee agrees not to compete directly or indirectly with any of the business activities or products of the Company during the period of employment and for a period of (NUMBER) years following termination from employment for any reason.

For purposes of this agreement, "not to compete" means that the Employee or former employee shall not own, operate, manage, or otherwise participate in the management or conception of a business that is the same as or substantially similar to or competitive with any of the present products or services of the Company, or any products or services the Company may add during the Employee's period of employment.

Further, the Employee may not use to his or her own benefit or disclose to any third party any confidential information (including trade secrets, customer information, and financial data) obtained during employment covered by this agreement.

This agreement is binding upon both parties, their successors, and assigns.

Date of agreement:

Employee name:

Employee signature:

Company representative name:

Company representative signature:

Confidentiality agreement

From Legal Office or Compliance Office to third party

(NOTE: Check with your legal department or outside legal counsel if you have any concerns about proper use of this release form).

The following contract between Consolidated Intergalactic (the Company) and the undersigned client, consultant, manufacturer, or other third party (the Recipient) summarizes the terms of a confidentiality agreement.

The Company proposes to disclose certain relevant confidential or proprietary information to the Recipient for a specific purpose as agreed to between the parties.

The term "confidential or proprietary information" is deemed to include any such information identified as such by the Company and conveyed or disclosed to the Recipient under notice that it falls within this category. In general, confidential and proprietary information includes financial information, customer data, technology, research, marketing plans, sales data, and other such information whether in written, printed, or electronic form or orally disclosed.

The Recipient agrees that any such information identified as confidential or proprietary is to be used only for the purposes agreed upon by the Company and the Recipient and is not to be used by the Recipient for its own advantage or disclosed to any third party in any manner without the prior written authorization of the Company. The Recipient may not assign this agreement or any interest contained within it without the Company's prior written consent.

At the request of the Company, the Recipient shall return all confidential or proprietary information (including any copies made) to the Company within five (5) days of written request.

The Recipient agrees not to disclose the fact that it has in its possession confidential or proprietary information or that it has signed a confidentiality agreement.

The term of this agreement shall begin on the date this agreement is signed and cannot be ended by the Recipient without the specific written permission of the Company. The obligations contained in this agreement cannot be breached as the result of bankruptcy or other financial reorganization, sale, or merger of the business of the Recipient, or as the result of any disagreement or termination of business relations between the Company and the Recipient.

If information included under terms of this agreement becomes public because of disclosure by the Company or by a third party, the Recipient shall have no further obligations regarding the specific confidential information that has become public.

This Agreement shall be governed and construed in accordance with the laws of the United States and the State of (STATE) and the Recipient consents to the exclusive jurisdiction of the state and federal courts in that region for adjudication of any dispute arising out of this Agreement. The Recipient agrees that in the event of any breach or threatened breach by Recipient, the Company may obtain, in addition to any other legal remedies which may be available, such equitable relief as may be necessary to protect the Company against any such breach or threatened breach.

If any part of this agreement is determined by an appropriate court to be invalid or unenforceable, all of the remaining terms of the agreement will remain in full force and effect as if such invalid or unenforceable term had never been included.

IN WITNESS WHEREOF, the parties have executed this Agreement as of the date first above written.

Date of agreement:

Recipient company name:

Authorized signatory for recipient:

Signature of authorized signatory for recipient:

Company representative name:

Company representative signature:

16 Crisis Management

Bulletins to Media Outlets

Bulletins and Notices to Employees and Customers

Bulletins to Media Outlets

Bulletin: Fire damages warehouse

From Media Relations to media outlets
E-mail Press Release to Media
Monday, May 21
6:15 A.M.

A fire has seriously damaged the main warehouse at the Lumbertown headquarters of Consolidated Intergalactic. Several members of the staff were injured.

The blaze, which broke out at approximately 1:10 A.M. this morning, appears to have been limited to the warehouse facility. Firefighters from Lumbertown as well as mutual aid companies from Eumonia and other area communities were on the scene almost immediately.

The late shift at Consolidated Intergalactic was evacuated from the building.

Further details will be released as soon as they are available.

Update on fire at warehouse

From Media Relations to media outlets
E-mail Press Release to Media
Monday, May 21
8:15 A.M.

Firefighters have extinguished the blaze at the main warehouse at the Lumbertown headquarters of Consolidated Intergalactic.

Three members of the Consolidated Intergalactic Security Office were injured in the initial response to the fire, which broke out at approximately 1:10 A.M. this morning. One of the staffers is in critical condition at Lumbertown Community Hospital; the other two injuries are described as minor and not life-threatening.

"We are thankful for the heroic efforts of our staff as well as area firefighters," said Consolidated Intergalactic President and Chief Executive Officer Daniel Keyes. "Our prayers and hopes go out to the families of the injured staff."

The Consolidated Intergalactic headquarters and plant in Lumbertown will be closed today. Employees are being notified by telephone and pager, and area news media are asked to assist in advising staff of the situation. An emergency hotline for employees has been set up at (727) 555-0101.

The fire appears to have been limited to the warehouse facility. Firefighters from Lumbertown as well as mutual aid companies from Eumonia and other area communities were on the scene almost immediately.

The late shift at Consolidated Intergalactic was evacuated from the building.

Further details will be released as soon as they are available.

Statement to the press about fatality in fire

From Media Relations to media outlets
E-mail Press Release to Media
Monday, May 21
11:30 A.M.

It is with great sadness that we report that Eugene Orsillo, a fifteen-year veteran of the Security Office of Consolidated Intergalactic in Lumbertown, died this morning as the result of injuries suffered in a fire at the main warehouse.

"A member of our family has fallen and we are heartbroken," said President and Chief Executive Officer Daniel Keyes. "Mr. Orsillo was injured doing his duty: evacuating others from the building in an emergency."

Two other members of the Consolidated Intergalactic Security Office received minor injuries in the initial response to the fire. All other members of staff in the building were able to evacuate safely.

The cause of the blaze is under investigation but appears to have been caused by an electrical problem in air handling equipment. The fire, which broke out at approximately 1:10 A.M. this morning, heavily damaged the warehouse and its contents.

Firefighters from Lumbertown and mutual aid companies from Eumonia, Central Square, and East Westfield fought the fire for more than three hours before bringing it under control. Damage was contained in the warehouse building and did not spread to the manufacturing or administrative sections of the headquarters.

Eugene Orsillo, fifty-seven, joined Consolidated Intergalactic in 1993. He is survived by his wife Amelia and his son Arthur.

The company will announce plans for a memorial service later this week.

Consolidated Intergalactic's headquarters is closed today. The Manufacturing and Technical Departments will reopen at 4 P.M. today and Executive Offices will reopen at ordinary hours on Tuesday.

Consolidated Intergalactic is the world's largest manufacturer and distributor of nonmetallic widgets, gadgets, and geegaws. The privately held company, headquartered in Lumbertown, employs more than 12,000 at factories and warehouses across the United States and in Canada, Japan, Luxembourg, and New Guinea.

Announcement of memorial service for employee killed in warehouse fire

Media Relations Office or Executive Office to media

Employees of Lumbertown-based Consolidated Intergalactic will gather Friday for a special memorial service honoring the memory of Eugene Orsillo, who died in a fire at the company's warehouse on May 21.

The memorial will be held Friday, May 25, beginning at 12:30 P.M. in a tent that will be set up in the south parking lot of the headquarters facility.

In attendance will be members of the family of Mr. Orsillo, the Board of Directors and executives of Consolidated Intergalactic, and several thousand employees of the company.

Daniel Keyes, president and chief executive officer of the company will make a special announcement of plans to honor Mr. Orsillo.

Note to Media: To arrange to bring satellite trucks and other broadcasting equipment to the ceremony, please contact Media Relations at extension 2348. Trucks can enter the south parking lot between 11:00 and 11:30 A.M. on May 25.

Announcement of memorial fund for former employee

Media Relations to media

At a memorial for fallen hero Eugene Orsillo, who died in a fire at Consolidated Intergalactic's warehouse on May 21, the company announced the establishment of the Orsillo Scholarship.

The award will pay full expenses for four years of college, and will be given every year to a child of a current or former employee of Consolidated Intergalactic. The first recipient of the award will be Arthur Orsillo, a graduating senior at Lumbertown High School and son of Eugene Orsillo.

"We could not think of a better way to honor the sacrifice of Eugene Orsillo than to help a child fulfill his or her dream of higher education," said Daniel Keyes, president and chief executive officer of Consolidated Intergalactic. "And though we wish this sad event had never happened, we are proud to be able to help Mr. Orsillo's own family with the first scholarship."

The Orsillo scholarship will be awarded each year on the anniversary of the fire, with the recipient selected by a committee that will include a company representative, a member of the Orsillo family, and an administrator from the Lumbertown School District. Each year's winner will be judged on the basis of his or her contributions to the community and their academic record.

In brief remarks at the ceremony, Amelia Orsillo thanked the company for its support. "My husband was very proud of his career at Consolidated Intergalactic, and I am sure he would be happy to know that CI has chosen to take care of his family in this way," she said.

Death of top executive

From Media Relations to media outlets
E-mail Press Release to Media
Wednesday, January 5
9:00 A.M.

Biff Isaak, chairman of the Board of Consolidated Intergalactic, died early this morning at Lumbertown Community Hospital.

Mr. Isaak, 80, had been taken to the hospital last night complaining of chest pains. According to his family, he passed away at about 5:15 A.M., apparently as the result of a heart attack.

"We join Mr. Isaak's family in this great loss," said CI's President and chief Executive Officer Daniel Keyes. "He will be deeply missed. Our thoughts and prayers are with his wife Karen and the rest of his family."

Death of top executive, details of memorial service

From Media Relations to media outlets
E-mail Press Release to Media

Consolidated Intergalactic employees will gather tomorrow morning, January 7, at 9 A.M. for a memorial service and remembrance of Biff Isaak, chairman of the Board, who died yesterday at Lumbertown Community Hospital.

Mr. Isaak had been a member of the Board of Directors of Consolidated Intergalactic for ten years. He joined the Board after retiring as senior executive vice president for sales and marketing. All told, he had worked for CI for nineteen years.

According to Daniel Keyes, president and chief executive officer of the company, Mr. Isaak had been responsible for many of CI's most innovative marketing practices, including our Web-based sales and order tracking.

Mr. Isaak, eighty, was born in Eumonia. He attended Lumbertown Community College and later obtained advanced degrees from Eumonia Technical Institute and the Massachusetts Institute of Technology. He was a fellow of the International Association of Organic Whirligig Manufacturing.

Active in a number of civic and charitable organizations, Mr. Isaak was on the Board of Directors of Lumbertown Cares.

He is survived by his wife Karen, his son Osborne, and two grandchildren.

The memorial service at Consolidated Intergalactic will be held in a tent in the south parking lot of the company. Family members and friends will join employees of the company.

Funeral arrangements are being handled by the family, and will be private.

Members of the media seeking to cover the memorial service at Consolidated Intergalactic are asked to call the Media Relations Department hotline at extension 2363 to arrange access to our facilities. Any satellite trucks must be in place no later than 7:30 A.M. on January 7.

Bulletins and Notices to Employees and Customers

Advisory to staff of closure of building because of emergency

From Human Resources or Office Services to employees
Emergency E-mail to staff
Monday, May 21
8:15 A.M.

All employees scheduled to work the day shift at Consolidated Intergalactic headquarters in Lumbertown today are advised that the facility will be closed and that they are not to report to work.

An overnight fire heavily damaged the main warehouse of the plant. Fire, rescue, and emergency crews are still on the scene.

Three members of the Consolidated Intergalactic Security Office were injured in the initial response to the fire. One of the staffers is in critical condition at Lumbertown Community Hospital; the other two injuries are described as minor and not life-threatening.

"We are thankful for the heroic efforts of our staff as well as area firefighters," said Consolidated Intergalactic President and chief Executive Officer Daniel Keyes. "Our prayers and hopes go out to the families of the injured staff."

An emergency hotline for employees has been set up at (727) 555-0101. Please also continue to check your e-mail or pager devices for updates throughout the day.

At this time, we expect to resume operations at the Lumbertown plant with the second manufacturing shift, beginning at 4 P.M.

Statement to employees about fatality at warehouse

From Human Relations or Executive Office to employees
E-mail Statement to Employees
Monday, May 21
11:30 A.M.

It is with great sadness that we report that Eugene Orsillo, a fifteen-year veteran of the Security Office of Consolidated Intergalactic in Lumbertown, died this morning as the result of injuries suffered in a fire at the main warehouse. Two other staffers are recovering from nonlife-threatening injuries.

"A member of our family has fallen and we are heartbroken," said President and Chief Executive Officer Daniel Keyes. "Mr. Orsillo was injured doing his duty: evacuating others from the building in an emergency."

Because the fire was contained in the warehouse, we will reopen the headquarters building at 4 P.M. today for manufacturing, maintenance, and Office Services personnel. Other staffers are asked to report for work at their regular hours tomorrow, Tuesday, May 22.

An emergency hotline for employees has been set up at (727) 555-0101. Please also continue to check your e-mail or pager devices for updates throughout the day.

Eugene Orsillo, fifty-seven, joined Consolidated Intergalactic in 1993. He is survived by his wife Amelia and his son Arthur.

The company will announce plans for a memorial service later this week.

Statement to returning staff after fire at warehouse

From Human Relations or Executive Office to employees
E-mail Statement to Employees

We return to work this morning with heavy hearts. We are thankful for the assistance of firefighters and emergency response workers who fought the fire in our warehouse yesterday, and we are grateful that more than 100 staffers were able to safely evacuate from our Lumbertown building early Monday.

But nothing can replace the loss of Eugene Orsillo, a dedicated employee who rushed toward the fire while everyone else was leaving the building. His efforts, as well as those of Fred Thomas and Brad Maas, were a demonstration of the highest level of bravery and dedication.

Fred and Brad are both recovering from minor burns and scrapes.

We have rented temporary warehouse space at the former Ace Moving Company building in downtown Lumbertown; we will also be relocating much of our shipping operations to that building. We expect that it will be at least six months before we can reopen the warehouse at headquarters.

I will be sending out a statement to all employees tomorrow with the details of a memorial service for Eugene Orsillo and other plans to honor his memory.

Announcement of memorial service for employee killed in fire

From Human Relations or Executive Office to employees
E-mail Statement to Employees

All employees are invited to attend a memorial service for Eugene Orsillo this Friday at 12:30 P.M.

Participants will include the Board of Directors, executives, coworkers of Mr. Orsillo, and members of his family.

We will be setting up a tent in the south parking lot for the event.

Death of top executive

From Media Relations to employees
E-mail Press Release to employees
Wednesday, January 5
9:00 A.M.

It is with the deepest of regrets that we must report that Biff Isaak, chairman of the Board of Consolidated Intergalactic, died early this morning at Lumbertown Community Hospital.

Mr. Isaak, 80, had been taken to the hospital last night complaining of chest pains. According to his family, he passed away at about 5:15 A.M., apparently as the result of a heart attack.

We join Mr. Isaak's family in this great loss. He will be deeply missed. Our thoughts and prayers are with his wife Karen and the rest of his family.

We will advise you of plans for the funeral and a company memorial service as soon as they are available.

Daniel Keyes, President and Chief Executive Officer
Consolidated Intergalactic

Death of top executive, details of memorial service

From Executive Office to employees

E-mail Press Release to employees

All employees and their family and friends are invited to attend a memorial service and remembrance of chairman of the Board Biff Isaak tomorrow morning, January 7, at 9 A.M.

The memorial will be held in a tent in the south parking lot of the company. Family members and friends will join employees of the company. Funeral arrangements are being handled by the family, and will be private.

We have made arrangements to have all telephones covered during the service by temporary workers.

Mr. Isaak had been a member of the Board of Directors of Consolidated Intergalactic for ten years. He joined the Board after retiring as senior executive vice president for sales and marketing. All told, he had worked for CI for nineteen years.

Daniel Keyes, President and Chief Executive Officer
Consolidated Intergalactic

Death of top executive, details of memorial service, for customers and vendors

From Executive Office to customers and vendors

All of us here at Consolidated Intergalactic suffered a great personal loss on January 5 with the unexpected death of Biff Isaak, chairman of the Board.

Mr. Isaak had been a member of the Board of Directors of Consolidated Intergalactic for ten years. He joined the Board after retiring as senior executive vice president for sales and marketing. All told, he had worked for CI for nineteen years.

"Many of our customers considered Biff a friend and partner," said Daniel Keyes, president and chief executive officer of the company. "He will be deeply missed by all of us."

Mr. Isaak, eighty, was born in Eumonia. He attended Lumbertown Community College and later obtained advanced degrees from Eumonia Technical Institute and the Massachusetts Institute of Technology. He was a fellow of the International Association of Organic Whirligig Manufacturing.

Active in a number of civic and charitable organizations, Mr. Isaak was on the Board of Directors of Lumbertown Cares.

He is survived by his wife Karen, his son Osborne, and two grandchildren.

In a statement issued by the Board of Directors of Consolidated Intergalactic, it was announced that Charles Dylan, head of the executive compensation subcommittee, will serve as interim chairman of the Board while a search committee seeks a new member.

17 Community Organizations: From Company and Individuals

From Company to Community Organization

From Individual to Community Organization

From Company to Community Organization

Support for community organization

From Human Resources, Executive Office, or department head to employees

Consolidated Intergalactic will be sponsoring "CI Day" at Lumbertown Stadium on Saturday, May 26, for the baseball game between the Lumbertown Jacks and the Eumonia Harmonics. First pitch is scheduled for 2 P.M.

Any employee can pick up free tickets for themselves and all members of their immediate family at the Benefits Office between now and 5 P.M. on May 25.

As part of Consolidated Intergalactic's commitment to supporting community organizations, the company has made a major donation to the Lumbertown Jacks. We hope to see a large turnout of CI employees at the ballgame; we'll all be seated along the right field line—hot dogs, popcorn, and soft drinks will be free for everyone in our section.

Offering donation of used office equipment

From Office Services to community organizations

Consolidated Intergalactic has several dozen computers, printers, copiers, and other pieces of used office equipment that we would be happy to donate to community organizations.

Each of the devices has been tested and found to be in working order, but we cannot make any further guarantees about their condition. All are supplied with all available cables, accessories, and software (where applicable).

In past years some community organizations have chosen to make use of this sort of equipment in their own operations, as tools in training courses, or as the source of spare parts for existing office equipment.

A list of the equipment is attached to this letter. If you are interested in obtaining any of these devices, please contact me at extension 3872. Distribution will be made on a first-come, first-served basis.

Announcing mentoring program in community

From Human Resources or Employment Office to community organizations

Continuing a twenty-year tradition of service to the community, Consolidated Intergalactic will once again offer the services of more than a hundred of its current and retired employees as mentors to young students and entrepreneurs.

For information about obtaining the assistance of a CI Mentor, please contact Human Resources at extension 4325.

Services are provided without charge during evenings and weekends. CI recognizes participants in the program with an annual banquet and special monetary awards for exceptional service.

Offering mentors for community businesses

From Human Resources to community organizations

Once again, Consolidated Intergalactic would like to lend a hand to area businesses.

Our annual Rent-a-Mentor program provides executives and professionals to meet with small businesses to offer advice on product and financial planning, insurance, banking, and other essentials for success.

There's no charge to "rent" one of our mentors, of course. We've developed this program in hopes of helping to keep the entire Lumbertown economy vital and growing, and we're very proud of our accomplishments over the past decade.

For information in obtaining assistance from one of our experts, please call Human Resources at extension 9823.

Announcing discounted products or services available to community organizations

From Human Resources or Employment Office to community organizations

Nonprofit organizations serving the greater Lumbertown area are invited to apply for a "CI Cares" account which allows purchase of any Consolidated Intergalactic product at a 50 percent discount.

Orders must be placed through a designated salesperson, and products must be picked up at a CI warehouse by the organization. CI Cares is open to any nonprofit, nonsectarian organization. For details, please contact the Special Sales Department at extension 1592.

Communicating information about community organizations through distributions made by Human Resources

From Human Resources or Employment Office to community organizations

Eligible community organizations are invited to submit proposals to distribute information about their campaigns and offerings to employees of Consolidated Intergalactic. Available options include inclusion of flyers in paycheck or direct deposit envelopes, posters in break rooms, and links on the CI Web site.

This program is open to nonprofit, nonsectarian, nonpolitical organizations. For information about communicating with our employees in this way, please contact the Payroll Services Department at extension 4749.

Responding to request for contribution from community organization

From Human Resources or Employment Office to community organization

Thank you for your request for a contribution from Consolidated Intergalactic. We are committed to assisting organizations in our community in any way we can.

For details on the criteria necessary for inclusion in our donation or matching grant programs, please contact the Payroll Services Department at CI at extension 2348. Organizations must meet IRS regulations as a nonprofit, and must not be political or religious in nature.

Seeking discount for company sponsorship

From Human Resources or Executive Office to community organization

Once again, Consolidated Intergalactic is prepared to sponsor a day at the ballpark for all of our employees and their families. We expect to purchase between 2,000 and 3,000 tickets and provide food for all attendees.

We would like to propose the same terms as last year. We ask that the Lumbertown Lumberjacks set aside at least 3,000 tickets in a contiguous section of the ballpark for a weekend day game in July or August. For our part, we commit to purchase at least 2,000 seats at $10 each and food coupons (for any item except alcoholic beverages) worth $10 for each seat purchased.

We will set a cutoff for distribution of tickets of three days before the ballgame and release any unused tickets beyond the 2,000 minimum at that time.

We are pleased to be able to support an important community organization in this way while also treating our employees and their families to a day at the ballpark.

I look forward to hearing from you soon to confirm your acceptance of our offer and to select a date for this special event.

Responding to request for company presentation at school

From to Media Relations or Executive Office to community organization

Thank you for your invitation to meet with the students of your business administration class. We would be happy to send one of our CI Mentors to an upcoming session; please contact me to discuss details.

Because we are a privately held company, our representative will not be able to discuss details of our financial results in specifics but will be able to discuss the corporate mission and business structure of Consolidated Intergalactic.

Response to request for company presentation at organization

From Media Relations or Executive Office to community organization

Thank you for your invitation to speak at an upcoming meeting of the Lumbertown Do-Gooders Club. I have been asked by the Public Affairs Office to represent the company, and I will be happy to meet with your members.

Please contact me to set up a date and to discuss details. I'd like to bring a laptop computer and a projector for a presentation about CI.

Response to request for executive as speaker

From Media Relations or Executive Office to community organization

Thank you for your invitation for a senior manager to meet with the members of the Lumbertown Executive Council. We are honored to be invited, and I have asked Frances Audrey to represent the company; Ms. Audrey is executive vice president for community affairs and an excellent representative for all of us here at Consolidated Intergalactic.

Please contact Ms. Audrey directly at extension 9782 to arrange details.

From Individual to Community Organization

Making financial contribution

From individual to community organization

Enclosed please find my gift to the building fund for the Lumbertown Community Hospital. I am pleased to be able to support such an essential part of our town, and I will be encouraging all of my friends and business associates to join me in offering a helping hand.

Making financial contribution in response to fundraising request

From individual to community organization

I am pleased to be able to join with others in Lumbertown in supporting the Community Cares program. Reading your appeal letter, I was very impressed with the broad reach of services provided to our community.

I would like to make a contribution at the Founder's Circle level. Enclosed please find a check in the amount of $500.

Declining financial contribution in response to fundraising request

From individual to community organization

I appreciate the letter you sent me inviting me to participate in the Lumbertown Community Hospital building fund campaign. Unfortunately, at this time I am not in a position where I can make a contribution.

Declining financial contribution in response to fundraising request, for cause

From individual to community organization

I appreciate the letter you sent me inviting me to participate in the Lumbertown Cares fundraising campaign. Unfortunately, at this time I do not care to contribute to an organization that includes among its members an organization that condones pharmaceutical testing on laboratory animals.

I will instead make direct contributions to organizations of my own choosing after investigating their political, ethical, and financial policies.

Resigning from Board position because of workload

From individual to community organization

I regret that I must resign my position as a member of the Board of Directors of Lumbertown Cares.

I do so not because of a lack of belief in the important role of the organization but for exactly the opposite reason. Lumbertown Cares is so critical to the well-being of our community that I feel I am hurting its success because of my inability to devote enough time to the Board.

My recent promotion to executive vice president at Consolidated Intergalactic has resulted in a significant increase in travel and other assignments that prevents me from devoting enough time to Lumbertown Cares. You will, though, have my continued support within my own company and my personal financial contributions.

Thank you for the opportunity to serve these past three years.

Resigning from community group

From individual to community organization

With regret, I am resigning from membership and all affiliation with the Lumbertown Chamber of Business Executives.

The organization's recent endorsement of H.R. 132, the Oil Shale Subsidy Act, is completely at odds with my personal beliefs about the need for our nation to address the accelerating threat of global warming. As the saying goes, we need to think global and act local.

I'm doing everything I can to reduce my personal contribution to wasteful energy practices, and I'm not going to support an organization that does not recognize the fragility of our environment.

Accepting formal invitation to event

From individual to community organization

Thank you for your invitation to attend the May 4 Lumbertown Cares meeting; I am pleased to be able to attend on behalf of the entire team at Consolidated Intergalactic.

In your letter you asked each participant to prepare a five-minute presentation about our organization's involvement with community groups. I would like to bring a PowerPoint presentation; will you have a projector and screen for that purpose?

Cancel appointment for cause

From individual to community organization

With apologies, I must cancel our scheduled appointment for next Thursday, May 4. I have just been assigned by the company to make a trip to New Guinea to meet with one of our key suppliers and as I am sure you understand this will keep me out of the office for more than a week.

I will be available any day during the week of May 22; if that works for you, please give me a call or send me an e-mail and we'll reschedule.

I'm sorry for any inconvenience.

Apologize for missing appointment

From individual to community organization

Please accept my deepest apologies for missing our appointment yesterday. As I explained on the phone my flight home from Chicago was delayed by six hours because of the snowstorm and I missed my entire schedule for the day.

I look forward to seeing you next Wednesday, January 16, at 2 P.M. I plan to stay out of Chicago and stick to Lumbertown between now and then.

Accept a formal invitation to a business-related social event

From individual to business organization

Thank you for the invitation to be your guest at the Honors Dinner for graduate students at Lumbertown Community College. I am pleased to accept.

We are all very proud of the accomplishments of the graduating class at LCC. As you know, Consolidated Intergalactic has been a long-time supporter of the college, and we look forward to continuing our backing in years to come.

Cancel acceptance of social event for cause

From individual to business organization

It is with regret that I have to cancel my plans to be your guest at the Honors Dinner for graduate students at Lumbertown Community College. I have just been asked to travel to Chicago on that day for an important business meeting and will not be back in time for the dinner.

If you would like a proposal for a replacement, can I suggest asking Justine Saul, our director of legal affairs? She is a graduate of LCC and has been involved in many programs at the college on behalf of Consolidated Intergalactic.

In any case, please accept my apologies for this unavoidable cancellation.

Accept an honor or award

From individual to business or academic organization

I am very pleased to accept your invitation to receive an honorary degree at the upcoming commencement ceremonies at Lumbertown Community College.

It is a great honor to be recognized for my work on behalf of Lumbertown Cares. In my work on behalf of community organizations I have seen the best of our town and the tremendous importance of LCC as a resource for students, businesses, and organizations here.

Accept an invitation to speak at an event

From individual to business organization

Thank you for the invitation to be a guest speaker at the May 4 meeting of the Lumbertown Circular Club. I am pleased to accept.

In your letter you asked me to speak about Consolidated Intergalactic's activities on behalf of environmental action. This is a subject that is very important to the company, and to me personally.

I would like to use a PowerPoint presentation at the luncheon. I will bring my own laptop; can you arrange for a projector and screen or should I ask CI's Information Resources Department to assist?

Decline an invitation to speak at an event

From individual to business organization

Thank you for the invitation to speak at an upcoming gathering of the Lumbertown Republican Club. I regret that I must decline; company policy does not permit involvement of executives in partisan politics of any type.

Declining invitation to speak because of travel

From individual to business organization

Thank you for the invitation to address the graduating class at Lumbertown High School. I am honored to be asked.

Unfortunately, I will be out of the country on company business for most of the month of June and will be unable to attend the ceremony.

If I can be of help in coming up with another speaker I would be happy to discuss other worthy candidates here at Consolidated Intergalactic as well as at other area organizations.

Accept an appointment to an honorary or volunteer position

From individual to community organization

I am pleased to accept your offer of a position on the Board of Directors of Lumbertown Cares. As community relations manager for Consolidated Intergalactic for the past eight years I have been very impressed with the accomplishments of LC, and I look forward to helping guide its efforts.

Decline an appointment to honorary or volunteer position

From individual to business organization

Thank you for your offer of a position on the Board of Directors of Lumbertown Cares. Unfortunately, I find that I am already over-extended.

I do not feel that I could devote sufficient time to this very important community organization.

I appreciate the fact that you thought of me. If I can be of any assistance in suggesting other possible candidates for the Board, please feel free to contact me.

Appreciation for donation as thanks

From invited speaker to Executive Office

Thank you so much for your gracious gesture of making a contribution in my name to Lumbertown Cares.

I enjoyed very much the opportunity to speak to your employees at your recent company meeting. I am all the more appreciative knowing that together we have helped others in the community through your donation.

18 Community Organizations: To Company and Individuals

From Community Organization to Company

From Company to Employees on Behalf of Community Organization

From Community Organization to Employees and Individuals

From Community Organization to Company

Requesting company presentation at school

From community organizations to Media Relations or Executive Office

I am a professor of business administration at Lumbertown Community College. I would like to invite a representative of Consolidated Intergalactic to come to a class to discuss your company's operations and business structure.

The class meets Mondays, Wednesdays, and Fridays at 11:10 A.M. for fifty minutes.

I hope CI will accept this invitation for an upcoming date; our students greatly benefit from such "real life" business examples.

Requesting company presentation at organization

From community organizations to Media Relations Office or Executive Office

On behalf of the Lumbertown Do-Gooders Club, I would like to invite a representative of Consolidated Intergalactic to make a presentation at an upcoming meeting. Our members want to learn about the products and services of local businesses and to seek ways in which we can cooperate to improve our community.

The club meets on the first Monday of each month at 7 P.M. at the Lumberman Diner on East Bank Street.

Requesting executive as speaker

From community organizations to Media Relations or Executive Office

The Lumbertown Executive Council would like to invite a representative of Consolidated Intergalactic to meet informally with our members at an upcoming luncheon.

The Executive Council is a national association intended to foster networking amongst senior managers of companies to help improve the economy and improve support of community organizations. We meet on the first Monday of each month; meetings are held at various restaurants and conference rooms owned or operated by participating companies.

From Company to Employees on Behalf of Community Organization

Seeking volunteers for fundraising phone bank

From Human Resources to employees

Once again, Consolidated Intergalactic is a leading supporter of Lumbertown Cares.

On Sunday, May 20, we'll be lending our telephone lines and other facilities to a community outreach fundraising campaign. We're looking for about fifty employees and family members willing to give at least two hours of their time to place calls to area residents on behalf of Lumbertown Cares.

We'll provide a buffet lunch and our deep thanks to all participants.

To register to participate, please contact Human Resources at extension 4890.

Thanking volunteers for fundraising phone bank

From Executive Office to employees

On behalf of all of us here at Consolidated Intergalactic, I want to thank all employees who contributed their time and money to the Lumbertown Cares fundraising event on May 20.

We had an outstanding turnout of more than seventy-five employees, family, and friends, and as you may know, Lumbertown Cares set a new record for the amount of money raised for community organizations.

We could not be more proud of our staff, for reasons including events like this.

Seeking volunteers to answer phones at public radio telethon

From Human Resources to employees

Saturday, September 30, will be Consolidated Intergalactic Day during KLUM-FM's fall fund drive. For more than a decade, CI has been a Gold Circle Underwriter of our town's public radio station.

We're looking for volunteers to work the phone bank at KLUM on September 30, answering pledge calls from listeners. We'll reward all CI employees (and friends and family) with a $50 donation in their name to KLUM and a gourmet buffet dinner at the station.

To register to participate, please contact Human Resources at extension 4890.

Seeking volunteers for fundraising community talent show

From Human Resources to employees

Here's your chance to strut your stuff, show off your pipes, and leave 'em rolling in the aisles.

All Consolidated Intergalactic employees, members of their family, and friends are invited to attend (and participate in) the Lumbertown Idol charity fundraiser on Saturday, March 17, at 7 P.M. at the Bijoux Theatre in downtown.

If you'd like to sing, dance, tell jokes (PG-rated, please), or show off some other talent that will surprise and impress your coworkers, please register with Debbie Debow of Human Resources at extension 3878 before March 9. You'll be assigned a time slot for the rehearsal earlier in the day on March 17 and be given a moment in the spotlight in the show.

Tickets for the fundraiser will be available through the Human Resources, Benefits, and Office Services Departments and at the door of the theater. We'd love to see all of our employees in the audience— or up on the stage—for this worthy event.

We'll have our own panel of "celebrity" judges including some familiar faces plus a few surprise guests.

All of the proceeds from the show will be distributed to member agencies of Lumbertown Cares. CI is underwriting all of the expenses of promoting, mounting, and staffing the show.

Seeking contributions of canned goods for food pantry

From Human Resources to employees

As we approach the holiday season, it is once again time for our annual Consolidated Intergalactic Cannery for the Community.

On Tuesday, December 21, members of the Board of Directors and senior executives of the company will be at all entrances to our Lumbertown offices collecting sealed cans and other packaged food to be redistributed through the Community Food Pantry.

Employees not at work on that day, and those of you at our sales and manufacturing offices around the world, are welcome to make cash donations; contact the Payroll Office at extension 5356 to arrange for an automatic deduction.

And thank you, in advance, for thinking of others less fortunate than us.

Discounted admission to local museum

Human Resources to former employees

Consolidated Intergalactic has become a Corporate Circle supporter of the Lumbertown Historical Association. We believe very strongly in the importance of collecting artifacts and researching the history of our hometown as a legacy for generations to come.

As a former employee of the company, we want to extend a special benefit to you: Please show the enclosed Consolidated Intergalactic benefits card to receive a 50 percent discount on admission for yourself and as many as three members of your family or friends.

From Community Organization to Employees and Individuals

Seeking volunteers for community agency, recruiting through Human Resources

From community organization to individuals

Can you lend us a hand? Lumbertown Cares is seeking volunteers to give the one thing money (at least our money) cannot buy: your time and expertise.

We're looking for volunteer teachers, mentors, advisors, and warm-hearted people of all description to spend time with those in need. You'll help people put their lives back on track, polish job skills, plan a business, and become a better citizen of Lumbertown.

Please contact us at (727) 555-0101 to set up an appointment.

Invitation to join business association

From community organization to executive

On behalf of more than one hundred of our town's most dynamic and successful executives, managers, and business owners, we'd like to invite you to join the Lumbertown Business Women's Association.

The LBWA offers education, networking opportunities, and a chance to participate in important community events as representatives of Lumbertown's business community.

We're holding an open meeting on Friday, May 18, at noon. We hope you'll join us as our guest for lunch at the Racetrack Café in Lumbertown.

If you have any questions, or would like to RSVP to tell us you're coming to the meeting, please call Rachel Sabado at (727) 555-0020.

Invitation to join professional association

From community organization to executive

The Lumbertown Facilities Engineering Association would like to invite you to a reception and dinner on Monday, July 18. We're looking for a few good men and women to join our professional organization.

We offer a wide range of training, certification, and career advancement courses as well as personal benefits including discounts on insurance and equipment. And we also are deeply committed to our community mentor program, offered as part of Lumbertown Cares.

Please call our membership chairman, Saul Curtin, to let us know you're coming to our meeting and to discuss any questions you may have.

Writing a fundraising letter

From community organization to individuals

Have you ever thought about what Lumbertown would be like without our own Community Hospital right here in town? Are you comfortable with the idea of an extra thirty-minute drive to Merriam when lives are on the line? Do you want to keep our best doctors living and working right here in town?

These are not fanciful questions, nor are we trying to scare you. The fact is that Lumbertown Community Hospital is at a critical juncture: It must expand its facilities and update its medical equipment within the next two years or it faces decertification by the state as a primary care hospital.

I'm writing to ask you to join your neighbors and business associates in making a contribution to the Lumbertown Community Hospital Building Fund. Attached is a brochure that discusses our plans and hopes for the hospital and outlines the special recognition we give to all of our donors, from supporters to Platinum Patrons.

Thanks to donor in response to fundraising letter

From community organization to individuals

I wanted to personally thank you for your generous gift to the Lumbertown Community Hospital Building Fund.

I look forward to seeing you at upcoming receptions honoring our Platinum Patrons and at the unveiling of the supporter's plaques in the new lobby of the hospital.

Seeking volunteers, recruiting through Human Resources

From Human Resources to employees

Consolidated Intergalactic wants to share its greatest natural resource with the community.

In your next paycheck envelope or direct deposit confirmation you will find a letter from Lumbertown Cares seeking volunteers to serve as teachers, mentors, and advisors for those in need.

It's a great program, and one that CI supports in many ways including corporate sponsorship. And, as we have in previous years, at the annual holiday party we will honor three CI employees for their special contributions in the community; awards include cash bonuses, paid vacations, and other benefits.

If you want to get in touch with Lumbertown Cares immediately, you can contact them at (727) 555-0101 to set up an appointment.

19 Accounts Payable

From Accounts Payable to Employee

From Accounts Payable to Third Party

From Accounts Payable to Employee

Clarifying policy on general expense accounts

From Accounts Payable or department head to employees

In an effort to reduce the expense of photocopying and storage of paper documents, the Accounts Payable Department would like to encourage all staffers to submit expense account forms in electronic form. Here is our suggested method:

Scan all receipts as PDF files;
Store the PDF file in an electronic folder on your computer;
Fill out the online expense report located on the Accounts Payable Web site, and use the "attach" command to electronically append the scanned document to your expense account.

Please retain the original paper copies of all receipts until you receive confirmation from Accounts Payable that your expense report has been accepted and payment has been made. After then you should use a paper shredder to destroy the original.

Requesting details of expenditure for temporary workers

From Human Resources, department head, or Accounts Payable to employee

Regarding your July 14 request for payment of an invoice in the amount of $1,562 for data entry services provided by an outside vendor, we need the following sections of the Temporary Labor Requisition Form (CI-TLR) fully filled out: #2 Reason for Expenditure, and #5 Details of Competitive Bids Received. Please feel free to contact me with any questions.

Requesting receipts for travel expense report

From Accounts Payable or department head to employee

We have received your expense account form for April and are missing several receipts for which you asked to be reimbursed. The missing items are highlighted on the attached form.

Please obtain copies of receipts for these expenditures and resubmit the form. If you cannot locate a receipt to cover the expenditure, please contact your credit card company for assistance in obtaining a duplicate.

Warning letter about expense account policies

From Accounts Payable or department head to employee

Please note that our corporate travel policy requires special approval for any per diem expenditure above $250 for hotel and meals.

On the attached request for reimbursement of travel expenses we note four days on which you exceeded this amount. Please discuss this matter with your supervisor and obtain approval for the indicated items.

Questioning element of expense report

From Accounts Payable or department head to employee

Regarding your May expense report, please provide an explanation of the charge in the amount of $124.67 for rental of formal wear in Chicago.

Please review the employee manual for a complete listing of our rules for allowable travel expenses.

Granting exception on expense report

From Accounts Payable or department head to employee

We have accepted your expense report for May and will be reimbursing you for the rental of formal wear on your recent trip to Chicago. Clothing costs are not ordinarily covered under our expense account rules, but we note this was associated with your representation of the company at the Awards Ceremony of the Midwest Widget Association.

Request to employee to obtain supervisor approval for expenditure

From Human Resources, department head, or Accounts Payable to employee

We have received your request for payment of an invoice for the hiring of six temporary workers from an outside accounting agency in preparation for our upcoming audit.

Before we can approve payment of the invoice, we must receive a Temporary Labor Requisition Form (CI-TLR) that explains the need for the expenditure and the request must be approved by a departmental manager or vice president of the company. Copies of the form are available on the Accounts Payable Web site.

Please feel free to contact me with any questions.

Disallowing expenditure on expense report

From Accounts Payable or department head to employee

Regarding the attached request for reimbursement of travel expenses, please note that corporate policy does not cover charges for in-room movies. We have deducted that amount from the reimbursement check that will be issued.

Notification of policies regarding petty cash

From Accounts Payable or department head to employee

We have received your request for reimbursement for petty cash expenditures for meals provided to members of your staff who were unexpectedly called upon to work overtime for a special project.

Please obtain approval, on the attached form, from your supervisor for this unscheduled expense.

Announcing end-of-year expense report deadline

From Accounts Payable or department head to employees

All employees are asked to file any outstanding expense reports by September 1 in order to allow processing and payment before the end of our fiscal year on September 15.

Department heads are reminded that expenses for the current fiscal year that are not reimbursed by September 15 will be deducted from next year's budget; this may adversely affect your ability to stay within your plan.

From Accounts Payable to Third Party

Requesting provision of tax-exempt certificate

From Accounts Payable or department head to outside supplier

We have received your invoice for wood supplies and are processing payment. Please note that under state law we are exempt from paying sales tax on this purchase since we will be reselling the materials as part of a finished product. Attached please find a copy of our tax-exempt certificate for your records.

Requesting taxpayer ID or SSN

From Accounts Payable or department head to outside supplier

In order for us to process your recent invoice for services, please fill out the attached IRS form to indicate your personal Social Security Number or your company's Taxpayer ID. Please return the form to Accounts Payable as soon as possible so that we can process payment as quickly as possible.

Questioning invoice from supplier

From Accounts Payable or department head to outside supplier

Regarding your June 21 invoice, number 6SJ7 in the amount of $14,231.12, we note a discrepancy between the bid received from your company and the purchase order we issued.

Our documents show that based on your bid we specified 2,000 pounds of pyrithione zinc at a price of $2,500 delivered. The invoice shows 2,200 pounds of the chemical were delivered, and a freight charge of $567 was added.

The purchase order we issued specifies that any discrepancies in quantities, quality, or additional charges must be approved in advance and that variances from the bid may result in rejection of invoices. Please provide an explanation for the discrepancy between the bid and invoice amounts.

Questioning prices from supplier

From Accounts Payable or department head to outside supplier

We have received your invoice (number 6SJ7, dated March 21) for provision of security services. The hourly labor price does not match the amount quoted on your bid for services.

I have attached copies of the bid and your invoice. Before we can make payment the amount of the invoice must be adjusted to match the bid, or we must receive an explanation for the discrepancy that is acceptable to us.

Offering apology for accounting error

From Accounts Payable or department head to outside supplier

I am writing to apologize for our delay in crediting your payment to your account. We have rectified the error.

Attached is a current statement that shows your payment.

Offering apology for delay in issuance of refund

From Accounts Payable or department head to customer or outside supplier

I want to apologize for the delay in issuing your refund check. We experienced a problem with our computer accounting system that resulted in a backup in issuance of payments.

We appreciate your patronage, and hope this sort of problem does not happen again.

Availability of electronic funds transfer for bill payment

From Accounts Payable or department head to customer or outside supplier

Effective June 1, Consolidated Intergalactic will be paying all bills electronically through our account at the Left Bank of Lumbertown.

We offer our vendors and suppliers two options:

- Electronic Fund Transfer. Funds will be transferred from our bank account to an account you specify, with payments scheduled to arrive on or before the business day nearest the due date for invoices. The EFT will include a code number keyed to the invoice or purchase order number.
- Electronic Checks. The bank will generate and mail to your Accounts Receivable Department a computer-generated check. Payments will be scheduled to arrive on or before the business day nearest the due date for invoice. Your Accounts Receivable or Accounting Department will be responsible for depositing the check in your account.

Please advise Consolidated Intergalactic's Accounts Payable Department of your company's preference for means of payment. If we do not receive instructions, we will make payment by electronic check.

Requesting early payment discount

From Accounts Payable to outside supplier

According to the contract we signed with your company for provision of waste disposal services, we are entitled to a 3 percent discount for payments made within ten days of receipt of invoices.

We have been making immediate payment and deducting 3 percent from invoices for the last four months, but the most recent statement from your company shows an outstanding balance in the amount of $1,232, which includes a 10 percent late payment fee.

Please remove the outstanding balance from our statement and inform your Accounts Receivable Department of the elements of our contract, which include the 3 percent discount for early payment.

Making second request for early payment discount

From Accounts Payable to outside supplier

I am writing again to insist that an improper outstanding balance be removed from our account with your company. According to the contract we signed with your company for provision of waste disposal services, we are entitled to a 3 percent discount for payments made within ten days of receipt of invoices.

We have been making immediate payment and deducting 3 percent from invoices for the last five months but the discount has not been credited against our account.

At this time we seek an immediate resolution to this problem. We are otherwise satisfied with your company's service, but if our account is not adjusted by July 1 we will consider the contract to be breached, and will seek service from another company.

I look forward to a satisfactory response within five business days.

20 Accounts Receivable

Requesting credit reference for new customer

From Accounts Receivable or Billing Department to third party

We have received an application for a new account from Diamond Music, Inc. Your company was listed as a credit reference.

Can you advise us whether Diamond Music had an account in good standing with your company?

Thank you.

Second request for payment

From Accounts Receivable or Sales Department to customer
Invoice: AEJ09235
Account: 6SJ7

As of this date we have not received payment on the above invoice, which was due on March 1.

We value you as a customer, and hope that you will pay immediate attention to this matter. If you have any questions about this invoice please contact me.

As per the terms of sale, we will apply a penalty fee for overdue invoices beginning on April 1.

Third request for payment, warning of turnover to collection agency

From Accounts Receivable or Sales Department to customer

I am writing to advise you that your account is now seriously overdue. As of this date, the outstanding balance is $12,894, which includes $300 in late fees.

This is our third request for payment. We ask that you take immediate action to pay this account in full.

Final demand for payment, warning of legal proceedings

From Accounts Receivable or Sales Department to customer

Your account with Consolidated Intergalactic is now in default. We have made three previous requests for payment and have received no response.

This letter is our final demand for payment. Unless we receive the full outstanding balance of $24,876 within ten days of the date of this notice, it is our intention to turn your account over to our Legal Office to initiate collection proceedings.

Collection fees, legal fees, and late fees can amount to a significant increase in your outstanding balance. And a negative rating on your credit report may result in higher interest costs in the future and difficulty in obtaining accounts with other companies.

We suggest you make immediate and full payment before the deadline.

Suspending credit because of past-due invoices

From Accounts Receivable or Sales Department to customer

We regret to inform you that due to the outstanding balance on your account, we will be unable to accept future orders that are not prepaid.

We will review your credit status once the outstanding balance has been fully paid. Please feel free to call me with any questions. Thank you.

Imposing late charge for past-due invoices

From Accounts Receivable or Sales Department to customer

We are writing to notify you that, in keeping with our sales contract, we are imposing a 5 percent late fee on the overdue balance in your account. The charge will be posted on March 1, and will be repeated on the first of each subsequent month in which there is an overdue balance.

We urge you to make full payment before we are forced to turn your account over to our Legal Office to initiate collection proceedings.

Collection fees, legal fees, and late fees can amount to a significant increase in your outstanding balance. And a negative rating on your credit report may result in higher interest costs in the future and difficulty in obtaining accounts with other companies.

Returning improperly filled-in or unsigned check

From Accounts Receivable or Sales Department to customer

Enclosed please find the check you sent on May 3 in payment for Account 6SJ7. The check was unsigned, and the numerical amount and the handwritten amounts are different from each other.

Please reissue a check with the proper payment amount, sign it, and return it as soon as possible.

Assessing fee for check returned for insufficient funds

From Accounts Receivable or Sales Department to customer

Your check #4572 has been returned by your bank for insufficient funds. We would appreciate your immediate attention to this matter.

Under terms of our sales contract, we are passing along our bank's charge of $25 for rejected checks. Your new balance on Account 6SJ7 is $1,758.32.

Making apology for unwarranted collection letter

From Accounts Receivable or Sales Department to customer

Please accept our apologies for the demand for payment letter you received on April 12. Your payment was apparently delayed in the mail and arrived in our offices after our letter was sent to you.

We value you as a customer and hope to continue to be a partner.

Offering payment plan for outstanding balance

From Accounts Receivable or Sales Department to customer

We note that your account is overdue for payment. We hope to be able to continue to do business with your company in the future.

Please contact me if you would like to discuss setting up a payment plan for the outstanding balance on your account. Doing so will avoid penalty charges and possible legal fees and adverse credit ratings.

Offering discount for early payment on invoices

From Accounts Receivable or Sales Department to customer

As a valued customer, we would like to offer you a special discount for early payment.

If full payment is made at the time an order is placed, we will discount the price by 5 percent. If full payment is made within ten days of delivery of an order and an accompanying invoice, we will issue a 2 percent credit to your account. The credit can be applied against any future purchases.

Please feel free to contact me to discuss this special discount offer.

Announcing suspension of early-pay discount

From Accounts Receivable or Sales Department to customer

Effective May 1, we will be discontinuing our 2 percent discount for invoices paid within ten days of receipt of invoice. We are doing this out of fairness to all of our customers; because of delays in shipping, postal service, and interbank transfers it is impossible to equitably treat customers located all across the country.

We will continue to offer a 5 percent discount for all orders paid in full at the time an order is placed.

Offering early-pay discount for electronic funds transfers

From Accounts Receivable or Sales Department to customer

Effective May 1, we will be changing our policy on early-pay discounts for Consolidated Intergalactic clients.

We will continue to offer a 2 percent discount for invoices paid by EFT (electronic funds transfer) within ten days of receipt of invoice. To arrange for payment by EFT, please contact your account manager at CI, or ask for assistance through our help desk at extension 9999.

We no longer offer a discount for invoices paid by standard check. We have discontinued that program out of fairness to all of our customers and because of unpredictable delays caused by the postal service.

We will continue to offer a 5 percent discount for all orders paid in full at the time an order is placed.

Notifying customer of overpayment and ask for advice

From Accounts Receivable or Sales Department to customer

We received a check from you on May 6 in the amount of $2,356.43 and have applied it to your account. The payment was $100 in excess of the outstanding balance on your account.

Please advise us whether you would like us to retain the $100 as a credit on your account to be used for future purchases or whether you would prefer we issue a check to you for the excess payment.

Notifying customer of incorrect payment amount and asking for balance

From Accounts Receivable or Sales Department to customer

Your recent payment (check #6809 dated May 23, in the amount of $670.23) has been received and credited to your account.

We note that the amount of the check was $200 less than the outstanding balance in your account. We would appreciate your immediate payment of the unpaid balance.

Responding to request for letter of credit reference

From Accounts Receivable or Sales Department to customer

We have received your request for a letter of credit reference for National Ukelele Corporation.

For privacy reasons we do not disclose the details of financial and other relations with customers. However, we can report that as of this date we have had no problems with timely and full payment from this client.

Requesting bids for collection services

From Accounts Receivable to collection agency

The Accounts Receivable Department of Consolidated Intergalactic is seeking bids from area collection agencies to assist in obtaining payment from outstanding commercial and individual accounts more than 90 days overdue.

We expect any bidder to provide written assurances that it will follow all federal and state laws in its business practices and will not harass or improperly pursue any of our clients.

Full details of the specifications of our request for bid plus a required nondisclosure agreement is available on request from the Accounts Receivable Department of Consolidated Intergalactic.

All bids are due no later than June 1, and we anticipate awarding a contract by July 1.

21 Payroll Services

Payroll Services to Employees

Payroll Policy Announcements to Employees

Payroll Services to Third Party

Payroll Services to Employees

Availability of paycheck direct deposit

From Payroll Services or Human Resources to employees

Payroll Services reminds all employees that direct deposit of paychecks is available. To arrange for automatic deposit of your check into any checking account, please fill out the forms that are available at our office; the forms can also be downloaded from the Payroll Services Web site.

Notification of error on direct deposit or paycheck

From Payroll Services or Human Resources to employees

Due to a clerical error, all paychecks or direct deposit statements issued today (dated June 21) include a minor error in calculation of Social Security tax withholding.

In most cases, the amount deducted from the paycheck was between $3 and $10 too high. We have determined the error, and all affected employees will see a credit and the correct deduction amount on their next paycheck or statement.

We apologize for any inconvenience this may have caused.

If you have any questions about this error, please contact the Payroll Services help desk at extension 2348.

Reminding employees to update tax form exemptions annually

From Payroll Services or Human Resources to employees

As Tax Day approaches, all employees are reminded that adjustments to the IRS W-4 form can be filed at any time during the year. You can increase or decrease the number of personal exemptions or ask that an additional amount of money be withheld from your paycheck for tax purposes.

Payroll Services can assist employees in filling out the form. If you have any tax questions, we suggest you consult a financial advisor or tax accountant of your own choosing.

Notification of inclusion of W-2 forms with paychecks this period

From Payroll Services or Human Resources to employees

The paychecks and direct deposit notification letters for this pay period, which will be distributed on Friday, January 27, will include your annual IRS W-2 form with details of the amount of federal and state taxes that were withheld in the prior calendar year.

If you want to make any changes to your personal exemption, Payroll Services has W-4 forms available. If you have any tax questions, we suggest you consult a financial advisor or tax accountant of your own choosing.

Announcing early deadline for timesheets because of holiday

From Payroll Services, Executive Office, Benefits Office, or Human Resources to employees

Because of the upcoming Memorial Day holiday, all hourly employees are advised to submit their timesheets for the current work period before the end of the business day on Friday, May 25. If you are due to work over the weekend, please file your work hours for those days on the next scheduled date for timesheets.

If your timesheet is not received before the holiday, your paycheck will not be available on its regularly scheduled distribution date of Wednesday, May 30, and will be delayed until the following Wednesday.

Paychecks for nonhourly salaried employees are not affected by the holiday.

Payroll Policy Announcements to Employees

Policy on charitable contributions and community organizations

From Executive Office, Benefits Office, Payroll Services, or Human Resources to employees

Consolidated Intergalactic is committed to being a good corporate neighbor in Lumbertown and everywhere else it conducts business.

We welcome suggestions from employees for charitable contributions by the company as well as ways in which we can help our workers conduct fundraising campaigns.

Our general policy declares that CI seeks to work with nondenominational faith-based or secular organizations. We exclude involvement with organizations aligned with political candidates, officeholders, or political parties.

For more details on CI's charitable giving program, please contact the Benefits Office.

Announcement of availability of direct charitable contribution from paycheck

From Payroll Services, Executive Office, Benefits Office, Payroll Services, or Human Resources to employees

We are pleased to announce that we have added the Lumbertown Food Bank to our list of approved local organizations for direct contribution from paychecks.

If you would like to contribute to this worthy organization, or any of the other approved groups, please contact the Payroll Services Office. A full list of organizations supported in this way by Consolidated Intergalactic can be found on the Payroll Services Web site; click on the Contribute from "Your Paycheck" icon for details.

Announcing policy on payroll advances

From Payroll Office, Executive Office, Benefits Office, Payroll Services, or Human Resources to employees

Consolidated Intergalactic permits a reasonable number of advances against upcoming paychecks for the following needs: medical expenses, unanticipated emergency housing costs, and job-related moving costs.

We permit a payroll advance of no more than 150 percent of the total value of unused vacation and personal days plus three weeks of anticipated salary or hourly wages.

For more details on this policy and an application for a payroll advance, please contact the Payroll Services Office.

Policy to request correction of error on paycheck or direct deposit

From Payroll Services, Executive Office, Benefits Office, Payroll Services, or Human Resources to employees

If you note an error on your paycheck or direct deposit confirmation, including the hourly or weekly rate, number of hours worked, tax withholding, insurance deductions, or the details of your name, address, or employee number, please immediately contact the Payroll Services hotline at extension 4012.

Payroll Services to Third Party

Seeking bid for payroll services

From Payroll Services to outside service provider

The Payroll Services Department of Consolidated Intergalactic is seeking bids from third-party service companies for the management, production, and audit of payroll checks.

This is part of a regular review of our contracts with outside service providers, conducted every two years. We may choose to accept a bid from a new provider or stay with our current provider.

A copy of the current specifications is available on request from the Payroll Services Department, at extension 2349.

All bids are due on or before September 1; award of the contract will be made on or before December 1, with the starting date for the contract January 1.

22 Office Services: Maintenance, Facilities, and Food Service

Facilities Notices and Policies to Employees

From Employees to Office Services

Food Services and Catering Notices and Policies to Employees

Janitorial and Recycling-Related Notices and Policies to Employees

Facilities Notices and Policies to Employees

Announcing policy for reservation of conference rooms

From Office Services to employees

Conference rooms at Consolidated Intergalactic may be reserved as much as thirty days in advance of a scheduled meeting. An online request for use of rooms can be found on the Office Services Web site. There are six available conference rooms.

- Conference Rooms A and B have a capacity of twenty-five persons.
- Conference Rooms C, D, and E can each accommodate forty-eight persons.
- Our largest facility, Conference Room F can be used by forty-eight persons in its ordinary configuration or ninety-six persons when its rear wall is retracted to make it an extension of Conference Room E.

In general, use of rooms is on a first-request basis. However, Office Services maintains the right to cancel a reservation when another meeting with a higher priority must be scheduled at the same time.

Conference rooms are ordinarily available for eighty-minute blocks of time; this is intended to allow ten minutes for clean-up and preparation between meetings. For meetings that will require more than ninety minutes, special approval is required from the Office Services Department.

All conference rooms include the following facilities: a projection screen for use with presentations, one or more amplified speakerphones for use in telephone conferences, and chalkboards or whiteboards.

Confirming reservation of conference room with details

From Office Services to employees

Your request for use of Conference Room B on Tuesday, April 30, has been approved.

The room will be available to you from 1 P.M. until to 2:20 P.M. Please plan on ending your meeting at that time and removing all materials before 2:30 P.M. to allow other staffers to use the room.

Reminder of reservation of conference rooms

From Office Services to employees

This is a reminder of your reservation of Conference Room B for tomorrow, April 30, from 1 P.M. until 2:20 P.M.

If your department's plans have changed, please notify Office Services immediately so that we can release the room for the use of other departments. Thank you.

Policy on use of off-site facilities for meetings

From Office Services to employees

All requests to use off-site facilities for meetings are required to be approved by the Office Services Department.

Consolidated Intergalactic has negotiated special rates at several area hotels and conference centers. We also have specific requirements for insurance coverage for our staffers as well as any service providers.

Approval of use of off-site facility for meeting

From Office Services to employees

We have approved your request for use of an off-site facility for a departmental meeting on June 17. The proposed contract with the Lumbertown Marriott has been signed and delivered to the hotel.

Please notify the department if the meeting is cancelled or postponed; note that penalties will be assessed by the conference center in that instance.

Denial of approval of use of off-site facility for meeting

From Office Services to employees

We are unable to approve your request for use of a conference room at the Knights of Columbus meeting hall on July 5. This facility is not on our list of pre-approved conference sites.

If you would like to request evaluation of that facility for future meetings, please provide a contact name and phone number and details on your expected requirements.

Please feel free to call the Office Services department to discuss other options for your meeting. Whenever possible, we prefer to use our own onsite facilities. Outside facilities are booked only when available meeting rooms are too small or are not available.

Personal letter regarding handicapped access to building

From employee to Office Services

Since I returned from work two weeks ago after my automobile accident, I have become aware of several obstacles put in the way of persons with permanent or temporary physical handicaps.

As a long-time employee of Consolidated Intergalactic, I am well aware of the company's commitment to supporting the needs of all employees, and I am certain CI has followed all of the elements of federal and state laws mandating accommodations for persons with disabilities.

However, I feel it is worth pointing out that I have found—from personal experience—that the curb cuts in the south parking lot are on a stretch of pavement that is not level, making use of a wheelchair very difficult. Further, the lunch counter at the CI Café is completely unusable for someone in a wheelchair and the otherwise friendly staff at the lunchroom have obviously not been trained in assisting someone in a wheelchair.

I would be happy to share my experiences with Office Services and assist in any way in improving access for all employees and visitors to Consolidated Intergalactic.

Response to letter about handicapped access

From Office Services to employee

Thank you for your thoughtful letter about deficiencies in access for the handicapped at our headquarters building.

You are absolutely correct that Consolidated Intergalactic is fully committed to supporting the needs of all employees. It is our hope that we far exceed the minimum requirements in federal and state law.

We do face several difficulties here at our Lumbertown headquarters. First of all, there is very little flat land anywhere on our property which means that we have slopes and stairs almost everywhere. Secondly, the main building itself is forty years old, predating the founding of our company.

I hope you have noticed that we have added a small asphalt berm alongside the curb cuts in the south parking lot that you mentioned, and we have also instructed the head of Food Services to assign at least one staffer in each shift to be available to assist persons with disabilities in the cafeteria.

As far as your offer to consult with Office Services on suggestions to improve our accommodations for persons with disabilities: We gladly accept. Please contact me at your convenience to schedule a meeting to begin the process.

From Employees to Office Services

Requesting reservation for conference room

From employee to Office Services

I would like to request use of Conference Room A or B on Tuesday, April 30, from 1 P.M. to 2:30 P.M. for a team meeting to discuss an upcoming product launch.

We will be using a laptop for a PowerPoint presentation and have requested use of an LCD projector from Information Technology.

Request from department for approval of use of off-site facility for meeting

From employee to Office Services

Enclosed please find a proposed contract for use of conference facilities at the Lumbertown Marriott on June 17 for an all-day training session for the Facilities Management Department.

The contract is based on the negotiated master contract between Consolidated Intergalactic and the hotel. The meeting includes a breakfast buffet at registration and a lunch buffet at midday.

Food Services and Catering Notices and Policies to Employees

Announcement of cafeteria hours and policies

From Food Services Department to employees

The CI Café has extended its hours in order to accommodate the increasing number of employees taking advantage of flextime schedules.

Effective May 1, the cafeteria will be open for breakfast snacks beginning at 7:45 A.M. daily. Lunch will be served from 11:45 A.M. until 2:30 P.M., and sandwiches and other snacks will be offered for the remainder of the day until 5 P.M.

Each day's menu will be posted on the CI Café Web site.

Announcement of outdoor picnic area

From Executive Department, Office Services, or Human Resources to employees

Now that warm weather has finally arrived, we are pleased to announce that we have added six picnic tables and umbrellas on the patio outside the CI Café.

During regular hours for the cafeteria, the emergency exit door just past the cashier's station will be unlocked to allow direct access to the patio.

Please help us keep the area clean by using the trash cans (divided into paper, plastic, and food bins), and please return all utensils, plates, and trays to the collection stations inside the cafeteria.

Policy on use of cafeteria and break rooms for meals

From Food Services Department to employees

Employees are reminded that company policy prohibits eating meals at your desk. You may bring your meal to the cafeteria and eat it there, or use one of the break rooms located on each floor of the headquarters building.

Policy regarding guests in cafeteria

From Food Services Department to employees

Employees are reminded that they are welcome to bring guests to the cafeteria; all visitors must register with the security desk when they enter the building.

Policy regarding catering of departmental meetings by in-house Food Services

From Food Services Department to employees

The CI cafeteria is available to offer catering for in-house meetings and seminars. Because the Food Services Department is subsidized by Consolidated Intergalactic, its prices are generally considerably lower than those charged by outside vendors.

Catering must be arranged at least forty-eight hours in advance; for details please contact the CI Café at extension 8383.

Policy regarding use of outside vendors to cater departmental meetings

From Food Services Department to employees

Consolidated Intergalactic recommends the use of our in-house Food Services Department to cater informal gatherings and meetings held on company premises. CI Café services are generally much less expensive than outside vendors.

If a department chooses to use an outside catering service for a function that takes place on company property, the company must be among those on the pre-approved vendor list maintained by the Office Services Department. The proposed contract for catering must also be approved by Office Services, and must show evidence of current workers compensation, liability, and other insurance as well as all necessary health department permits for food service.

Policy regarding special meal requests for medical or other reasons

From Food Services Department to employees

CI Café is pleased to offer meals to employees with special needs or requirements. These include low-fat, low-salt, gluten-free, kosher, halal, and other diets. In some cases the meals will be prepared by an outside vendor and shipped frozen to the cafeteria for reheating.

Arrangements for such meals require a minimum of one week's advance notice. Please call the cafeteria at extension 8383 to request special meals.

Janitorial and Recycling-Related Notices and Policies to Employees

Procedure to request emergency clean-up

From Janitorial Services, Office Services, or Maintenance to employees

If you require assistance in cleaning up a spill or liquid or other substances in the workplace, please call the Janitorial Department at extension 2348. There are "danger" cones located in closets located next to the elevator banks that can be used to mark slippery areas before the janitorial staff arrives.

Procedure to request after-hours emergency clean-up

From Janitorial Services, Office Services, or Maintenance to employees

If you have need for emergency assistance in cleaning up a liquid or other spill after ordinary office hours, please contact the Security Office at extension 9111. Depending on the nature of the spill, we have twenty-four-hour coverage from an outside vendor.

Policy regarding spills of toxic or dangerous substances

From Janitorial Services, Office Services, or Maintenance to employees

Employees are asked to be careful when handling toxic or dangerous substances including solvents, toner cartridges, and certain cleaning supplies. If any of these items spill or are otherwise released, please immediately contact the Security Office at extension 9111. That department will coordinate response by the janitorial staff or by outside specialists.

Limited janitorial services during holiday period

From Office Services to employees

Although our offices will be open during the three-day New Year's weekend, please be advised that there will be only limited janitorial and maintenance services available.

Restrooms and break rooms will be cleaned once daily, during the night shift. Office equipment services, including maintenance and repair of copying machines, printers, and computers will only be available on an emergency basis and will be provided at the discretion of the on-call Office Services supervisor.

Any employee who comes to work during the holiday weekend is required to enter through the main lobby entrance and to check in with the security desk on arrival and departure.

Request for weekly cleaning of refrigerators in break room

From Janitorial Services, Office Services, or Maintenance to employees

The Janitorial Services Department reminds all employees who use the facilities of the break room that they are expected to clean up after themselves. Please deposit all trash in the provided receptacles and clean up any spills in the microwave and on the tables.

All food stored in the refrigerator must be labeled with the name of its owner. Any food left in the refrigerator after 5 P.M. on Friday of each week will be thrown away.

The janitorial crew will clean the rooms once each night.

Policy on recycling of paper

From Office Services to employees

Consolidated Intergalactic is committed to supporting the environment through recycling of paper products. The Office Services Department has begun distribution of special bins that will be located near copying machines and in central locations throughout the building.

In the first phase of our program, we will concentrate on recycling office paper (the type used in copy machines, laser printers, and inkjet printers). We ask all employees to make a special effort to separate this type of paper and place it in the marked bin.

Departments that use paper shredders can also deposit cut paper of this type in the bins.

Policy on recycling of toner cartridges

From Office Services to employees

As part of our recycling effort, we ask all employees to store emptied laser printer, photo copier, and inkjet cartridges in special containers that have been placed near these machines in all departments.

Recycling these cartridges helps prevent release of dangerous chemicals and substances. In addition, Consolidated Intergalactic will receive an estimated savings of as much as $10,000 per year.

Installation of recycling bins in break rooms and cafeteria

From Janitorial Services, Office Services, or Maintenance to employees

Consolidated Intergalactic is committed to reducing waste and helping the environment. All break rooms and the CI Café are now equipped with recycling bins for deposit-back cans and bottles, and recyclable cans and bottles.

Please make use of the appropriate bins.

All monies received from the return of bottles and cans with deposits will be contributed to local charities.

Installation of recycling bins near photocopy centers, printers

From Janitorial Services, Office Services, or Maintenance to employees

Please make use of the recycling bins near all photocopy machines and printers in the office. There are separate bins for white paper, colored paper, and ink or toner cartridges.

23 Office Services: Supplies and Equipment

Policy advisory on office supplies

From Office Services to employees

All employees are advised that orders for office supplies must be placed with an approved vendor. Consolidated Intergalactic has negotiated contracts with most of the major local and national supply companies.

If a particular product is not available through an approved vendor, please contact the Office Services Department and request assistance in obtaining preferred pricing.

The Accounts Payable Department will not authorize payment to unapproved vendors.

Implementing policy to account for assets, including bar codes and valuations

From Office Services or department head to employees

We have begun a program to account for all physical assets of the company valued at $25 or more. This includes office equipment, computers, and furniture.

In coming weeks, members of the Maintenance Department will be visiting every department to record details of equipment and to apply bar codes. We would appreciate any assistance staffers can provide in identifying equipment.

Effective immediately, the employee manual is amended to include the following:

"No employee is to remove or deface an identification bar code applied to any physical asset of the company."

Notification of approved vendors

From Office Services to employees

Attached is a list of approved vendors for office supplies, updated as of this date. Please be aware that the Accounts Payable Department will not authorize payment to vendors that are not pre-approved.

Contact the Office Services Department if you have any questions about the vendor list.

Notification of unapproved vendors

From Office Services to employees

Please be advised that the companies on the attached list are no longer on the approved vendor list for Consolidated Intergalactic.

The Accounts Payable Department will not authorize payment to unapproved vendors. If you have questions about the vendor list, contact the Office Services Department at extension 2390.

Policy to request stocking of specific products not on approved list

From Office Services to employees

Our master contracts with approved office supply vendors list specific types of products; if you have need for an item not included under these agreements please contact the Office Services Department. Certain items may require pre-approval by a supervisor or departmental head before they are added to master contracts with suppliers.

Policy regarding use of office equipment for personal purposes

From Office Services to employees

All employees are reminded that office equipment, including photocopiers, printers, fax machines, scanners, postage meters, and all other devices are not to be used for personal purposes or in support of outside organizations including religious and political groups or causes.

The only exception to this rule involves officially endorsed fundraising or publicity campaigns. For information about Consolidated Intergalactic's procedure to seek approval for a company contribution of equipment, supplies, or employee time to community groups please contact Human Resources. You can also read details of our policy on the HR Web site; look for the "CI in the Community" icon and select, "How to Propose a Community Initiative."

Warning about improper use of office equipment for personal purposes

From Office Services or Human Resources to employee

(As an initial warning, this memo does not make any accusations and does not include specifics of any possible violation.)

It has come to our attention that you may have violated the company policy against use of office equipment for personal purposes.

Office equipment, including photocopiers, printers, fax machines, scanners, postage meters, and all other devices are not to be used for personal purposes or in support of outside organizations including religious and political groups or causes.

If you have any questions about our policies in this area, please contact the Office Services Department or your supervisor.

Telephone answering protocols

From Office Services or Training Department to employees

Whenever you answer the telephone, you are the voice of Consolidated Intergalactic. We ask that all employees identify themselves and offer a courteous, helpful introduction to the company in all interactions on the phone.

Please review the following guidelines for proper telephone etiquette.

Calls that are not placed to a specific extension or are not handled by our automated telephone attendant will be directed to the main switchboard during ordinary business hours. The proper greeting is: "Good morning. This is Consolidated Intergalactic. How may I help you?"

If a call comes in to a departmental receptionist, please identify the department and yourself: "Human Resources. This is Janice Keefe. How may I help you?"

And it is acceptable to assume that calls that ring through to your own phone are being made by someone who has specifically asked to speak to you. You may answer, "Hello. This is Janice Keefe. How may I help you?"

Here are some further details on proper telephone protocol:

- If you are answering on behalf of someone else, please do not give specifics about where that person is. Do not say, "He is out to lunch," or "She is out sick." Just tell the caller that the person he or she has asked for is unavailable. Then ask if there is someone else who could help the caller, or offer to transfer the caller to the voicemail system to leave a message.
- To avoid privacy issues and to avoid disturbing other members of staff, limit the use of speakerphones. Ask the caller if it is acceptable to broadcast a call in this manner. Speakerphones are appropriate when a group of people seek to communicate with an individual or another group.
- Although all telephones at Consolidated Intergalactic have Caller ID displays, it is not safe to assume that you know the identity of the person who is calling. The ID usually displays the name of the company or the subscriber; anyone may be using a particular phone.
- Always ask permission before transferring a call or putting someone on hold.

If you have any further questions about telephone protocol, please consult the online manual available on the Office Services Web site or call the help line at extension 8942.

Training session on voicemail system

From Office Services or Training Department to employees

A representative of the BelloPhone automated telephone system will be at Consolidated Intergalactic on Tuesday, August 5, to offer seminars on newly installed upgrades and updates.

Mary Reinhardt will present ninety-minute sessions at 9 A.M., 1 P.M., and 3 P.M. in Conference Room A.

All members of the Office Services staff are required to attend one of the sessions. Departmental managers are asked to assign receptionists to attend. And any other members of staff who wish to attend a session are invited to attend; please consult with your supervisor or manager so that departments are able to maintain adequate levels of staffing on the training day.

Guidelines on use of copying machines

From Office Services to employees

Each year, Consolidated Intergalactic spends more than $340,000 on supplies for copying machines and laser printers.

That's a significant portion of the supplies budget for the company, and each department must bear its own share of the cost based on usage. There are a number of ways we can all work together to reduce our expenditures in this area.

First of all, it is important to understand that a laser printer is more expensive to operate (and generally slower) than a copying machine. And the least expensive printing method for orders that require more than a thousand copies is a commercial printing shop. Here's what that means to us as users:

- If you need only one or a few copies of a document produced on your computer, you should send the document to a laser printer;
- If you need to produce dozens or hundreds of copies of a document, create an original on a laser printer and then have copies made on one of our high-speed high-efficiency copying machines.
- If you need thousands of copies—for sales and marketing purposes or for an essential form—consult with the Office Services help desk for advice on using a commercial printer already under contract with Consolidated Intergalactic.
- And finally, ask yourself the question: Does this document actually have to be produced on paper, or can it be transmitted, stored, or acted upon electronically? A page that is not printed does not cost money for paper, toner, file folders, and filing cabinets.

Notification on standardized filing procedures

From Office Services or Legal Office to employees

(NOTE: Review with your in-house or outside legal counsel.)

The Legal Office has advised that properly archived electronic copies of most forms and documents can be used instead of paper originals.

Therefore, we have instituted the following policy:

Scan all contracts, receipts, invoices, and other financial documents immediately upon receipt and store the file as a PDF document on your local workstation and maintain appropriate electronic backups of the files.

Retain the original paper documents for eighteen months.

Verify the existence of the electronic file before paper documents are shredded.

Any legal, tax-related, or personnel-related paper documents should be delivered to the appropriate department. An electronic file copy may be retained in the department, providing proper security and privacy procedures are followed.

Policy on availability of special project support staff

From Office Services or Human Resources to employees

As we approach the busy product introduction season, departments are reminded of the availability of special project support staff. In years past, Consolidated Intergalactic has temporarily reassigned as many as 100 employees from regular duties to assist other departments on an as-needed basis.

For information on the program, please contact your department head. Further details are also available on the Human Resources Web site; click on the icon labeled "Special Project Support."

Policy on hiring of temporary workers for special projects

From Office Services or Human Resources to employees

Managers and department heads are reminded that any hiring of temp workers for special projects must be pre-approved by Human Resources.

The HR Department offers special project support for certain short-term tasks, reassigning staff from other departments as needed. It is also company policy to use employees for a reasonable amount of overtime before bringing in temporary workers who may need special training or who may be less productive than our own staff.

In addition, the company has negotiated master contracts with several area temporary employment agencies for general office labor and specialized assignments to accounting, information technology, and manufacturing.

Policy on rental of special equipment for projects

From Office Services to employees

All requests for lease or rental of special equipment for projects must be pre-approved by Office Services. The company may be able to temporarily shift equipment it already owns or make other special arrangements that are less costly than short-term rentals.

For details, please contact the Office Services support desk at extension 8942.

General cover letter for faxes

From Office Services, Information Technology, or Executive Office to employees

Fax Transmittal Cover Sheet

From: _____   at Consolidated Intergalactic

Department:

Mailing Address:

Voice Telephone Number:

E-mail Address:

Date Sent: Time Sent:

Number of Pages (including this cover sheet):

Please Deliver to: (name of intended recipient)

Company Name:

Department:

Telephone Number:

E-mail Address:

Fax Number: _____   (number the fax is sent to)

Description/Remarks:

This fax is intended only for the person named above under "Please deliver to"
If you receive this fax and it is not intended for you, please call the phone number above.
If there are any problems with this transmission, please call the phone number above.

General cover letter for faxes, alternate version

From Office Services, Information Technology, or Executive Office to employees

Fax Cover Sheet

To: From:

Recipient's Fax Number: Sender's Fax Number:

Recipient's Voice Telephone: Sender's Voice Telephone:

Pages (not including cover sheet):

Date Sent: Time Sent:

Subject:

CC:

❏ Urgent   ❏ For Review   ❏ Please Comment   ❏ Please Reply

Comments:

This fax is intended only for the person named above under "To."
If you receive this fax and it is not intended for you, please call the phone number above.
If there are any problems with this transmission, please call the phone number above.

Use of energy-saving light bulbs required in office areas

From Office Services to employees

Beginning today, Office Services will be substituting high-efficiency compact fluorescent bulbs for standard incandescent bulbs throughout the enterprise.

We'll begin by replacing any failed incandescent bulb with a fluorescent, but over the coming year we expect to completely change all such lighting. The bulbs we have chosen deliver a close match to the color of daylight; in fact, they are closer to sunlight than the more orange hue of older bulbs.

According to industry studies, Energy Star qualified bulbs use about 75 percent less energy than standard incandescent bulbs and last up to ten times longer.

Seeking suggestions for saving money

From Office Services to employees

With thanks to Ben Franklin: In a business, as in life, a penny saved is a penny earned.

Once again, the Office Services Department is offering the Chairman's Award for the best suggestion of ways to save money on supplies, services, or operations. In previous years, winning suggestions have included the use of compact fluorescent light bulbs, recycling packing materials from incoming packages for use with our own shipments, and an idea from the manufacturing line that helped reduce our use of certain very expensive natural oils.

The deadline for submission of ideas is December 1, and the winner is announced at the annual company meeting later in the month. We'll award a check worth more than a few pennies, and a place on the wall of honor in the entrance lobby.

24 Office Services: Mailroom, Library, and Transportation

Mailroom Notices to and Policies for Employees

Library and Archives Notices and Policies

Transportation-Related Notices and Policies to Employees

Mailroom Notices to and Policies for Employees

Mailroom policy regarding use of express and overnight services

From Mailroom or Office Services to employees

Because of the significant expenses for use of express and overnight mail delivery services, we have instituted the following policies:

All requests for overnight or express mail shipping must go through the Mailroom's online portal, which includes links to the U.S. Postal Service as well as private delivery companies.

A billing code and reference number must be entered for each letter or package shipped.

The billing code will be used to charge the cost of shipments to the sending department; the reference number will be provided to the department for tracking costs for particular projects, clients, or suppliers.

Please note that under no circumstances are overnight or express mail services to be used for the shipment of documents between domestic offices of Consolidated Intergalactic. Instead, such documents should be placed in an interoffice envelope and delivered to the Mailroom before 4 P.M.; the Mailroom will consolidate all packages sent to other CI divisions into single envelopes or boxes.

Mailroom policy regarding use of intraoffice mail

From Mailroom or Office Services to employees

Intraoffice mail, intended for delivery from one part of the Lumbertown office to another, is picked up twice daily. The first pick-up is at 8 A.M. and the second at 2 P.M.; it is our goal to deliver all intraoffice mail within two hours of receipt.

If you have an urgent need to get documents from one department to another at other times and it is not convenient to dispatch a staffer to deliver the package personally, please call the Mailroom at extension 9727 to arrange a special pick-up.

Mailroom policy disallowing personal use of outgoing mail services

From Mailroom or Office Services to employees

Consolidated Intergalactic prohibits the use of postage meters or overnight package delivery services for personal mail. Violation of this policy may be considered grounds for immediate dismissal.

There is an outgoing mailbox in the Mailroom where employees may leave personal mail that carries stamps. This mail is picked up by the U.S. Postal Service each day at approximately 4:30 P.M.

Mailroom policy disallowing acceptance of personal packages

From Mailroom or Office Services to employees

It is against company policy for the Mailroom to accept personal packages sent to employees. We recommend the use of a private mailbox company or other similar services.

Advisory of postage rate increase

From Office Services to employees

As you may be aware, the U.S. Postal Service will be raising rates for all classes of postage on Monday, May 14. On average, the cost of postage will increase by about 5 percent.

We recommend all departments with planned mass mailing of statements, catalogs, and promotional materials make special efforts to get their items into the mail before the new rates go into effect. The Mailroom will stay open an extra hour on Friday, May 11, to accept mail at the older rate.

Library and Archives Notices and Policies

Policy on loan of Library items

From Library or Archives to employees

All books, publications, and electronic media (including CDs, DVDs, and videotapes) in the CI Library are available for loan to employees. Items can be borrowed for one week; the loan period can be extended by request.

Items are not to be removed from the office without specific permission of the Library, and in no case are they to be loaned or given to any nonemployee.

We are in the process of digitizing most of our research materials so that they can be accessed online. As documents are scanned we are removing the original versions from circulation.

If you have any questions about Library policy, please contact us at extension 9192.

Notice of overdue borrowed Library item

From Library or Archives to employee

According to our records, a book you borrowed on May 12 has not been returned to the company Library.

The details of the borrowed book are as follows:

Title:

Item number:

Due date:

If you have need for an extension, please contact the Library at extension 9192.

Request for suggestions for Library acquisition

From Library or Archives to employees

The Library invites requests for acquisitions of books, journals, and electronic media that would be of value to employees of the company.

To make a suggestion for an acquisition, please contact the Library at extension 9192. We would appreciate as much information as possible about the item, including its title, author, ISBN or other identifying number, and publisher.

Announcement of central registry of newspaper and magazine subscriptions

From Library or Archives to department heads and employees

As part of our efforts to reduce unnecessary expenditures, the Library is compiling a list of all magazines and newspapers that are currently received by individuals or departments within the company. It is our goal to encourage sharing of publications where possible, and to maintain a central collection of publications for use by others.

Please respond to this e-mail with a list of any publications which are currently shipped directly to your mail stop.

Request for donation of Library or archival items

From Library or Archives to employees

All departments are asked to notify the Library before any books, periodicals, or electronic media are thrown away. We have an ongoing program of digitizing one-of-a-kind printed documents and would appreciate the opportunity to evaluate materials held by the company.

Policy on use of copyrighted material

From Library, Archives, or Legal Office to employees

Consolidated Intergalactic is committed to full observance of U.S. copyright laws.

In general, you may photocopy, scan, or otherwise duplicate a copyrighted document for your own use. However, you may not make use of a document held under copyright by another for commercial purposes, including presentations to clients or training without the specific permission of the copyright holder.

The same rules apply to copyrighted material that is published in electronic form on a Web site, CD, DVD, or database.

The CI Library staff can assist in determining the copyright status of materials. If you have any questions about proper use of copyrighted material, please contact the Counsel's Office at extension 6666.

Policy on access to materials over intranet

From Library, Archives, or Legal Office to employees

The corporate intranet, available only to employees and other specifically authorized customers, suppliers, and consultants, is owned and operated by Consolidated Intergalactic and held under copyright.

Documents and other information on the intranet is not to be redistributed, copied, or otherwise given to unauthorized persons.

Research materials available on the intranet, including periodicals and utilities, remain the copyrighted property of their owners and may be used only for activities that are included in CI's license.

If you have any questions about the intranet, please contact the Library at extension 9192.

Policy on access to institutional Archives

From Library, Archives, or Legal Office to employees

We are pleased to announce the completion of a six-month project to digitize the institutional Archives of Consolidated Intergalactic, dating all the way back to our company's formation in 1948 as a small maker of rubber novelty items.

Access to files, including patents, designs, advertising and marketing materials, and office documents is available to all authorized employees of the company through the Archives portal on the Library Web page.

Note that sales records, confidential financial information, and personnel files can only be viewed by staffers with appropriate clearance.

For information on using the Archives, please contact the Library at extension 9192.

Requirement to advise archivist before disposal of documents

From Library, Archives, or Legal Office to employees

The Counsel's Office advises all departments that the corporate archivist must be given ten days advance notice before any of the following paper documents are destroyed or otherwise disposed:

- Personnel records
- Customer records
- Financial records including purchases, sales, loans, and stock transactions
- Tax records
- Accounting records
- Correspondence related to patents, trademarks, copyrights, licenses, and so on
- Any document related to potential or ongoing legal actions

The archivist may choose to take possession of these documents or convert them to digital form.

If you have any question whether a particular document or group of papers not included in the above list should be archived, please contact the Library at extension 9192.

Policy on availability of professional researchers

From Library or Archives to employees

The Library Department has posted on its Web site a list of approved professional researchers who can be hired for special projects. Details about Consolidated Intergalactic's policies regarding use of outside researchers are also posted.

In general, researchers working on any subject considered proprietary to the company (including patents, processes, and financial matters) must be approved in advance by the Library. Clearances for such sensitive research are reviewed every three months and are subject to termination at any time.

Announcing access to interLibrary loan

From Library or Archives to employees

The Consolidated Intergalactic Library Department has joined the Gadget Consortium, which permits the sharing of nonproprietary documents, publications, and online electronic documents.

For information about access to information held by the consortium, please consult the Library Web site or call extension 9192.

Policy on use of scanners to record paper documents

From Library, Archives, Information Technology, or Legal Office to employees

The Library, in cooperation with the Information Systems Department, offers electronic scanning of paper documents. All such documents are recorded as PDF files which can be archived, shared, or transmitted but are protected against alteration by the recipient. Details of the scanning program can be found on the Library Web site.

All departments are reminded that special procedures are required to safeguard any document related to a pending or ongoing legal action or investigation by a government agency. If you have any questions in this regard, please contact the Legal Office at extension 6666.

Transportation-Related Notices and Policies to Employees

Announcement of parking policies

From Office Services to employees

The Office Services Department has issued revised regulations for the use of the company parking lot. The full set of rules, which are now incorporated within the employee manual, can be found by visiting the Office Services Web site and clicking on the "Parking Lot" icon.

Here are the highlights of the regulations:

> Every vehicle must be registered with the Office Services Department, and employees must affix a CI Parking Permit to the back of the rear-view mirror.

> Vehicles cannot be left in the parking lot overnight or over the weekend without advance notification to the Office Services Department; permission will be granted only when the employee is traveling on company business or is working on-site during time periods beyond ordinary hours.

> All employees are required to park in designated spaces and not in areas marked for use of visitors or handicapped drivers.

Enforcement of handicapped parking rules

From Office Services to employees

The Office Services Department advises all employees that effective May 1, unauthorized vehicles in any of the handicapped parking spaces will be towed and owners will be required to pay a $150 service charge in order to retrieve their car.

Handicapped parking permits are issued by the City of Lumbertown and are available at City Hall weekdays from 8:30 A.M. to 4:30 P.M.

Consolidated Intergalactic will also honor handicapped parking permits issued by other governmental agencies.

If you have any questions about parking policies, please call the Office Services help line at extension 2552.

Award of special parking space to employee of the month

From Office Services or Human Resources to employees

The Office Services Department has installed markings and a sign directly in front of the main entrance noting the location of the "Employee of the Month" parking space.

Beginning June 1, Human Resources will honor one employee each month for special achievements or services. Among the benefits that come with the award is a placard that allows use of the special space.

We hope you will join us in congratulating each month's winner and respect the use of the special space.

Advisory about towaway zones in parking lot

From Office Services to employees

There's a sign we've seen in a resort town: "Don't Even Think of Parking Here."

We're not going to be that blunt, but we do need to advise all employees that effective immediately we will be strictly enforcing the parking regulations in the company lot. All employees are required to advise Office Services of the make and model of their vehicle and the license plate.

Any vehicle left in a handicapped parking spot or in one of the spaces marked for the use of visitors is subject to towing; vehicles removed in this way will be taken to an area garage and owners will be charged a $50 fee.

Notice of bicycle and motorcycle parking area

From Office Services to employees

We are pleased to announce that we have set up a dedicated parking area for bicycles and motorcycles in the southwest corner of the main lot at our Lumbertown facility.

We have installed four racks that allow locking bikes, and the motorcycle spaces are safely protected from intrusion by four-wheel vehicles.

As a reminder, all vehicles must be registered with Office Services and are not allowed to be left overnight in the parking lot without specific permission obtained from the Security Office.

Announcing closure of section of parking lot and opening of satellite lot

From Office Services to employees

Work will begin on August 1 on our new warehouse expansion on the south side of the main building.

We're all proud of the success of our facilities here in Lumbertown, but our growth will come at a cost: We're going to lose about 100 parking spaces in the main lot.

To deal with this problem, we are offering two solutions:

- We have opened a satellite parking lot about half a mile north of the main entrance to our building, with an entrance on Liberty Street near the intersection with Daniels Avenue. Any employee who registers to park a car at the satellite lot will receive a monthly bonus of $50 in his or her paychecks.

The satellite lot is an easy walk to the main entrance, but we will also offer shuttle van service every weekday between 7:30 A.M. and 9:30 A.M., and again between 4:30 P.M. and 6:30 P.M.

It is our intent that the parking lot be used by employees who work ordinary day shifts. However, if you do find yourself at work late into the night, the Security Office will provide after-hours van service to the satellite lot on request.

- In cooperation with the Benefits Office, we are offering a double bonus to any employee currently in possession of a parking permit for the main lot who turns in that pass and instead enrolls in either a CI-sponsored car pool or purchases a Lumbertown transit pass; please contact the Benefits Office at extension 3421 for details.

Announcing lottery for preferred parking spaces

From Office Services to employees

With the completion of construction of the new east entrance to our Lumbertown facility, we have added twenty-four new parking spaces in that area.

In fairness to all employees, we have decided to conduct a lottery for a dedicated parking space near the east door. Any employee who wishes to participate must register with Office Services before June 1; the lottery will be conducted on June 2 and winners will be notified on that date.

To register, please send an e-mail to *lottery@officeservices.consolidatedintergalactic.com*.

As always, Consolidated Intergalactic is committed to the needs and rights of all of its employees. A full set of handicapped parking spaces is available to the right of the main entrance to the Lumbertown offices.

Purchase of leased vehicle by employee

From Office Services to employees

Any employee currently driving a company-provided vehicle is advised that we offer the opportunity to them to purchase their car at the end of the standard leasing period (usually three years) for the contract's residual value plus a transfer fee.

In most instances, this will allow you to purchase a well-maintained young car at or near its wholesale price.

If you are interested in purchasing your company-provided vehicle under this program, please contact the Office Services automotive desk at extension 2342. Arrangements for such purchases must be made at least sixty days before the end of a lease term.

Availability of leased vehicles for purchase by employee

From Office Services to employees

Consolidated Intergalactic will offer all permanent employees the opportunity to purchase vehicles from our fleet before they are returned to leasing agencies or sold to dealers.

Beginning August 1 and continuing on the first business day of every month thereafter, we will post on the Office Services Web site a list of available vehicles that are due to reach the end of their lease period within sixty days. Employees may purchase any listed vehicle for the lease's residual value plus a transfer fee.

In most instances, this will allow you to purchase a well-maintained young car at or near its wholesale price.

The current driver of any leased vehicle will have first priority in purchasing a car. If they do not offer to purchase the vehicle before it is posted by Office Services, we will accept the first offer received.

If you are interested in purchasing a company-leased vehicle under this program, please contact the Office Services automotive desk at extension 2342.

Announcing auction of company-owned vehicles

From Office Services to employees

The Office Services Department is offering any permanent employee of Consolidated Intergalactic the opportunity to purchase cars, trucks, and other vehicles being retired from the fleet.

A full list of available vehicles is now available on the Office Services Web site at *http://automotive sales.officeservices.consolidatedintergalactic.com.*

You'll find details about each vehicle, including its mileage and maintenance records, on the listing.

The company will conduct an auction of the vehicles on Saturday, May 19, at 9 A.M. in the south parking lot. The starting price for each vehicle will be the wholesale "blue book" value; vehicles which do not receive a bid at or above this price will be sold to a dealer.

If you have questions about the auction, please contact the Office Services automotive desk at extension 2342.

Solicitation of bids for leased vehicles

From Office Services to automotive leasing company

Consolidated Intergalactic is seeking bids from leasing companies and automotive dealers for provision of a fleet of at least 100 mid-sized passenger cars for delivery on September 1.

All vehicles must be new, must have four doors, automatic transmission, and air conditioning. Each must include a full manufacturer's warranty and be supported by a dealership within 50 miles of our Lumbertown headquarters.

The term of the agreement must be thirty-six months, and it must be set up as a $0 down payment, closed-end lease. Each lease must include the option for the company, or a permanent employee of the company, to purchase the vehicle for its residual value plus a reasonable transfer fee, at the end of the lease period.

Full details of specifications for the bid are available at the automotive desk of the company's Office Services Department. For a copy, please call extension 2343.

Policy on use of personal vehicle for company purposes

From Human Resources, Legal Office, or Office Services to employees

Employees of Consolidated Intergalactic are not required to use their own vehicles for company business, although we recognize that there are situations where it is more efficient for a staffer to drive to a client or supplier as part of their trip to or from the workplace.

Such use of a personal vehicle for business purposes requires approval from your supervisor. In order to avoid the possibility of rejection of your request for reimbursement, we recommend you seek advance approval.

After the completion of a trip, the employee must file a report with starting and finishing odometer readings. Reimbursement will be made on the basis of the current Internal Revenue Service mileage rate which is intended to include the cost of gasoline, insurance, and usage of the vehicle.

Employees are encouraged to consult with their personal auto insurance agents or carriers to confirm they have proper coverage for such use of their vehicles. Consolidated Intergalactic does not assume any additional liability for use of personal vehicles.

Request for reimbursement for use of personal vehicle for business purposes

From employee to Human Resources, Legal Office, or Office Services:

I hereby submit a request for reimbursement for use of my personal vehicle for business purposes.

1. Date of use of vehicle: _____

2. Vehicle license number:_____

3. Purpose of trip:_____

4. Starting odometer mileage: _____

5. Ending odometer mileage:_____

Signed (Employee)_____

Supervisor Approval_____

Policy on use of company vehicle for personal purposes

From Human Resources, Legal Office, or Office Services to employees

In general, it is against company policy for an employee of Consolidated Intergalactic to use a company vehicle for personal purposes.

Company vehicles are intended to be used for sales and service calls or deliveries. Certain employees may be permitted to drive their company vehicle to their place of residence if they have need to make sales or service calls from their home.

Policy on use of company vehicle for personal purposes

From Human Resources, Legal Office, or Office Services to employees

Although we discourage use of company vehicles for personal purposes, employees may request such usage in special circumstances. Prior approval must be granted by a supervisor and employees must fill out a Company Vehicle Reimbursement Form that accounts for all mileage driven.

Under current guidelines from the Internal Revenue Service, employees must reimburse the company for all personal usage of company vehicles at the rate of 48.5 cents per mile driven.

If you have any questions about this policy, please contact the Office Services help desk at extension 1238.

25 Office Services: To Vendors

Soliciting bid for services

From Maintenance Department, Procurement, or Office Services to outside company

Consolidated Intergalactic is soliciting bids for the repaving of its parking lot and access roads on its property at its main facility in Lumbertown.

We would like to invite you to submit a bid for the job. Full specifications for the job, and details of the bidding process, are available through the Maintenance Department.

All bidders must fully comply with state and federal laws regarding hiring practices, hourly wages, and other labor issues. In addition, successful bidders must provide evidence of worker's compensation and other required insurance and bonds as stated in the bid specification.

The deadline for submitting a written bid is June 1.

Request for references for contractor

From Offices Services to outside company

We have received your offer to provide landscaping services for our facility in Lumbertown. Can you provide the contact names and phone numbers for at least three area businesses for which you have provided similar services?

Please also note that all contractors must fully comply with state and federal laws regarding hiring practices, hourly wages, and other labor issues. In addition, successful bidders must provide evidence of workers compensation and other required insurance.

Requesting clarification of bid for services

From Maintenance Department, Procurement Department, or Office Services to outside company

We have received your bid for repaving of the parking lot and access roads at our main facility in Lumbertown.

In reviewing your bid, we do not see mention of repair of potholes and broken curbs. Both of these items are included in the list of jobs in the specification.

Please respond no later than June 1 to indicate inclusion of these essential jobs in your bid or to make any necessary changes to the submitted bid.

Rejecting bid for services because of high price

From Maintenance Department, Procurement Office, or Office Services to outside company

Thank you for submitting a bid to repave and repair the parking lot and access roads at our main facility in Lumbertown.

We have decided to accept the lower-priced bid of another company.

We hope to have the opportunity to work with you in the future. Consolidated Intergalactic is committed to hiring local companies whenever possible.

Confirming oral agreement and bidding procedure

From Office Services or Procurement Office to outside company

I am writing to confirm the terms of our agreement, as reached on the telephone yesterday.

Consolidated Intergalactic will engage Lumbertown Parking Lot Stripers to redo the markings in the employee parking lot. The agreed-upon cost was $5,000 for surveying, painting, and directional marking in the lot. You will use high-density Ultra Yellow 6SJ7 acrylic paint for the job.

The work will commence on Saturday, May 1, and will be completed by 5 P.M. on Sunday, May 2; the parking lot will be closed to traffic during that period but will be in a condition usable by employees on Monday, May 3.

You will provide evidence of all required licenses and permits for the work as well as evidence of current workers compensation coverage for all of your employees who will be on our property.

You will generate a contract based on the above specification for approval by our Purchasing Department no later than April 1.

Appointing representative for real estate or rental negotiation

From Office Services or Legal Office to outside company

This is to confirm our appointment of your agency as our representative in negotiations related to the leasing of commercial office space in Houston for a regional sales office. We have agreed to pay a finder's fee of 10 percent of the first year's annual rent, upon execution of an acceptable lease agreement.

The specifications for the office we are seeking as well as the standard elements of any lease agreement we require are included in the attached memo from our legal counsel.

Please advise the Consolidated Intergalactic Real Estate Department of any developments in the search for office space.

Request for bids on transportation services

From Office Services to outside company

Consolidated Intergalactic seeks bids from area businesses for transportation of employees to or from its Lumbertown headquarters or residences in the area to or from the Broome County International Airport.

We estimate an average of about twenty roundtrips per month.

We seek bids on a flat-rate basis for all trips within a 25-mile radius of our Lumbertown office, and an additional per-mile rate for trips that are farther than that distance.

Bids are due in the Office Services Department by 5 P.M. on Monday, April 30. All bidders must provide evidence of proper liability, workers compensation, and other applicable forms of insurance as well as meet all requirements for licensure as a limousine service.

Follow-up on bid for transportation services

From Office Services to outside company

Thank you for your bid to provide transportation services for employees to and from the Broome County International Airport.

Your offer did not address one of the elements of the request for bids: the price for transportation for employees who live beyond a twenty-five-mile radius around the airport. Please clarify your bid to include a per-mile cost for such services, or indicate if there is no additional charge for employees who live within Broome or Licking County.

Your revised bid is due in the Office Services Department by 5 P.M. on Monday, April 30. All bidders must provide evidence of proper liability, workers compensation, and other applicable forms of insurance as well as meet all requirements for licensure as a limousine service.

Request for bids on local delivery or courier service

From Office Services to outside company

The Office Services department of Consolidated Intergalactic seeks bids from any qualified area business for local delivery and courier services.

Full details of the required services can be found on the attached Request for Bids #6SJ7.

Bids are due in the Office Services Department by 5 P.M. on Monday, August 15. All bidders must provide evidence of proper liability, workers compensation, and other applicable forms of insurance as well as meet all requirements for licensure for provision of freight and courier services.

Follow-up on bids for local delivery or courier service

From Office Services to outside company

Thank you for your bid for local delivery and courier services for Consolidated Intergalactic.

In order for us to proceed with a review of your bid, we require evidence of workers compensation and liability insurance as well as state licensure.

We must receive this information in the Office Services Department before the deadline for bids of 5 P.M. on Monday, August 15.

Request for bid for catering in workplace

From employee or department to outside vendor, request for bid for catering in workplace

We are seeking bids for provision of an informal catered working lunch for Human Resources at Consolidated Intergalactic. The lunch is to be served on Wednesday, December 5, at 12:30 P.M.

If you are interested in bidding, please provide your bid no later than 5 P.M. on November 15. Note that all outside vendors are required to have workers compensation and liability insurance as well as all required health department permits.

Full details of the requested food items are attached, along with a copy of guidelines for bidding for provision of services to Consolidated Intergalactic.

Follow-up on bid for catering in workplace

From employee or department to outside vendor

Thank you for your bid to provide a catered luncheon for Human Resources at Consolidated Intergalactic. We will be making a final decision on the bid by November 22.

The current bid specifies food for fifteen persons. Can you please advise the adjustment to the price if we were to increase or decrease the number of staff members at the meal?

Acceptance of bid for catering in workplace with details

From employee or department to outside vendor

We are pleased to accept your bid to cater a working luncheon at Consolidated Intergalactic on December 5. The executed contract is attached.

Please call Office Services at extension 3457 at least one day in advance of the dinner to discuss parking and set-up procedures for catered meals.

Request for credit for problem with catering in workplace

From employee or department to outside vendor

Your company provided catering services to Human Resources on December 5. We were generally pleased with the quality of the food, but we were disappointed that the meal did not include the chocolate cake that was specified in the contract.

I am writing to request a credit in the amount of $40, the contracted price for the dessert. We would appreciate your immediate attention to this matter.

Request for proof of proper workers comp insurance for service in workplace

From employee or department to outside vendor

We have received your bid for provision of catering services at Consolidated Intergalactic.

In order for us to certify your company as qualified to offer these services in the workplace we require evidence of current workers compensation and liability insurance as well as county health department certificates.

I look forward to receipt of these details.

26 Information Technology: General Policies

From Information Technology to Employees

Announcement of scheduled downtime for computer network maintenance

From Information Technology or Office Services to employees

All employees are advised that the corporate computer network will be shut down on Sunday, April 29, from 7 A.M. until noon to allow for scheduled maintenance and upgrade of equipment. We have chosen this date and time in hopes of having the least impact on operations.

If you have any questions about the shutdown, or any special need for assistance during that period, please call the IT hotline at extension 6666.

Announcement of scheduled unavailability of resources because of updates

From Information Technology or Office Services to employees

The Human Resources's benefits database will be unavailable for online access all day Tuesday, April 10, beginning at 8 A.M. to allow for installation and testing of new software.

Employees who need information regarding health benefits, vacation and personal days, and other related information are advised to make inquiries before the end of business on April 9. If you have any questions about this update, please contact the Benefits Office at extension 4443.

We apologize for any inconvenience.

Notice of system-wide update for all workstations

From Information Technology or Office Services to employees

Information Technology will be applying a system-wide update to software over the weekend of September 14 and 15.

All PCs and workstations currently running Microsoft Office XP will be upgraded to the newer and improved Microsoft Office 2007 applications suite.

None of your data files will be affected by the update. However, the new applications suite uses a different file format for storage; the format requires less storage space and is more resistant to infection by viruses in macros embedded in text or spreadsheet files.

Once you begin using the new application suite it will automatically use the new file format, which gives all files a new filename extension of .DOCX. You will continue to be able to use older files with a .DOC filename extension.

However, if you are preparing a file that will be given or transmitted to a customer or client using an older version of Microsoft Office, you will need to do one of the following two things: 1) save your file as a "compatible" file for older versions, or 2) advise the recipient of your file to visit the Microsoft Web site to download a free conversion utility that permits them to use files created under the new system.

If you have any questions about this upgrade to your computer, or seek instructions on using the new applications suite, please call the Information Technology help desk at extension 6666.

Policy on file naming conventions

From Information Technology to employees

Information Technology requests all employees to follow a standard file naming convention for all electronic files. This will improve our ability to locate and index data, and will assist in tracking versions of files as they are edited and changed collaboratively.

You may use any allowable name for the identification portion of your file. Following the identification, please add your initials and the date the file was first created in a six-digit number. For example:

name of file CDS060208

Our system will automatically add the proper filename extension (.DOC, .DOCX, .TIF, etc.) to identify the type of file.

If you have any questions, please call the IT help desk at extension 5501.

Use of computers for personal purposes (prohibition on commercial, religious, political use)

From Information Technology or Legal Office to employees

All employees are reminded that it is prohibited to use a company computer or laptop for any personal commercial purpose including stock trades, online auctions, or shopping. Further, it is not allowed to use computer equipment on behalf of any religious or political organization.

Policy regarding use of office telephone for personal purposes

From Information Technology or Office Services to employees

Employees are asked to refrain from unnecessary use of the company's telephone system for personal purposes.

Further, it is specifically against company policy to use the phone system on behalf of political or religious organizations or for illegal purposes including gambling.

Policy regarding use of company-provided cell phones

From Information Technology or Office Services to employees

Employees are reminded that company-provided cell phones are intended for use solely for business purposes. All accounts are subject to auditing.

Members of staff who are traveling on company business are permitted a reasonable number of personal calls.

Policy regarding use of personal cell phones in the workplace

From Information Technology or Office Services to employees

It is prohibited to use personal cell phones in the workplace. Employees may make and receive calls or messages only during lunch breaks or, with approval of a supervisor, for emergency purposes.

Prohibition on use of personal cell phone cameras in the workplace

From Information Technology or Office Services to employees

For security and personal privacy reasons, it is prohibited to use cell phone cameras, digital cameras, video cameras, or other forms of recording devices in the workplace without the specific permission of a supervisor.

Soliciting requests for training

From Information Technology or Training Department to employees

The Information Technology Department welcomes suggestions from all employees for training and refresher courses on use of the corporate IT system, laptops, and personal data assistants.

Classes can be offered as seminars, or with the approval of department heads individualized courses can be arranged for employees performing specialized tasks or using nonstandard software or hardware.

Please submit your suggestion to Mary Sobotnik at extension 3457.

Requirements for approval for new software installation

From Information Technology or Office Services to employees

Employees are reminded that it is against company policy to install any software without specific approval from the IT department. This includes commercial software packages as well as downloaded shareware and utilities available on the Internet.

This policy is in effect to protect the enterprise from computer viruses, security leaks, and other problems that may arise from use of nonstandard software.

If you have need for a particular software package not already installed on your machine or on corporate servers, please contact the IT help line at extension 6666.

Requirements for approval for installation of new hardware

From Information Technology or Office Services to employees

The Information Technology Department reminds all employees that permission is required for installation of any new hardware on a company-owned workstation, desktop, or laptop computer. This includes external devices which plug into USB, eSATA, or FireWire ports, as well as adapters that require internal installation.

This policy is in place to prevent the possible corruption of operating systems and applications, or the introduction of computer viruses as part of device drivers and software that support the new hardware.

If you require the use of specialized hardware or an upgrade to your system, please consult the IT help desk at extension 3467.

Policy on e-mail accounts

From Information Technology or Office Services to employees

E-mail accounts are intended exclusively for business purposes. Please do not use your e-mail address for any other purpose.

Employees are reminded that all messages on the corporate system are subject to monitoring by the company. Improper use of the e-mail system, including disclosure of confidential financial or personnel information as well as transmission of improper data or images, is grounds for immediate dismissal.

E-mail privacy warning

From Information Technology, Office Services, or Legal Office to employees

(Attached as a signature to all outgoing e-mails.)

This message is a private communication. If you are not the intended recipient, please do not read, copy, forward, use it, or disclose its contents to others. Please notify the sender by replying to this message and indicating the message was improperly sent to you, and then delete it from your system. Thank you.

Policy on maintenance of e-mail files

From Information Technology, Library, Archives, or Legal Office to employees

All employees are advised that all incoming and outgoing e-mail is automatically archived on servers here and at our Internet service provider.

In addition, employees are instructed that it is company policy that under no circumstance is it permissible to alter the contents, or change time and date or other details of any document sent using corporate facilities. Documents that are not critical to the performance of our mission statement may be deleted on users' e-mail accounts, but will be retained in the Archives.

Finally, the Legal Office advises that any e-mail related to a pending or ongoing legal issue including lawsuits or investigations by a government agency must be maintained without relocation or alteration. If the Legal Office is aware of a legal issue, you will be notified of proper safeguards for e-mails which may become an element of a legal action; if you are advised by a third party of a legal challenge or action you are directed to immediately notify the Legal Office at extension 6666.

Availability of corporate discounts for computer purchases by individuals

From Information Technology or Office Services to employees

Information Technology advises all personnel that as part of our master procurement agreement for desktop and laptop computers, employees are eligible for discounts on purchases of these devices and accessories for personal use. Equipment will be shipped directly to your home.

For information, please contact Matt Ziff at extension 9812.

Availability of corporate discounts for cell phone purchases by individuals

From Information Technology or Office Services to employees

AllCellTel, the supplier of cell phone services to the company, has extended an offer to all Consolidated Intergalactic employees for specially discounted cell phone plans for personal use.

For details, please contact AllCellTel and provide them with discount code CONINTER and your employee number.

Policy on disposal of outdated computer hardware

From Information Technology or Office Services to employees

Outmoded or failed computer equipment must be collected by Information Technology for proper disposal.

Where possible, retired computer equipment will be donated to area schools and community groups. Any disposal will be done in an environmentally appropriate manner.

Availability for purchase of used equipment by staffers

From Information Technology or Office Services to employees

Information Technology will be offering recently retired desktop and laptop computers, monitors, and other electronic equipment at a silent auction event on Friday, May 15. Equipment will be on display in Conference Room C, near the IT Department offices.

Employees can place a bid for equipment on that day between noon and 3 P.M.; successful bidders can pick up the equipment at the end of the day.

In keeping with company policy, 10 percent of the proceeds of the sale will be contributed to the Lumbertown Boys and Girls Club for ongoing activities.

Policy on use of integrated calendar software

From Information Technology or Office Services to employees

All employees are reminded to use CON-SCHED, the online calendar and scheduling program. Please record all appointments on your personal page and consult it regularly.

Supervisors and department heads are able to consult staff calendars to allow them to schedule meetings and training sessions. In addition, company-wide meetings or events are automatically added to calendars and the computer will automatically generate and send an e-mail message if you have a conflict between an appointment you have set up and a meeting that has been added to your calendar.

Training course on PowerPoint presentations

From Training Department and Information Technology to employees

Want to learn how to PowerPoint like a pro? The Information Technology Department, in cooperation with the Training Department, will be offering a six-part course in designing and delivering an electronic presentation.

The course, appropriate for beginners and experts alike, will be offered Wednesdays from September 26 to October 31 at 4 P.M. in Conference Room B.

Participants will be taught how to bring together text, art, animation, and sound for presentation before large audiences, small conferences, or as preprogrammed shows for transmission over the Web or as self-running demonstrations for sales and marketing.

The course is open to any CI employee. Please seek permission from your department head before enrolling; contact the Training Department at extension 2323 to reserve your space.

Announcement of recall of laptop batteries

From Information Technology to employees

According to our records, you are currently using a Innodelgate SmartPass laptop computer issued by Information Technology for use in your business travels.

Innodelgate has just issued a bulletin recalling the lithium batteries used in all current models of their laptop computers because of a rare but dangerous defect that could cause a fire. The affected models are those in the TS8xx series, numbered from TS800 through TS852.

Please immediately stop using your laptop on battery power. Remove the battery and set it aside to prevent inadvertent problems; we will advise you on proper disposal procedures in a subsequent e-mail.

You may continue to use your laptop with the supplied AC adapter. Information Technology has been informed by Innodelgate that replacement batteries for these models of laptop have already been shipped to Consolidated Intergalactic and should be available for distribution to users within a week.

If you have any questions about this recall, please contact the Information Technology help desk at extension 2347.

Process to replace laptop batteries

From Information Technology to employees

Information Technology has received a supply of replacement batteries for Innodelgate SmartPass laptop computers affected by a safety recall. According to our records, your company-issued laptop is included among the models that require a change of batteries.

If you are located in the Lumbertown headquarters office, please visit the IT help desk on the second floor of the east wing any time between 8 A.M. and 6 P.M. this week to obtain a new battery for your laptop; we will collect your machine's old battery at the same time to permit proper disposal.

If you are traveling or located away from Lumbertown please call our office at extension 2347 or send an e-mail to *batteryrecall@IT.consolidatedintergalactic.com* to arrange for shipment of a replacement battery and return of the original device.

As a reminder, until you receive your new battery please do not use your laptop on battery power. Remove the battery and set it aside to prevent inadvertent problems. You may continue to use your laptop with the supplied AC adapter.

Availability of amplified telephones

From Information Technology to employees

Information Technology is pleased to offer to employees a special telephone with a built-in amplifier; the devices are appropriate for any person with moderate to severe hearing loss.

To request issuance of the phone, please contact the Medical Office help desk at extension 2932. They will put through the necessary work order and Information Technology will arrange for installation and training on the device.

Availability of privacy filters for laptop computers

From Information Technology to employees

Information Technology has received a shipment of privacy filters that can be used with most models of company-issued laptops. These special screens attach to the laptop display and prevent viewing of information by anyone except the person directly in front of the device.

Consolidated Intergalactic requires all users of company-issued laptops to safeguard the security of the information contained within or displayed by these devices. Security measures include fingerprint authentication, password protection, and privacy filters.

To arrange for installation of a privacy filter, please contact the Information Technology help desk at extension 4235.

Information Technology to Third-Party Vendors

Request for written bid for corporate cell phone service

From Information Technology or Office Services to third-party vendor

Consolidated Intergalactic is seeking bids for cell phone equipment and service for a minimum of 250 employees (up to a maximum of 750). We are seeking equipment and plans that include the following specifications:

- Free cell phone to cell phone service;
- Full national coverage without roaming charges, and
- Electronically searchable individual reports on each phone account.

Full details on the requirements for submitting a bid to Consolidated Intergalactic, including all required insurance, bonds, and guarantees, are listed on the attached Bidding Guidelines.

The deadline for submission of a bid is June 5 at 5 P.M. in the Procurement Office of Consolidated Intergalactic in Lumbertown. The company reserves the right to accept any, or none, of the submitted bids.

Follow-up on bid for corporate cell phone service

From Information Technology or Office Services to third-party vendor

We have received your bid for provision of cell phone service for Consolidated Intergalactic.

In reviewing the bid, we find that it does not include the following essential element: the provision of electronically searchable individual reports on each phone line provided.

Please clarify, no later than the end of business on June 10, whether you are able to provide this service as part of your bid. At this time we are unable to accept any other alterations to your bid, including any change to the charges per line.

27 Information Technology: Security and Maintenance

Security Notices from Information Technology

Announcement of mandatory training courses on security

From Information Technology or Training Department to employees

All employees are asked to attend one of six upcoming seminars on Information Technology Security.

The ninety-minute sessions, to be held in Conference Room A, will include a review of our corporate policies on data security and basic training on the new enterprise-wide electronic scheduling calendar.

Seminars are offered on different days at varying times of the day; please choose the class that best meets your schedule. Requests for specific classes must be approved by your department head or supervisor in order to assure that all departments have adequate staffing during the seminar period.

Policy on confidentiality of electronic information

From Information Technology to employees

Consolidated Intergalactic is committed to protecting the privacy of confidential personal, salary, and business-critical data.

Employees are not to disclose their login name or password to any other person for any reason. If you have any reason to believe that your password is being used by others or that your account is in any way compromised, please immediately contact the Information Technology hotline at extension 6666.

Prohibition against back-dating of documents, computer monitoring

From Information Technology, Legal Office, or Compliance Office to employees

All employees are advised that it is against company policy to attempt to change computer clocks or to manually alter dates on files. The purpose of the computerized clock is to assist the company in maintaining an audit trail for all documents, including financial, personnel, and technology.

Computer security software will automatically detect any such attempt and altered files will be logged.

Policy regarding travel with laptop

From Information Technology or Office Services to employees

All employees who use a company-issued laptop or personal digital assistant (PDA) are advised that each such device must be inspected by the IT department at least once a month to assure that proper security measures are in place to protect the contents of the hard drive or other storage medium and that passwords and logins are safeguarded.

The inspection can be performed automatically by attaching the laptop or PDA to the corporate intranet, connecting to the IT Web site, and selecting the Laptop Security Check-up option. The security check requires about an hour and runs unattended.

All new laptops must include a built-in fingerprint recognition system; the IT Department is also outfitting existing laptops with an external fingerprint recognition device.

If your laptop is lost or stolen, or if you have any reason to suspect that its security has been compromised, you are required to immediately notify the IT hotline at extension 6666.

Policy regarding use of PDAs

From Information Technology or Office Services to employees

Employees are required to seek certification from Information Technology for any personal data assistant (PDA) they use to access corporate information. It is required that any PDA be password-protected to prevent unauthorized access to our systems by outsiders and to prevent viewing of data stored on the device itself.

Certain older-model PDAs are no longer supported by the IT Department because of security shortcomings. Such models will no longer be allowed to access the corporate data systems and must be replaced.

Notification of monitoring of Web usage

From Information Technology or Legal Office to employees

Employees are reminded that all data passing through our corporate network is subject to monitoring by Information Technology. It is not safe to use a company computer for personal banking or other personal confidential information.

Notification of blocked Web sites

From Information Technology or Legal Office to employees

Information Technology has added a program that blocks access to certain known sites that are considered unacceptable or dangerous to corporate security. These include, but are not limited to, sites featuring adult content, gambling, and games.

In addition, the system will block certain sites based on monitoring of data transmitted by the site. The system will log any attempt to visit a blocked site.

If you find that the system is blocking your access to a legitimate site, or if you have a business reason to visit a blocked site, please contact the IT hotline at extension 6666.

Notification of monitoring of e-mails

From Information Technology or Legal Office to employees

All employees are advised that the company e-mail system is considered proprietary property of Consolidated Intergalactic. All messages are subject to monitoring, inspection, and storage.

Our purposes in monitoring the e-mail system include assuring that we follow all of the provisions of federal laws regarding insider trading and financial disclosure, protecting against leaks of proprietary company information including financial data and patents, and protecting against intentional or accidental release of confidential personal information of our employees.

We strongly advise all employees to limit their use of the e-mail system to appropriate purposes. If you have any questions about our e-mail policies, please contact Information Technology.

Policy on mandatory use of antivirus and antispam software

From Information Technology or Office Services to employees

All workstations, desktop computers, and laptops that are used to access the corporate information system must use the EnGarde Antivirus Antispam system. This software is automatically installed on all systems, and is updated on a daily basis.

Any user who attempts to sign on to the corporate system without EnGarde installed and enabled will be denied access, and a security alert will be logged in the system.

If you have any questions about the use of the antivirus or antispam system, or if you have difficulties accessing the system with the proper software installed, please call the IT hotline at extension 6666.

Warning against opening unsolicited attachments and files

From Information Technology or Office Services to employees

We're under attack: On an average day the Consolidated Intergalactic information technology e-mail servers detect and remove about fifty attempts to spread viruses, worms, and other nasty attempts to infiltrate our system.

Even with the best efforts of our automated antivirus and firewall facilities, we cannot guarantee 100 percent protection for every incoming message, every time.

For that reason, all employees are advised that they should always take extra care when accepting or considering opening of any file sent as an attachment to an e-mail. If you don't know the sender, are not expecting an attachment, or if you have any reason to suspect that a file sent to you may not be legitimate, STOP. Call the IT Department help line at extension 4532 and ask for advice.

Don't worry about "bothering" us. We'd much rather spend a few minutes walking you through the process or scanning an unknown file rather than having to spend hours or days cleaning out a virus or worm that has made its way inside our system.

Emergency procedure if you suspect a virus in your computer

From Information Technology or Office Services to employees

What do you do if—despite following all of the advice and instructions for safe computing—you suspect that your computer has been infected by a virus, worm, or other unwanted intruder?

Stop what you're doing. Don't attempt to fix anything yourself. Don't send any messages. Pick up your telephone and call the IT Department help line at extension 4532.

If it appears that your computer is busily sending out copies of the virus to others (that's the way many of these nasty pieces of electronic graffiti work) turn off your computer. Don't worry about shutting down your system in its standard, orderly process: Just turn it off or unplug it. We'll repair any problems to your operating system once your computer has been disconnected from the office network and properly disinfected.

Reminder of company-wide required password changes

From Information Technology or Office Services to employees

Employees are reminded that passwords are required to be changed on the first business day of each month; if you do not sign in to the system on that day, you will be prompted to change your password the first time you use the computer that month.

For tips and suggestions on how to create a safe password and how to set up a system to help you remember it as it changes from month to month, please visit the IT Web site and click on the "Password Wizard" icon.

Company policy on creation of password and proper safeguards

From Information Technology or Office Services to employees

We have posted a new Password Wizard on the Information Technology Web site that helps generate high-security passwords for use with all company workstations, desktop, and laptop computers. Use of this wizard will help you create a password and allow for secure storage of that password on the IT system in case it is forgotten.

Users are reminded that all passwords must be between eight and twelve characters long and must include at least one number. Please do not use passwords based on your name or anyone in your family, your phone number, your license plate, or any other piece of publicly available information. Further, do not write down your password and attach it to your desk or computer.

The Password Wizard will help you make selections based on places or objects that are obvious only to you, and will display customized hints on your screen to help you remember each month's entry code.

If you have any questions about the use of passwords, please call the IT hotline at extension 6666.

Policy regarding release of e-mail addresses to outsiders

From Information Technology or Office Services to employees

Your personal e-mail address should be given only to clients, suppliers, and others with a specific need to contact you.

Please do not give or distribute e-mail addresses of other Consolidated Intergalactic employees to outsiders without the permission of the account holder.

You will receive an automatically generated report each morning that lists any e-mails sent to your address that have been flagged as possible "spam" by our system. If you see an e-mail inappropriately placed on the spam list, use the system to mark the sender as legitimate; that message will be immediately moved to your inbox and future mail from that sender will be allowed.

If you have any questions about use of the e-mail system, please contact the IT help desk at extension 3457.

Policy regarding release of company phone directory to outsiders

From Information Technology or Office Services to employees

The internal printed telephone directory and its online electronic version are the property of Consolidated Intergalactic and are not to be given to unauthorized persons.

Customers and suppliers are free to call directly to employees; our automated phone answering system will direct callers who do not know the internal phone extension of members of staff.

Policy forbidding unauthorized use of copyrighted material

From Information Technology, Legal Office, or Library to employees

Employees are reminded that it is against company policy to include any copyrighted text or images in e-mail, presentations, or other documents without permission from the owner of the material. This is becoming an increasingly significant problem for all organizations because of the lack of proper safeguards on Internet Web sites.

If you find material on a Web site that bears a copyright notice, you cannot reuse that material without permission. If a Web site does not post a copyright notice, that is not a guarantee that the producer of that Web site owns the rights to the material or is able to grant rights to you or to Consolidated Intergalactic for reuse.

If you have any questions about proper use of material, please consult the corporate archivist, at extension 7923. If you have any reason to be concerned about material that has already been used, please immediately contact our in-house counsel at extension 9998.

Procedure to seek permission to use copyrighted material in presentations

From Information Technology, Legal Office, or Library to employees

Attached is a form that can be used to request permission for the use of copyrighted material in presentations, e-mails, and other publications. A properly executed form must be on file with the Legal Office before any reuse of copyrighted material is made; the form must be signed by the owner of the copyrighted material and approved by the Legal Office.

If you have any questions about this policy please contact the corporate archivist, at extension 7923.

Policy on use of data projectors for presentations

From Information Technology or Office Services

Information Technology has purchased four data projectors that can be used with PowerPoint and other computer-based presentations; the devices are intended for use in conference rooms with projection screens.

Users can reserve a projector as much as two weeks in advance; first-time borrowers are required to take a fifteen-minute online training course in use of the devices and proper preparation of presentations.

For details about the use of the data projectors, please contact the IT help desk.

From Information Technology Regarding Support and Repair Services

Procedure for troubleshooting and repair of computer equipment

From Information Technology or Office Services to employees

The Information Technology help desk has extended its regular hours to offer assistance to users between 6:30 A.M. and 6:30 P.M. CST. If you have need for assistance outside of that time period, a phone call to the help desk (extension 3457) will be automatically forwarded to an employee on-call twenty-four hours a day.

If you are traveling away from the office with a company-issued laptop or personal data assistant, the help desk will be able to assist in arranging for emergency repairs or replacement of equipment if necessary.

Employees are reminded that it is against company policy to seek or obtain repair or troubleshooting assistance from unauthorized sources.

Availability of outside consultants for special projects

From Information Technology or Office Services to employees

Information Technology has retained the services of a technology consultant who is available to assist with planning and implementation of special projects that make use of our computer resources.

Please contact the IT help desk if you feel you or your department could make use of specialized training or planning services of this sort.

Policy on upgrading or replacement of computer equipment on an individual basis

From Information Technology or Office Services to employees

It is company policy to replace computers on a four-year cycle, with no more than 25 percent of the company's machines being changed each year. All computers are tracked through an online database.

If you have a specific need for an upgrade to your present computer, please contact the IT help desk. Exceptions to the four-year replacement cycle require approval by your departmental head.

Announcement of outsourcing of computer maintenance services

From Information Technology or Office Services to employees

Effective June 1, maintenance on installed computers, workstations, and laptops will be outsourced to a local consultancy, Lumbertown 'Lectronics. This will allow Information Technology to concentrate on supporting applications and managing the flow and use of data in the company.

Management of repair and upgrade services will continue to be handled by Information Technology. To request service, please call the IT help desk at extension 2231; the department will arrange for service by the consulting company. Please do not call Lumbertown 'Lectronics directly; they are not authorized to accept work orders directly from employees.

Announcement of in-house maintenance of computers

From Information Technology or Office Services to employees

Information Technology will take over maintenance and upgrade of all installed computers, workstations, and laptops effective January 1.

The department will be adding two full-time technicians to work on computers, and additional part-time staff will be on-call as needed. Emergency service will be available through the IT Department at all times. Employees traveling away from headquarters on company business can call for assistance and may be referred to repair services under contract to the company.

To request service, please call the IT help desk at extension 2231. For emergency service during off-hours, call the same number and press the 7 key and # on your telephone to page an on-call technician.

28 Office Medical Services

Emergency health needs: whom to call first

From Security Office or Medical Office to employees

In case of medical emergency, please call the Security Office immediately at extension 9111. The officer on duty will coordinate with our Medical Office to provide the fastest response with our own staff, and will summon an ambulance and EMTs if necessary.

If a hospital or EMT is contacted directly by an employee, please also call the Security Office so that we can be prepared to assist.

Advisory on policy for noncritical health care in the workplace

From Security Office or Medical Office to employees

For noncritical health care issues, please call or visit the Medical Office at extension 2375. On-duty nurses can assist with basic first aid and coordinate necessary medical care.

Calls placed to the Medical Office after regular office hours will automatically be forwarded to the Security Office.

Policy regarding workplace injuries and workers compensation

From Medical Office or Benefits Office to employees

It is essential that any injury, major or minor, that takes place on company property be promptly reported to the Medical Office. Failure to do so could jeopardize your eligibility for workers compensation or result in a denial of claims by your health care provider.

If you have any questions about this important policy, please contact the Medical Office at extension 2345.

Requirement of notification of medical condition that will impact ability to perform job

From Medical Office or Human Resources Office to employees

Any employee who is injured or develops a medical condition that will impact the ability to perform his or her job is required to immediately notify the Medical Office. This applies whether the injury or condition developed on the job or on your own time.

Consolidated Intergalactic is committed to maintaining a safe and secure workplace for all employees. When necessary, we will seek to make special accommodations for an injured or ill employee including adjustment to work tasks and hours.

Requirement of notification when employee is taking medication that may affect ability to perform job

From Medical Office or Human Resources to employees

Any employee who is prescribed a medication that may affect the ability to perform his or her job is required to notify the Medical Office immediately. Such medications include, but are not limited to sleep aids, painkillers, and certain cold or sinus treatments.

Consolidated Intergalactic is committed to maintaining a safe and secure workplace for all employees. When necessary, we will seek to make special accommodations for employees who should not be operating machinery or driving vehicles because of prescription medication. Such accommodations may include adjustment to work tasks and hours.

Advisory on intestinal flu outbreak

From Medical Office to employees

As most employees are aware, a number of members of staff at our headquarters here in Lumbertown have been sickened by a stomach bug in recent days.

Symptoms include mild to severe nausea, diarrhea, and associated dehydration. The illness typically lasts twenty-four to forty-eight hours.

Health experts say the disease is spread by contact and not by airborne transmission. We have asked the Maintenance Department to clean doorknobs, railings, sinks, and other fixtures several times each day.

In addition, the Medical Office asks all employees to observe the following guidelines:

- If you are ill at home, please do not come in to work until symptoms have completely ended.
- If you become ill at work, please contact the Medical Office to seek our assistance in arranging transportation to bring you home or to seek medical care if necessary.
- To help limit the spread of the disease, please regularly wash your hands, especially after using restroom facilities. The Medical Office will also be distributing bottles of antibacterial hand cleaners to all employees and will have bottles at all entrances to the building.

If you have any questions or need any assistance, please call the Medical Office hotline at extension 4323. After ordinary hours, the same phone number will automatically be rolled to the Security Office.

Cancellation of conferences because of intestinal flu outbreak

From Medical Office to employees

As a precaution to help stop the spread of a stomach flu currently affecting some employees here at our Lumbertown headquarters, the Medical Office asks all department heads to cancel or postpone conferences, training sessions, and other such gatherings scheduled for the next week.

Medical authorities say that our current efforts, including sanitizing of door knobs and railings and bathroom facilities should limit the course of the disease to about a week.

We have previously asked all employees to stay at home, or leave the office, if they become ill. In addition, we have distributed antibacterial hand cleaners throughout the building and ask that they be used regularly.

If you have any questions or need any assistance, please call the Medical Office hotline at extension 4323. After ordinary hours, the same phone number will automatically be rolled to the Security Office.

Policy on company's right to conduct random drug testing

From Medical Office or Legal Office to employees, policy on random drug testing

Consolidated Intergalactic is committed to the establishment and maintenance of a safe and secure workplace. All employees are reminded that we reserve the right to conduct random and unannounced drug tests at any time, and to require a drug test any time a worker is involved in an accident or incident in the workplace.

Policy on disposal of syringes, other medical supplies

From Medical Office or Benefits Office to employees

The Maintenance Department has installed medical syringe disposal boxes in bathrooms on each floor of the Lumbertown facility. An additional disposal box is located in a treatment room next to the Medical Office.

No employee is to dispose of an approved medical syringe in common waste receptacles or anywhere else on company property.

Use of these approved boxes is intended to reduce the possibility of accidental transmission of disease or injury to others. For further information about use of the boxes, please contact the Medical Office at extension 2345.

Reminder to update emergency notification forms

From Executive Office, Office Services, or Medical Office to employees

All regular full-time and part-time employees are required to have on file a current listing of emergency contact information for themselves.

The form requests telephone and cell phone contact numbers and addresses for yourself, any family members you choose to have listed, and medical information such as physicians and hospital preference. All such information is held confidential by the company.

Please review your form as soon as possible. The information is available by signing in to the Human Resources Web site. (Locate the "Personal Notification Update" icon on the toolbar on the left side of the screen.)

Reminder to update medical forms to indicate allergies and medications (confidential)

From Medical Office to employees, reminder to update health records

The Medical Office reminds all employees to update their medical form to include any new medications they are regularly using and to indicate any recently discovered allergies. This will assist the medical staff and any emergency responders in dealing with health problems at work.

The medical form is confidential and used for this purpose only.

Policy on confidentiality of health information

From Medical Office to employees

Under the provisions of the Health Insurance Portability and Accountability Act (HIPAA), all personnel records related to health and medical issues are confidential and not to be disclosed to any third person with permission. We have made necessary improvements to the security of our computer files here at CI, and have added confidential meeting rooms in the Medical Office and the Benefits Office where employees can discuss medical issues and questions in privacy.

Commendation to employee for handling emergency

From Executive Office, Medical Office, or Office Services to employee

On behalf of all of us at Consolidated Intergalactic, please allow me to thank you for your recent exemplary performance in assisting an employee who was suffering a medical emergency.

According to our health staff, you made all the right decisions: notifying emergency services, making the employee comfortable, and administering basic first aid until the EMTs arrived on the scene.

A copy of this commendation will be placed in your personnel file, and I expect to be taking special notice of your actions at the annual company meeting in May.

Announcement of health fair

From Benefits Office or Medical Office to employees

Lumbertown Hospital will conduct a health fair in the main parking lot on Saturday, October 5, from 8 A.M. to 4 P.M.

All employees and their dependents are encouraged to attend this event, which is subsidized by Consolidated Intergalactic. Attendees can receive a free cholesterol test and basic screening for diabetes, hypertension, and other conditions.

Physicians and nurses will also be available to answer questions on health concerns, diet, and physical conditions. For information, please call the Benefits Office help desk at extension 3456.

Announcement of flu shot clinic

From Benefits Office or Medical Office to employees

The Medical Office will offer a free flu shot clinic for all employees on Friday, November 15, from 8 A.M. until 6 P.M.

Please call extension 2375 to arrange for an appointment. If you have any medical concerns about the flu shot please consult your personal physician.

Announcement of blood donation clinic

From Benefits Office or Medical Office to employees

The American Red Cross Bloodmobile will be in the main parking lot on Thursday, January 8, from 8 A.M. until 6 P.M.

As a token of our appreciation for any Consolidated Intergalactic employee who makes a blood donation that day, we will offer a $25 dinner certificate at Danziger's Restaurant in Lumbertown.

Availability of confidential counseling on substance abuse

From Medical Office to employees

Consolidated Intergalactic is committed to helping all of our employees establish and maintain a healthy lifestyle. The Medical Office offers confidential counseling on matters of substance abuse, including referrals to area support organizations and medical treatment. No information disclosed in a counseling session may be used in any disciplinary action against an employee.

Training on emergency first response medical

From Human Resources, Manufacturing Department, or Medical Office to employees

Members of the Medical Office will meet with each shift of the Manufacturing Department during the week of May 1 to review proper first response procedures for medical emergencies including illness and injury.

Depending on the workload during the training period, division managers may choose to schedule thirty minutes of overtime for the training, or remove workers from the factory floor in shifts that will not disrupt ongoing production.

As a general reminder, all staffers are asked to immediately call the Medical Office at extension 9111 in case of emergency; health professionals will coordinate in-house response and summon an ambulance if necessary.

Seeking volunteers for emergency response staff

From Medical Office to employees

Help is on the way: All of us here at Consolidated Intergalactic spend our days at work comforted by the knowledge that emergency medical response is just a phone call or an emergency call button away. Our medical staff and the Security Office are staffed twenty-four hours a day, every day of the year.

Each shift includes a trained nurse and one or more staffers with certification as an Emergency Medical Technician (EMT).

But when it comes to protecting the health and safety of our staff and visitors there's no such thing as "good enough."

We're looking for ten to fifteen new recruits to receive training and serve as auxiliary members of our emergency response team. We'll provide the training and supplies; classes are given on the weekend (about twenty-four hours over a three-week period, with annual eight-hour refresher courses) and we'll credit all training to your accrued vacation time account.

If you're interested, please contact the medical office by May 1; courses will begin on Saturday, May 12. Call extension 9998 to register.

Accepting volunteer for emergency response staff

From Medical Office to employees

Thank you for volunteering to become an auxiliary member of the CI emergency response team. We're happy to include you in our next training session.

Courses are held at the Lumbertown YMCA from 8 A.M. to 4 P.M. for three Saturdays beginning May 12.

Please visit the Medical Office before May 7 to pick up the training manual. As part of the course you will be working with basic first aid supplies, automated external defibrillators, and other equipment. After graduation you will be assigned to an emergency response team, divided by floors and departments in the headquarters building.

Declining volunteer for emergency response staff

From Medical Office to employees

Thank you for volunteering to become an auxiliary member of the CI emergency response team. The response has been overwhelming—in fact, we have too many volunteers at this time. For that reason, we have decided to divide the training into multiple groups.

The first set of classes will be conducted in May, and all fifteen slots in that group have already been filled.

We expect to start a second set of classes in July and we will contact you by June 10 to see if your schedule will permit participation at that time.

CPR training course offered

From Medical Office or Training Department to employees

Beginning August 1, the Medical Office will offer a free course in CPR and use of automated cardiac defibrillation equipment to any employee. Four classes will be conducted Wednesdays at 3:30 P.M.

Consolidated Intergalactic encourages all departments to release employees from other duties to take the course if they choose.

Please call the Medical Office at extension 2345 to register.

Deployment of automated AED devices

From Medical Office to employees

We want to advise all employees that the Medical Office, in cooperation with Office Services, has completed deployment of automated external defibrillator (AED) devices throughout our Lumbertown offices. Each is marked with a bright red triangular AED sign with a heart-shaped logo.

More than 100 Consolidated Intergalactic employees, including every member of the Medical Office and the Security Office have received training on use of the devices. We will also be offering regular courses on their use to any interested employee.

Even without training, the AED devices are intended to be useable by anyone. Step-by-step instructions are plainly displayed on the devices and there is also automated recorded verbal instruction. The devices are designed so that they will only administer a shock if one is medically needed and the AED is properly in place.

As with any emergency in the office, we ask that employees call extension 9111 immediately to alert health and security staff.

OSHA occupational safety training

From Manufacturing Department or Training Department to employees

All full-time and part-time employees in the Manufacturing, Shipping, and Maintenance Departments are instructed to sign up for one of six Occupational Safety and Health Administration (OSHA) training seminars scheduled during the first week of June.

Please see your department head to choose one of the available sessions; a limited number of slots will be available for each meeting.

Consolidated Intergalactic is committed to the safety and security of all of its employees and fully supports all of OSHA's regulations.

Request for training suggestions

From Medical Office or Training Department to employees

The Medical Office requests suggestions for any health-related training or seminars. Please contact the office at extension 2345 with your ideas.

29 Security Office

Announcement of early shutdown because of weather

From Security Office or Office Services to employees

Because of the forecast for heavy snowfall beginning around 4 P.M., all employees at the Lumbertown offices are encouraged to leave for the day at 2:30 P.M. Staff will receive their regular day's pay.

If it is necessary for you to work after the early dismissal time, please contact the Security Office to let them know you are still in the building. We will make every effort to keep the parking lot clear of snow but authorities have issued a weather alert advising all area companies to close before the storm begins to affect travel.

Telephone number for weather advisories, weather closings

From Security Office or Office Services to employees

Employees are reminded that Consolidated Intergalactic maintains an automated telephone line and Web site to advise of any weather-related closings or delays. For information at any time, please call the main number and select extension 9158 or consult the Office Services Web site and select the "Weather Advisory" icon.

Announcement of advance notice of closing because of weather

From Security Office or Office Services to employees

All employees are advised that Consolidated Intergalactic will not be open for business tomorrow because of the anticipated blizzard that is expected to arrive overnight.

Salaried employees will receive their regular pay for the day; hourly employees will be given the opportunity to work overtime during the next week to make up for the lost hours.

For further details on the weather-related closing, please call the Office Services desk at extension 9158.

Announcement of early shutdown because of technical problem

From Security Office or Office Services to employees

Consolidated Intergalactic will close its Lumbertown facility today at 3:30 P.M. because of the failure of the company's air conditioning system. We anticipate a normal working schedule tomorrow; for updates, employees can call the Office Services desk at extension 9158.

All employees will receive credit for a full day's work.

Announcement of advance notice of closing because of technical problem

From Security Office or Office Services to employees

Alert to all employees: The Lumbertown offices will be closed tomorrow, May 5, because of a failure of the facility's fire sprinkler system. No staff will be allowed inside the building until the safety of the facility has been assured.

It is anticipated a normal working schedule will resume on May 6.

Salaried employees will receive their regular pay for the day; hourly employees will be given the opportunity to work overtime during the next week to make up for the lost hours.

Policy on emergency procedures: whom to call first

From Security Office or Office Services to employees

Employees are reminded that in case of a medical, fire, or safety emergency it is company policy that the first call for help be made to the Security Office at extension 9111.

Remember that the Security Office is the closest source of help for any point on company property. The office is prepared to coordinate with outside responders, assisting them on arrival.

If a call is made directly from an office telephone or cell phone to local ambulance, police, or fire departments please follow up with a call to our Security Office so that they can assist.

Notification of fire and evacuation drill

From Security Office or Office Services to employees

All employees are advised that there will be a mandatory fire and emergency drill at the Lumbertown headquarters on Wednesday, March 14, at 11:30 A.M. The drill will be announced over the office-wide intercom and will also interrupt all computer and telephone equipment with an announcement.

Please do not schedule any appointments or meetings for that time; the drill is expected to last about thirty minutes.

Please review the employee manual's section about procedures for evacuation of the building. All designated safety monitors are expected to be at their stations to assist.

Follow-up on fire and evacuation drill

From Security Office or Office Services to employees

We want to thank all employees for their participation in the fire and emergency evacuation drill held earlier today.

We were pleased to note that the entire building was emptied within ten minutes, which is our goal. We noted a few areas of congestion and delay, and our safety committee will be working on necessary modifications to evacuation routes to improve our plans.

Disaster preparedness planning

From Security Office, Office Services, or Training Department to employees

The Security Office asks each department head to designate two representatives to attend a two-hour planning session on disaster preparedness to be held Monday, November 1, at 1 P.M. in Conference Room A.

The purpose of the meeting is to solicit input from all departments in the preparation of a comprehensive disaster preparedness manual for the company. We will cover plans to deal with fire, floods, earthquake, severe storms, and damage caused by electrical outages and breakdown of air conditioning, heating, and communications networks.

Full details of the agenda for the briefing are posted on a special Security Office Web page. To view the agenda, visit *http://disasterpreparedness.security.consolidatedintergalactic.com*.

Because of the sensitive nature of this Web site, all users must have a User ID and password. To request issuance, please call the Security Office help desk at extension 2453.

Request for appointment of departmental captains for disaster preparedness

From Security Office, Office Services, or Training Department to employees

The Security Office asks each department head to designate two departmental captains to receive special training on disaster preparedness.

We are asking this as one of the results of the November 1 planning session.

Departmental captains will be asked to represent their office in all future meetings on disaster preparedness and to inform coworkers about any special planning necessary for specific operations with which they are involved.

We ask that where possible the departmental captains do not share the same or substantially similar job descriptions.

Please inform the Security Office help desk of the names and contact information for departmental captains. This can be done by e-mail to *captains@security.consolidatedintergalactic.com* or by calling extension 2453.

Security training offered

From Security Office, Office Services, or Training Department to employees

The Security Office asks each department head to designate two representatives to attend a sixty-minute briefing on office safety to be held Thursday, September 15, at 1 P.M. in Conference Room A.

The session will include discussion of updates to the company's "Eyes and Ears" campaign that is intended to extend observation of visitors to headquarters. Each attendee will be asked to conduct an informal briefing in their own department.

Full details on the campaign as well as the agenda for the September 15 briefing are posted on the Security Office Web site; click on the "Eyes and Ears" icon.

Escorts offered to parking lot after hours

From Security Office or Office Services to employees

Any employee may request an escort from the main lobby to their car in the company parking lot at any time by calling the Security Office assistance line at extension 7676. Staffers who arrive at the parking lot and seek an escort to the lobby may call the assistance line after they pass through the passkey gate.

Policy on after-hours in the workplace

From Security Office or Office Services to employees

All staffers are required to swipe their ID card in the computer readers at any entrance to the building.

In addition, any staffer who enters the office before or after ordinary office hours (8 A.M. to 6:30 P.M.) is required to log in with the security officer on duty when they arrive.

These procedures will prevent the inadvertent triggering of security alarms and allow the Security Office to adjust its patrols to include visits to your work area during off-hours.

Requirement to notify security of after-hours in office

From Security Office or Office Services to employees

Staffers who stay in the workplace after the end of ordinary work hours are asked to call the Security Office at extension 7676 to advise the night staff of your presence in the building.

These procedures will prevent the inadvertent triggering of security alarms and allow the Security Office to adjust its patrols to include visits to your work area during off-hours. Please log out at the Security Office when you leave the building.

Policy prohibiting delivery of food to individuals during ordinary hours

From Security Office to employees

Please note that company rules prohibit the delivery of prepared food to individuals during ordinary working hours. The Security Office is instructed to turn away deliveries except for pre-arranged catering for meetings.

Procedure for delivery of food to individuals after ordinary working hours

From Security Office to employees

For staffers who are at work between 5:30 P.M. and 6 A.M., the Security Office will accept deliveries of food; please call the security desk at extension 9112 to advise them of an expected delivery. When the food is delivered, you will be called and asked to pick up the package.

Policy on ID cards

From Security Office or Office Services to employees

Every employee of Consolidated Intergalactic is required to display his or her company ID card at all times while on company property; the card can be worn on a lanyard around the neck or clipped to a shirt pocket. The card must be swiped through the security gate when you arrive and leave.

Policy on renewal of ID cards

From Security Office or Office Services to employees

Every employee must turn in their current ID card and obtain a new one during the month of January. After February 1, current ID cards will no longer be accepted at entrances to the building.

The new ID cards will include an advanced printed barcode as well as a magnetic stripe to identify employees. Security staff will be able to visually check the card and view an electronic image on monitors at all entrances.

Requirement to notify security of lost ID cards

From Security Office or Office Services to employees

For your protection, your ID card remains the property of Consolidated Intergalactic at all times. If it is lost, stolen, or damaged you must notify the Security Office immediately; failure to do so may be considered grounds for immediate termination.

Policy on keys and passcards

From Security Office or Office Services to employees

Any employee who is issued a special key or passcard to enter storage areas, warehouses, or other secure locations is responsible for maintaining possession. If the key is lost or stolen, the Security Office must be notified immediately.

In the instance of passcards, the electronic coding can be changed by computer from the Security Office. Lost keys require changing of locks.

In no instance is an employee to lend a key or passcard to another person.

Requirement to notify security of lost keys or passcards

From Security Office or Office Services to employees

If an employee realizes a key or passcard is missing from their possession, they must immediately notify the Security Office. The hotline is open twenty-four hours a day, every day, at extension 9111.

Requirement of sign-in of guests

From Security Office or Office Services to employees

Any invited guest or business visitor must sign in at the security desk at the main entrance and receive a temporary badge which must be returned when they leave the building. Visitors must be escorted at all times by an employee of the company.

To avoid inconveniencing your guest, please arrange for someone to monitor your telephone if you are away from your desk at the time of your guest's expected arrival.

How to notify security of accidental alarms

From Security Office or Office Services to employees

If you accidentally set off a security alarm at an exit door or elevator, please immediately notify the Security Office at extension 9111. Be prepared to identify yourself by name and employee ID number; an officer will respond to reset the alarm and log the details of the incident.

Required notification of incidents in the office

From Security Office or Office Services to employees

Immediately notify the Security Office, at extension 9111, of any actual or potential physical altercation in the workplace. Describe the incident and let the officer decide whether outside assistance is required.

Please do not try to handle a possibly dangerous situation without assistance from the Security Office.

Procedure for handling bomb threats or other threats

From Security Office or Office Services to employees

Please review the employee manual for details of recommended procedures for handling threats of any sort received by telephone.

Employees are asked to remain calm and seek to obtain as much detail as possible from the caller. If there is a threat of a bomb or other device, ask where it is located. When will it be discharged? Make notes about any details you detect about the caller: type of voice, accent, age, exact phrasing of the threat.

Immediately notify the Security Office at extension 9111 and inform an officer of the details of the call. Allow the Security Office to coordinate contact with outside responders.

Reporting theft in the workplace

From Security Office or Office Services to employees

Please notify the Security Office, at extension 9111, of any apparent theft of personal or company property that may have taken place on the premises or parking lots.

The department will coordinate, if necessary, with local police.

If a theft or other loss of company property takes place away from our premises, please contact local police authorities and file a report. After the report is filed, contact the Consolidated Intergalactic Security Office so that they can follow up.

Policy banning weapons in workplace

From Security Office or Office Services to employees

It is against company rules to bring a weapon of any type into the building or parking lot. Violation of this rule may result in immediate termination from employment.

If you are aware of the presence of any weapons on company property please immediately notify the Security Office at extension 9111. Do not attempt to confiscate the weapons or confront any person by yourself.

Policy banning possession of drugs or alcohol in workplace

From Security Office, Medical Office, or Office Services to employees

Consolidated Intergalactic has a zero-tolerance policy regarding the possession, use, or sale of alcohol or illegal drugs anywhere on company property. Violation of this rule is cause for immediate termination from employment.

If you are aware of the presence of alcohol or illegal drugs on company property, please immediately notify the Security Office at extension 9111. Do not attempt to confiscate the material or confront any person by yourself.

Any employee who requires medication during the work day must keep the prescription in its original packaging with the name of the pharmacy or doctor indicated.

Outsourcing of parking lot and shuttle bus security staff

From Security Office or Executive Office to employees

Effective June 1, the guards who patrol the parking lot and staff the security gate at the entrance to the Lumbertown headquarters will be provided by a private security company. The same company will also operate the shuttle bus that travels from our main parking area to the satellite lot on West Main Street.

We are making this change to comply with new state regulations mandating the licensure and insurance requirements for Security Offices that extend beyond private property onto public roads and land.

There will be no changes within the offices and manufacturing facilities of Consolidated Intergalactic in Lumbertown. We will maintain our own security force, and we anticipate no changes in the staffing levels of full-time employees in that department.

30 Training Services

Training offered, general notice

From Training Department or Human Resources to employees

The Training Department has scheduled a series of courses on information technology, including advanced database management, PowerPoint presentations, and word processing. A full list is available by contacting the department.

Courses are open to any full-time employee with relevant job requirements or those seeking advancement within the company. Permission from your supervisor is required in order to be excused from your ordinary work assignments; in certain circumstances you may be asked to make up time devoted to the classes by performing overtime.

Class size is limited, and all applications are subject to approval by the Training Department. Please note the application deadline for each class.

Mandatory sales seminar scheduled

From Training Department, Human Resources, or Sales Department to employees

The Sales and Marketing Department has scheduled a special seminar entitled "How to Get Past 'No': Secrets of a Superstar Sales Rep."

The seminar, presented by bestselling author Janice Keys, will be presented Friday, June 6, at the Lumbertown Sheraton in Meeting Room C. A continental breakfast will be offered from 8:30 until 9:15 A.M.; the seminar will begin promptly at 9:30 A.M. and continue until noon.

All employees in the Sales and Marketing Department are expected to attend the seminar. We will make special arrangements to cover telephones during the event.

A packet of reading material and a reminder will be sent to you one week in advance.

If you have any questions about the seminar or if you have a scheduled conflict, please contact your supervisor.

Notification of training seminar on Accounts Payable procedures

From Training Department, department head, or Accounts Payable to employees

All members of the Accounts Payable staff are asked to attend an all-day seminar on Wednesday, June 12, to be trained on our new accounting software and changes to our tracking procedures.

The seminar will be held at the Lumbertown Marriott in Conference Room A. Please check in between 8:30 and 9 A.M.; classes will continue until 4:30 P.M. We will provide a buffet breakfast at check-in and a buffet lunch.

The Lumbertown Marriott is located on Canal Street, two blocks from Consolidated Intergalactic headquarters. Attendees can park at the hotel or leave their cars in their usual parking space at CI. If you require assistance in getting from the office to the seminar, please advise Marylou Carben in the Training Department and she will arrange transportation.

Seeking suggestions for training

From Training Department, Human Resources, or Employment Office to employees

The training office of Human Resources is putting together a schedule of advanced courses on office proficiency, sales techniques, and managerial skills for the coming months.

Consolidated Intergalactic is committed to the success and productivity of its employees in all their endeavors.

We welcome suggestions for topics and skills related to current and proposed job tasks and products and services of the company. Please submit your proposals to Mary Vandermeer in the Training Department by June 1.

Request for additional financial training subjects

From Training Department or department head to employees

As we put together the schedule for our upcoming training session, all employees are invited to suggest topics in any area related to Accounts Payable. Most of our day will be devoted to training on new accounting software, but there will be time slots for several workshops and question-and-answer sessions.

Please submit your suggestions to Marylou Carben in the Training Department no later than May 20.

Notification of availability of training on Accounts Receivable procedures

From Training Department, department head, or Accounts Receivable to employees

The Accounts Receivable Department will be offering a full-day refresher seminar on computer-based tracking and accounting procedures.

All members of the department are asked to attend the session, scheduled for Monday, April 5, from 9 A.M. to 4:30 P.M. at the Lumbertown Marriott. Please check in between 8:30 and 9 A.M.; a buffet breakfast and lunch will be provided.

Attendees can park at the hotel on Canal Street, two blocks from Consolidated Intergalactic headquarters. Or they can leave their cars in their usual parking space at CI. If you require assistance in getting from the office to the seminar, please advise Marylou Carben in the Training Department, and she will arrange transportation.

In preparation for the session, please review the course materials that will be distributed to all employees. There will also be computer-based instruction posted on the departmental intranet beginning March 29.

Request for additional Accounts Receivable training subjects

From Training Department, department head, or Accounts Receivable to employees

The Training Department has asked for suggestions for specialized training and refresher courses for staffers in the Accounts Receivable Department. These could include accounting practices, computer training, and organizational skills.

Please submit your ideas for training to Vijay Patel, at extension 2367.

Training on public speaking skills offered

From Training Department to employees

Is having to speak in front of 500 strangers one of your recurring nightmares? You open your mouth, and feathers fly out instead of words?

Or are you an experienced speaker, but wish you could be better and more comfortable in front of an audience?

Either way, we'd like to help.

On Friday, October 5, the Training Department will offer a three-hour seminar called "Before You Say A Word: A Guide to Preparation and Presentation for Public Speakers." The session, to be held from 1 P.M. to 4 P.M. in Meeting Room A, will be conducted by Miles McGuirk, a professional speech coach.

You'll learn how to plan a presentation, prepare handouts, and conquer your fears.

The course is open to any CI employee. Please seek permission from your department head before enrolling; contact the Training Department at extension 2323 to reserve your space.

Availability of new presentation tools

From Training Department to employees

The Training Department is pleased to announce the addition of a new electronic tool available to all departments for their in-service educational efforts.

Conference Rooms A and B now include wireless controls for the computer-based LCD projectors. The wireless devices allow presenters to roam the room while still being able to advance PowerPoint slides, click on-screen icons or controls, and perform other actions. In addition, the same wireless controllers also include a laser pointer that can be used to highlight projected images.

For information on how to use the wireless controllers, please see the following page on our corporate intranet: *http://training.wificontrol.consolidatedintergalactic.com*.

You can also call the help desk of the Training Department at extension 2223 any time during ordinary business hours.

Availability of online training tools

From Training or Information Technology Departments to employees

The Training and Information Technology Departments have added software and networking tools that permit creation of prerecorded instructional programs, PowerPoint presentations, and self-guided tutorials for distribution within the company on our intranet.

The first user of this new facility was Consolidated Intergalactic's Marketing Department which produced a twenty-minute training program to introduce our new line of environmentally safe three-quarter obscurantists. Viewers are shown the product line and then are able to put them to use in a series of simulations of field applications.

The Training Department has produced a program that demonstrates how the system works. To view the instructional Web site, please visit *http://training.demonstrationsoftware.consolidated intergalactic.com*.

You can also call the help desk of the Training Department at extension 2223 any time during ordinary business hours to arrange for personalized instruction.

31 Travel Office

Travel Office Policies and Letters to Employees

From Employee to Travel Office

Travel Office Policies and Letters to Employees

Notification of change in policy on travel expense reimbursements

From Travel Office or Accounts Payable to employees

Effective May 1, we are making the following changes to corporate travel policies.

Because of special discounts negotiated by the company with preferred airlines, all airline reservations must be made through our approved travel Web site portal, *www.travel.consolidatedintergalactic.com*.

If the suggested schedules presented by the program do not meet your needs, you can contact the Travel Office help desk at extension 4444 during regular working hours for assistance. There is also a special 24-hour hotline available for emergency travel arrangements or for unexpected changes to travel that is already underway; that number is listed on the travel Web site portal.

After May 1, Consolidated Intergalactic may choose to refuse reimbursement for any airline tickets purchased by employees outside of the travel Web site portal.

Please review these new policies carefully.

Per diem expenses for travel

From Travel Office to employees

Based on the latest cost analysis prepared for the company by our travel consultant, we are adjusting the per diem reimbursement rates for company authorized travel.

The base allowable rate for travel is $160 per day. This includes as much as $110 per day for lodging and $50 per day for meals and incidental expenses. The per diem for the first and last days of travel allows 75 percent of the meal and incidental expense rate and only includes lodging expenses if necessary.

Meals and incidental expenses are defined as including meals, snacks, tips, and applicable taxes. Consolidated Intergalactic does not reimburse for entertainment (unless related to a sales call and pre-approved by a supervisor) or personal expenses such as clothing, dry cleaning or laundry services, or sundries.

All common carrier travel, including airline, train, and bus service as well as car rentals must be pre-arranged by the Travel Office. Local travel, including taxis, will be reimbursed on the basis of receipts submitted to the Accounts Payable Office.

The following locations have an allowable per diem of as much as 150 percent of the base rate for lodging and 150 percent of the base rate for meals and incidentals: Albany, Columbus, Denver, Detroit, Newark, and Tampa.

The following locations have an allowable per diem of as much as 200 percent of the base rate for lodging and 150 percent of the base rate for meals and incidentals: Boston, Chicago, Los Angeles, New York City, and San Francisco.

For international travel, and if you anticipate or encounter exceptionally high costs on a particular business trip please contact the Travel Office help desk at extension 3231 before you incur expenses that may not be allowable.

Car rental policies

From Travel Office to employees

Any employee who rents a car for business purposes is asked to adhere to the following company rules:

- Make reservations through one of the four authorized rental agencies with which Consolidated Intergalactic has master contracts and use our discount code for direct billing. The four companies (Badgett, Evis, Harts, and International) offer vehicles in more than 95 percent of the airports in the United States. You must obtain pre-approval from the Travel Office to book through another agency.
- The standard rental class for business travel is a midsized car. You must obtain pre-approval from the Travel Office to rent a full-size or specialty vehicle (including vans).
- Decline all additional insurance packages on vehicle rentals made through one of the four authorized agencies. Our master contract applies corporate insurance coverage to rentals.
- Decline prepaid gasoline plans; return all rental vehicles with a full tank of gas.

Notification of preferred travel providers

From Travel Office or Accounts Payable to employees

Effective immediately, we have made changes to our preferred travel providers including airlines, car rental agencies, and hotels.

Attached to this memo is a list of approved companies including discount codes that must be provided at the time any reservation is made. It is each employee's responsibility to assure that proper procedures are followed as outlined on the list.

If you experience any difficulty in making travel arrangements before a trip begins or once it is underway, please contact the Travel Office help desk at extension 4444 during regular working hours, or the special twenty-four-hour hotline listed on the travel Web site portal. Any arrangements that involve an airline, hotel, or car rental agency not on the CI Preferred Travel Provider list must be approved in advance by the Travel Office or the hotline.

Policy on unauthorized travel expenses

From Travel Office to employees

All employees who travel on behalf of Consolidated Intergalactic are advised of the following adjustments to the employee manual that describe certain expenses that will not be reimbursed by the company:

- Personal entertainment, including theater tickets, sporting events, and other shows except as pre-authorized by a department head for salespersons and executives meeting with current or potential clients.
- In-room video entertainment including premium television channels and DVD or videotape rentals.
- Personal sundries and dry cleaning or laundry services with the following exception: employees traveling for more than seven consecutive days may increase their allowable per diem by $20 to include such items as necessary.

If you have any questions about allowable expenses on business travel, please contact the Travel Office help desk at extension 3231 before you incur expenses that may not be allowable.

Notification of contract with outside travel agency for transportation reservations

From Travel Office or Accounts Payable to employees

Effective immediately, all reservations for airline and train travel, car rental, and hotels are to be made through Go Away Travel Services (GATS), a professional corporate travel service.

GATS will ensure that Consolidated Intergalactic receives the best available negotiated rates with travel providers and assist all employees in following guidelines. Agents for GATS will be authorized to grant exemptions to per diem rates for lodging when necessary.

All employees are asked to communicate with GATS through the Consolidated Intergalactic Travel Office. Calls to extension 3737 will be connected to an agent at GATS.

In addition, any employee who needs emergency assistance while on company travel because of changes in appointments, cancellations or delays of flights, or other reasons can call a twenty-four-hour hotline at GATS. The phone number will be listed on your travel confirmations.

Request for more details of travel plans

From Travel Office or Accounts Payable to employee

Regarding your request to travel to the Global Gadget Trade Show in Geneva, Switzerland in May: Your presentation is scheduled for May 2 and your proposed itinerary includes a return on May 10.

Please advise whether there is any other company business that necessitates your staying in Geneva for an additional week.

If you choose to stay in Geneva for personal reasons, please contact Human Resources to arrange for use of your available vacation days. Reimbursement for hotel and meal expenses would end on May 3.

Policy on attendance at conference or seminar

From Travel Office or Accounts Payable to employees

Please be aware that the company reserves the right to limit the number of attendees at national or international trade shows; all travel to such events must be pre-approved by departmental supervisors.

We will make an effort to rotate assignments to major trade shows so that each employee who might benefit from attending receives a chance at least once every other year.

Approval of attendance at conference or seminar

From Travel Office or Accounts Payable to employee

Your request to attend the Global Gadget Show has been approved. Please contact the Travel Office to make arrangements; because of the large number of attendees from the company, we will be seeking to book blocks of hotel rooms near the convention site.

Requesting more information about conference or seminar before approval

From Travel Office or Accounts Payable to employee

Regarding your request to attend a seminar on international trade tariffs, please provide more information on how it pertains to your job assignment here at Consolidated Intergalactic. As your supervisor, I am required to approve any international travel before arrangements are made by the Travel Office.

Denying attendance at conference or seminar

From Travel Office or Accounts Payable to employees

I have reviewed the information you have provided and have determined that it would not be a good use of our limited resources to send you to Istanbul to attend the seminar on international trade tariffs.

I appreciate the fact that you are looking for ways to increase your background and skills, and hope we can find another opportunity of this sort in the future.

Proposed travel plans for approval by employee

From Travel Office to employee

Please review the attached proposed travel arrangements for your upcoming trip to Paris. We have made a few modifications in flight schedules and shifted your hotel to a location more convenient to the convention center.

We will make final bookings on May 5; please advise us of any problems with the suggested itinerary before that date.

Approval of conference registration

From Travel Office or Training Department to employee

This is to notify you that we have confirmed and prepaid your registration at the Global Gadget Show in Geneva in May. Your credentials and schedule will be sent directly to you within the next two weeks.

Confirming details of approved trip, with details of travel policy

From Travel Office or Training Department to employee

We have approved your request for travel to Geneva in May. Please note that because you have chosen to extend your stay in Switzerland for a week, using vacation time, we are unable to book your flights in business class. Company policy only permits use of business class for trips that do not include such personal days.

Approval of travel plans

From Travel Office or Accounts Payable to employees

Your request for travel to Geneva, Switzerland for a trade show has been approved. Please review the attached itinerary to make sure it meets your needs; advise the Travel Office help desk of any proposed changes before April 15.

Qualified approval of travel plans

From Travel Office or Accounts Payable to employees

We have received your request for approval of an international trip in May. In the paperwork you included, you proposed flying out of Chicago to Geneva on April 30; our travel consultant suggests that the total cost of the trip would be considerably less if you departed on a Sunday and stayed over a night in Switzerland. Is this acceptable to you?

From Employee to Travel Office

Request for approval of travel plans

From employee to Travel Office or Accounts Payable

As per the regulations of the employee manual, I am writing to seek approval for an international trip. I have been invited to make a presentation at the Global Gadget Trade Show in Geneva, Switzerland in May.

Details of the trip are attached, as is approval from my departmental supervisor.

32 Sales and Marketing: To Customers

From Sales and Marketing to Customers

From Customer to Sales and Marketing

From Sales and Marketing to Customers

Welcome to new customer, invoice cover letter

From Sales Department, Accounts Payable, or Executive Office to new customer

Thank you for your recent order. We want to welcome you as a new customer of Consolidated Intergalactic. Your account number is: 6SJ7. To ensure quick posting of payments, please include reference to that number on checks or electronic drafts.

Invoices are due within twenty-one days of receipt.

Thank you again.

Acknowledgment and acceptance of order

From Sales Department or Marketing Department to customer

Thank you for your order; the details are listed below for your review.

Production is scheduled to begin on May 16, and we would anticipate shipping no later than May 21.

Please note that orders cancelled after the start of production are subject to a 25 percent penalty; orders cancelled after shipping are subject to a 25 percent penalty plus the cost of freight.

Request for tax-exempt certificate

From Sales Department or Accounts Receivable to outside supplier or customer

We have received your request for exemption from the payment of sales tax on products purchased from Consolidated Intergalactic.

As required by state law, in order to meet your request we must receive a current copy of your tax-exempt certificate and we must verify its status with the state Department of Revenue. Please send your certificate to my attention.

Acknowledgment of cancellation of order

From Sales Department or sales employee to customer

Account 6SJ7
Order #MAR3728

We have received your cancellation of the above order and will halt shipment. The contract for purchase of the geegaws includes a 20 percent cancellation fee for orders already in production.

Because you are a long-time customer of Consolidated Intergalactic, we have decided to waive the cancellation fee for this order. We appreciate your business and look forward to future orders.

Acknowledgment of cancellation of back order

From Sales Department or Marketing Department to customer

We have received your cancellation of back-ordered merchandise; the details of that order are listed below for your review.

We apologize for any inconvenience caused by the unavailability of these items. As your sales representative explained, we have been experiencing difficulties in obtaining raw materials from New Guinea for this product. Various substitutes we have tested do not meet our quality control requirements.

Follow-up to customer (after phone call)

From Sales Department or Marketing Department to customer

Thank you for your interest in products and services offered by Consolidated Intergalactic. As we discussed on the phone, our Web site at *www.consolidatedintergalactic.com* includes pictures and specifications; I have also included some printouts with more detailed descriptions of some of the geegaws we discussed.

I would be happy to set up an account for your company. And, as we discussed, all new customers are eligible for a special introductory offer: free shipping on their initial order.

I look forward to working with you.

Follow-up to customer (after sales call)

From Sales Department or Marketing Department to customer

Thank you for the opportunity to meet with you and discuss the line of products and services offered by Consolidated Intergalactic. I would be happy to set up an account for your company.

As a new customer, you would be eligible for free shipping on your first order and a free sampler kit of twenty of our most popular geegaws, widgets, and doodads.

Please let me know if there are any questions I can answer or for assistance in placing your first order.

Formal offer of pricing for sale of goods

From Sales Department or Marketing Department to customer

Thank you for your request for pricing for Consolidated Intergalactic products.

Based on current pricing, we would be able to provide 222 reverse-thread geegaws (Model 6278) at a per-unit price of $0.68, or a total of $150.96.

I would point out that our quantity discount rate structure reduces the price for orders of 250 to 500 units of this model to $0.60. Therefore, I would suggest you increase the size of your order to 250 units; the total price would be $150.00 for the larger quantity.

In addition, you would be eligible for a special offer of free shipping for initial orders from new customers.

Please feel free to call me with any questions. I look forward to working with you.

Formal offer of pricing for provision of services

From Sales Department or Marketing Department to customer

We have received your request for pricing for maintenance service on geegaws. We can offer two tiers of service:

"Round the Clock" service. This includes dispatch of a technician within three hours of a call at any time of the day, every day of the week. Covered equipment will be repaired or replaced without any charge for parts or labor. Pricing for this premium service is based on the number of units in service at the time the contract is put in place; please see the attached quote.

"Value" service. We will dispatch a technician within three hours of any call placed between 8 A.M. and 3 P.M. on weekdays. Covered equipment will be repaired or replaced without any charge for labor. Parts still under warranty will be repaired or replaced without charge; parts that are no longer covered by warranty will be replaced for a flat fee equal to the current single-unit price for new equipment. Pricing for this value service is based on the number of units in service at the time the contract is put in place; please see the attached quote.

Please feel free to call me with any questions about this offer for maintenance service. I look forward to working with you.

Introduce new employee as part of team for customer

From Sales Department, Marketing Department, or Customer Service to customers

I am pleased to tell you of a new addition to our customer support team here at Consolidated Intergalactic.

Mary Maen has been appointed premier customer advocate. What does that mean? You'll still have access to me as your sales representative, and we'll continue to provide all of our other engineering, maintenance, and repair services to you. But if you have a problem with any order or any products you have already purchased, Mary is your designated "fix-it" person. Her assignment is to keep our best customers happy—and coming back for more.

You can expect to hear directly from Mary soon, but you can go ahead and add her name to your address book right now. I've enclosed her business card which includes her telephone number here at CI, her cell phone, and e-mail address.

I'm sure you will be pleased with this enhancement to our services. Please let me know if there is anything else we can do for you at this time.

Letter of introduction from new salesperson

From salesperson to customer

I'm writing to introduce myself as your new sales representative at Consolidated Intergalactic.

As I'm sure Charlie Lydon has informed you, he will be retiring on May 30 after more than twenty years as one of our most professional and productive salespersons. (He promises not to play too much golf; two rounds a day will be plenty, he says.)

I promise to do my best to give the highest level of service. I will be calling you soon and hope that I can make an appointment to come and meet you to introduce myself in person.

In the meantime, I would like to extend to you a special offer: free shipping on your next purchase.

Letter of reference about new representative, from former salesperson

From salesperson to customer

As you know, I'm putting down my order book and picking up my titanium driver. (Okay, maybe it's not the first time I've played golf, but this time I'm going to try to learn how to do it right.)

I hope you will welcome my replacement, Jock Fleming. He is a very capable and accommodating young man. And he was smart enough to allow me to eke out a win at the Lumbertown Country Club last week; he was way ahead until that unfortunate quintuple bogey on the eighteenth hole.

I have enjoyed working with you these past twelve years as your sales representative here at Consolidated Intergalactic, and I wish you and your company the best in years to come.

Announcement of price reduction

From Sales Department or Marketing Department to customers

Consolidated Intergalactic is pleased to announce a price reduction for our entire line of silver-plated involuted doodads.

The new prices are in effect immediately. As a courtesy to our customers, any orders that are currently in process or that have been shipped to customers in the past sixty days will be adjusted to reflect the reduced prices.

Advisory on price increase

From Sales Department or Marketing Department to customers

Due to an unexpected rise in the cost of raw materials, we regret to inform customers that effective May 1 we will be forced to increase the price of gold-flaked convoluted geegaws by 20 percent.

Any orders already in process will be charged at the current rate. As a courtesy to our existing customers, we will also accept orders between now and May 1 at the existing rate.

We apologize for any inconvenience this change in prices may cause.

Advisory of special pricing (sale)

From Sales Department or Marketing Department to customers

Our annual Spring Fling sale begins on April 10 and continues through May 1. During that period, we will issue rebates of 5 percent off all prices for standard-specification doodads.

As a courtesy to our customers, any orders that are currently in process will be adjusted to reflect the 5 percent rebate.

Advisory of new discount program

From Sales Department, Marketing Department, or Accounts Payable to customers

Consolidated Intergalactic is pleased to announce a discount for prepaid orders. Effective immediately, customers who pay in full at the time of their order will receive a 5 percent rebate.

Payment can be made by electronic funds transfer, credit card, or through use of credits on account with the company.

Advisory of new quantity purchase discount

From Sales Department, Marketing Department, or Accounts Payable to customers

Consolidated Intergalactic is pleased to introduce a new Mix and Match discount program.

Our existing pricing schedule offers a 5 percent discount for orders of at least 500 units of a particular item number.

Effective July 15, customers who place an order for at least 500 items, in any combination of item numbers, will receive the same 5 percent discount. This program will be in effect through December 31 of this year.

This discount is available to any CI customer with an account in good standing.

Denial of request for discount

From Sales Department, Marketing Department, or Accounts Payable to customers

We regret to inform you that we are unable to offer you a 5 percent rebate on your recent offer under the Mix and Match discount program because your account is currently more than ninety days late in payment.

Your order is now on record, but will not be fulfilled until your account is paid in full. Please feel free to call Accounts Receivable with any questions.

Confirmation of inclusion in discount program

From Sales Department, Marketing Department, or Accounts Payable to customers

We are pleased to inform you that your company is now eligible for Preferred Pricing for all products and services of Consolidated Intergalactic.

The Preferred Pricing program offers discounts above and beyond standard pricing programs for our best customers based on past order levels and payment history.

For information on the program, please contact your sales representative at extension 1212.

Availability of same-day priority shipment and delivery

From Sales and Marketing Departments to customers

We won't break the speed limit, but we'll do just about anything else to help our most valued customers in a pinch.

Consolidated Intergalactic is pleased to announce the introduction of a special program for same-day shipment and delivery of certain of our most popular products.

The CI Instant Response program will begin on September 1.

Here's the way the plan will work:

- We will make it a priority to keep in stock a week's supply of our top fifteen to twenty-five products in their most commonly ordered configurations and colors.
- Eligible customers must be located within 75 miles of our warehouse in Lumbertown, and must be able to accept shipments as late as 5:30 P.M.
- Customers must have established accounts with Consolidated Intergalactic and good credit records, and must place orders directly through their account executive (not online, and not through the general Customer Service desk).
- Orders must be received no later than 12 noon.
- Account executives will immediately check with the warehouse to determine that ordered products are in stock and confirm acceptance of the order.
- Orders will be assessed a $200 priority handling fee, plus shipping costs calculated at $5 per mile from our loading dock to the customer.
- All items will be priced at contract rates. No further discounts or special offers can be applied to Instant Response orders.

It will be our intention to have all same-day orders delivered to customers by 3 P.M., with a deadline of 5:30 P.M.

If for some reason we miss our deadline, we will refund the priority handling fee and arrange for delivery by 8 A.M. of the following day. We'll do everything we can to never have to say "we're sorry."

Thanks to customers for patronage

From Sales Department, Marketing Department, or Executive Office to customer

Happy Anniversary! According to the computer wizards in our Sales Department, your first order with Consolidated Intergalactic was placed exactly ten years ago today.

Thank you for your patronage over all of these years.

In recognition of your importance to all of us here at CI, we are offering a 10 percent discount on your next order placed between now and July 1. Please indicate discount code ANNIVERSARY10 on your order.

Seeking to reopen dormant account

From Marketing Department to customer

We've missed you . . . and your business.

It has been some time since we have received an order from your company. Please let us know if there was a problem in the past, or if you have need for a particular product or service that was not available previously.

We have introduced a number of exciting new and improved products in the past year, and we'd like to tell you about them.

I would be very happy to speak with you on the telephone or make a sales call and show you our current product line. I look forward to hearing from you soon.

Seeking to reopen dormant account with special offer

From Marketing Department to customer

Thank you for speaking with me about our current line of products and services. We would very much like to once again do business with your company.

As a special courtesy to a valued former customer, we would like to offer the following: 15 percent off your first order plus free standard shipping.

I look forward to hearing from you and assisting you in any way we can.

Special thanks to customer for large order

From Sales Department, Marketing Department, or Executive Office to customer

On behalf of all of us here at Consolidated Intergalactic, I want to thank you for your recent major order. All of our customers are important to us, but we are especially pleased when one of our partners demonstrates such a significant trust in our company.

Lauren Jamison, President

Requesting participation in customer survey

From Marketing Department to customers

We'd like your opinion.

As a valued Consolidated Intergalactic customer, we'd like to invite you to fill out a short survey about our products: past, current, and future.

We want to make sure that we are meeting your needs today, and we want to find out how better we can serve you.

As a token of our appreciation, we will make a $100 donation in your name to your choice of any of the Lumbertown charities or community organizations on the attached list.

Please send the survey back to us in the prepaid envelope.

Thank you.

Requesting participation in consumer test panel

From Marketing Department to consumers

We'd like to invite you to give us a piece of your mind—and get paid for the privilege.

Consolidated Intergalactic is planning a series of market research test panels that will be conducted in Lumbertown in June. We'll be showing some of our latest products, and prototypes of products under development, to small groups of consumers.

The questions will be quite simple: What do you like? What don't you like? And how can we make our geegaws, doodads, and whirligigs better?

The panels will be held in the meeting room of the Lumbertown Miracle Mall on each Tuesday in June, with sessions at noon, 3 P.M., and 7 P.M. Each panel will take about ninety minutes.

We will provide a light snack, free product samples, and pay you $25 for your time. If you'd like to participate, please call the Marketing Department at extension 4382 before May 25 to choose an available session that is most convenient for you.

Thank you.

Announcement of change in fee

From Sales Department, Marketing Department, or Manufacturing Department to customer

Due to increased manufacturing costs, we are forced to increase the set-up fee for custom logo printing on gold-leaf convoluted geegaws from $50 to $100. We apologize for any inconvenience this may cause.

Any orders already in process will be charged the current set-up fee. As a courtesy to our existing customers, we will also accept orders between now and May 1 at the existing rate.

Apology for error in catalog

From Sales Department, Marketing Department, or salesperson to customer

Due to a printing error, the specifications for Model G-39 Silver-plated Doodads are listed incorrectly in the April catalog. The proper weight per doodad is 3.2 grams and the thread depth is .01786 inch.

Our online catalog, available at our Web site, has been updated with the correct specifications.

We apologize for any inconvenience caused by this error. Please call your sales representative if you need to make any changes in orders placed or already received.

Informing customers of error in promotional materials

From Sales Department or Marketing Department to department heads and employees

Please be aware that there was an error in the sales promotion letter sent out earlier this week to our most valued customers. In the promotion entitled "Spring Fling," the image of our featured product, the Left-handed Chromium Deflaker, was inadvertently printed in reverse.

A corrected version of the promotion letter is attached. We apologize for any inconvenience this error may have caused. Any customer needing to adjust an order because of the error should contact their CI sales representative as soon as possible; we will waive all return fees related to the error.

Apology for lack of availability of product

From Sales Department, Marketing Department, or salesperson to customer

We apologize for the continued lack of availability of W-32 nonmetallic geegaws. Our suppliers in New Guinea have been adversely affected by the recent tsunami.

Some of our customers have found they can substitute N-56 nickel-plated nonpareils in many of their products. We would be happy to supply a sample quantity of that item for testing.

Announcing new sales office

From Sales Department, salesperson, Marketing Department, or Executive Office to customer

Consolidated Intergalactic is pleased to announce the opening of a new sales office in Chillicothe, Ohio, to better serve our customers in southern Ohio, West Virginia, and Kentucky.

Greg Champlin, an experienced CI sales representative who has many accounts in the area, will head the sales office. He can be reached through the CI main number, or directly at (740) 555-0100.

Announcing new distributor

From Sales Department, salesperson, Marketing Department, or Executive Office to customer

We are pleased to announce a new distributor to serve our customers in Belgium and The Netherlands. Belgische Trinket, in the beautiful city of Bruges, will handle the full line of Consolidated Intergalactic products.

For information on Belgische Trinket, please visit the Distributors page of our Web site at *www.consolidatedintergalactic.com.*

Submission of bid for sale of goods

From Sales Department, Marketing Department, or Manufacturing Department to outside company

In response to your request for bids (RFP AJ6SJ7) for provision of nonmetallic antistatic nonslip geegaws, attached please find an offer for sale of goods from Consolidated Intergalactic.

The attached package of files includes full specifications on our product along with details of packaging and shipping. You'll also find a copy of our standard warranty as well as information about maintenance and repair options.

Please let me know if you have any questions about our bid. We would be happy to work with your company on this and future orders.

Submission of bid for provision of services

From Sales Department, Marketing Department, or Manufacturing Department to outside company

Enclosed please find our bid for maintenance and repair of twelve inverse screw impellers currently installed at your location.

The attached bid includes basic twenty-four-hour on-call service minimums, plus prices for replacement parts. The proposed contract guarantees labor and part prices for twelve months, twenty-four months, or thirty-six months, depending on the option you choose.

We have also attached certificates indicating current workers compensation and liability insurance policies as well as a copy of our state and local licenses for handling and disposal of hazardous materials.

At Consolidated Intergalactic, we are fully committed to customer satisfaction. Our Service Department has received industry awards and recognition for the past five years in a row.

Please let me know if you have any question about our bid.

Acknowledgment of receipt of suggestion for new product, with Legal Office response

From Legal Office, Sales Department, Marketing Department, or Customer Relations to customer

Thank you for your suggestion for a new product. At Consolidated Intergalactic, our entire business is built around meeting the needs of customers, and I hope we can do exactly that here.

However, before we can proceed, I need to have on file a legal release from your company so that we can avoid any possible problems regarding patents, copyrights, and other issues of intellectual property. I have attached a letter drafted by our counsel that you can use for this purpose; if you have any questions about the release, please call Tony Quill at extension 6666.

I look forward to working with you.

Response to letter of rescission

From Sales Department or Marketing Department to customer

We have received your letter of rescission for Purchase Order JUN0408-2845. The order has been cancelled and your account has been credited.

We hope we will have the opportunity to work with you again soon.

Request comments on price schedule

From Sales Department, Marketing Department, or Manufacturing Department to employees

Attached please find a copy of the proposed new price schedule for brass-plated inverse screw impellers. Please review all of the elements of the price list as well as changes to quantity discount rates and custom design surcharges.

It is our plan to notify existing customers of the change in price schedule on June 1, with the new rates taking effect on July 1.

Please send me your feedback on any element of the attached document before May 15.

From Customer to Sales and Marketing

Suggestion for new product (from customer)

From customer to Sales Department, Marketing Department, or Customer Service

As you know, we've been a customer of Consolidated Intergalactic for many years. Our most successful product, the Flava-jam Home Jellymaker, depends heavily upon custom parts we purchase from your company.

I'm writing to suggest a new product we hope you'll add to your line.

We're looking for a rotating assembly to hold three to five nonmetallic osmotic filters; the system would allow near-continuous use of a fruit strainer without the need to shut down the device to clean filters.

I can promise you we'll be a steady customer if we can obtain this sort of device from CI. I would be happy to discuss our needs with one of your engineers.

Cancellation of order

From customer to Sales Department

Account 6SJ7
Order #MAR3728

Please cancel the above order for six gross of reverse-thread geegaws. Our client has changed specifications for their new product and we will need to use different widgets.

Request for product manual

From customer to Sales Department, Marketing Department, or Customer Service

We are considering purchase of several of your latest chromium-plated screw reversers. To help us evaluate the system, we would appreciate a copy of the instruction manual and a full set of specifications for the various models in the line.

Request for copy of sales invoice

From customer to Warranty Services, Repair Department, Marketing Department, or Customer Service

Our tax department has requested a copy of the sales invoice for the Chromium-plated Screw Reverser (Serial number 74824-ETAOIN) we purchased in 2006. Can you please assist us by providing a copy of that invoice?

Letter of rescission

From customer to Sales Department or Marketing Department

I hereby rescind my agreement to purchase products from Consolidated Intergalactic included in Purchase Order JUN0408-2845, under the contract signed on June 4, 2008.

This formal notice has been mailed to you within the three-day period provided for under State and federal law.

Please confirm receipt of this notice.

33 Sales and Marketing: To Partners and Employees

From Sales and Marketing to Employees

From Sales and Marketing to Partners

From Sales and Marketing to Employees

Invitation to coworker to attend business meeting

From Marketing Department or Manufacturing Department to department heads and employees

I'd like to invite you to attend an upcoming meeting of the Marketing Department's Steering Committee to share some of your observations on the front line. As one of our top sales representatives you have the best possible credentials to give us your opinion on several new products and services now under development.

We've already done the research and development, and we know the costs of manufacture and the expenses involved in delivery of services. What we'd like to know from you is your opinion about how the companies you deal with would respond.

The Steering Committee meetings are quite informal, held over lunch in the Chairman's Dining Room. Can you join us on Monday, October 4, at noon? Please let me know as soon as possible.

Confirm attendance at a business meeting

From department head or employee to Marketing Department or Manufacturing Department

Thank you for your invitation to attend the Steering Committee meeting; I would be happy to meet with the group to brainstorm about new products and services. Unfortunately, however, I will be out of the office on an important sales call that day.

However, my schedule is clear for lunch for the remainder of that week and the week of October 11. Please let me know if one of those dates will work for you and the group.

Sales lead from employee

From employee to Sales Department or sales employee

One of our service customers, Lefty's Automotive Recycling, has expressed an interest in obtaining a large quantity of reverse-thread geegaws for a major new project they are undertaking.

I thought you might want to make a sales call; my contact there is Lefty Pettite. Ask him about the Red Sox and I think you'll seal the deal.

Letter noting award of incentive for employee-generated sales lead

From Sales Department or Marketing Department to employee

The Sales and Marketing Department welcomes sales leads from CI employees. Each month, we will choose one such submission and award a dinner for two at a gourmet Lumbertown restaurant.

Please submit any leads by e-mail to *salesleads@consolidatedintergalactic.com* or by calling extension 5612.

Thanks to employee for sales referral

From Sales Department or Marketing Department to employee

Thank you for passing along the sales referral from Buffalo Coin Slot Manufacturing. They just placed an order for parts to support a new line of products.

We have entered your name in our monthly contest that offers rewards to employees who assist sales with referrals.

Announcing sales contest

From Sales Department or Marketing Department to sales representatives

We're approaching the end of the fiscal year, and we'd like to clear out the inventory before the accountants invade the warehouse.

Between now and September 30, every commission-based sales representative is automatically enrolled in the Clean Sweep contest. Cash prizes of $500, $1,000, and $1,500 will be awarded to the representatives who book the highest total orders in the period. An additional $500 award will be given to the representative who brings in the largest order from a new customer.

Announcing winner of sales contest

From Sales Department or Marketing Department to sales representatives

Please join me in congratulating Jock Fleming as the winner of this year's Clean Sweep contest. Second prize was awarded to Arlene Calderon, and third prize to William Cogle. The special award for the representative who brought in the largest order from a new customer was taken by Janice Henry.

The Sales Department will celebrate the completion of the fiscal year and the ceremonial handing-over of the award envelopes at a reception on Friday, October 1, at 1 P.M. Be sure to leave room for dessert.

From Sales and Marketing to Partners

Offer of cooperative effort with area company

From Sales Department or Manufacturing Department to area company

Our custom manufacturing division has received a rush order for some equipment that will require special efforts for delivery and installation. We would like to invite your company to meet with our manager of special projects to see whether there are ways in which we can cooperate to fulfill this large and important order.

Specifically, we are seeking assistance in rush deliveries of raw materials to our plant and extra-wide heavy-load flatbed trailers to transport manufactured devices from our plant to the customer about 50 miles from Lumbertown.

Full details of the request for bid are attached to this letter.

We hope you will be able to work with us on this and future contracts.

Follow-up on offer of cooperative effort with area company or organization

From Sales Department or Manufacturing Department to area company

Thank you for your recent offer of engaging in a joint venture with Consolidated Intergalactic.

Although because of time and material constraints we were unable to do this particular project with your company, we appreciate the offer and hope that there will be other opportunities to work together in the future.

Thanks for customer referral

From Sales Department or Manufacturing Department to area company

I wanted to thank you for your recent referral of Diamond Music. We are happy to have them as a customer, and appreciate the fact that you sent them our way.

I hope we can do the same for you in the future.

Pass along a noncompetitive sales lead

From Sales Department to individual at another company

One of our customers, National Chopped Vegetables, recently asked us about a special packaging tool that is outside of our area of expertise. I thought you might want to see if one of your products would meet their needs.

The contact at NCV is Charlie Applewhite in their shipping company.

I hope it works out for you.

Thanks to a speaker for presentation at a Board or company meeting

From Sales Department or Executive Office to individual

On behalf of Consolidated Intergalactic, I want to thank you for your inspiring presentation at our recent sales conference. Your well-researched and energetic lecture produced discussion groups that continued for more than an hour after you left, and we are convinced our sales force came away with several excellent new approaches to the way we do business.

We hope we can invite you to another meeting in coming years.

Holiday greetings to customers and business partners

From Sales Department, Procurement Office, or Executive Office to customers and business partners

On behalf of Consolidated Intergalactic and our 3,276 employees, I would like to wish you and your company a joyous holiday season and a prosperous and successful new year. We are very grateful to have you as a partner.

Request for media kit for advertising

From Marketing Department or Advertising Department to media outlet

Please send a media kit. We are considering advertising our products and services on your radio station. After we have examined the kit and pricing, we may choose to call to request a visit by a salesperson from your station. Thank you.

Request for bid for services by advertising agency

From Marketing Department or Advertising Department to advertising agency

Consolidated Intergalactic is seeking bids from area agencies to handle our print and electronic media advertising and special promotional efforts. We would appreciate an information kit about your company and its services.

We will be examining proposals and presentations from agencies during the month of July. We welcome requests to meet with our Marketing Department before then.

34 Manufacturing, Warehouse, and Shipping Offices

From Manufacturing or Warehouse to Employees

Acknowledging receipt of suggestion from employee

From department head or Manufacturing Department to employee

Thank you for your recent idea about improvements to our quality control process, submitted through our online suggestion box.

It's a good idea, and we will be appointing a study group to see how we might implement it here. The committee will invite you to discuss your suggestion in more detail.

And, of course, all suggestions are considered for our monthly Bright Idea award and one will be selected for the annual Idea of the Year honor.

Response to substance of suggestion from employee

From department head or Manufacturing Department to employee

We have begun research into the feasibility of your very clever suggestion for our Quality Control Department.

Have you seen this particular process in use elsewhere? Is it based on any published research?

We'd appreciate any further leads as we prepare to evaluate your idea. And, as you know, you will be invited to participate in the study group once it has been formed.

Policy on uniforms

From Human Resources, Manufacturing Department, or Medical Office to employees

All employees in the Manufacturing Department are required to wear company-issued uniforms as part of our commitment to the safety of all of our workers and to the quality of all of our products. The uniforms are designed to resist the build-up of static electricity and are made of a synthetic fabric that will not react with the specialized solvents used in the production of nonmetallic doodads.

We will be changing uniform suppliers in March, and all workers in the Manufacturing Department will be issued new clothing during the week of March 2. Each employee will receive three sets of clothing. One set is to be kept as a spare in the staffer's personal locker and the other two sets are to be worn on alternate days; our uniform supplier will pick up soiled clothing at 6 P.M. every day, returning cleaned and pressed clothing at the same time.

If you have any questions about the uniforms or any special needs, please contact Manufacturing Services at extension 9734.

Policy on safety equipment

From Human Resources, Manufacturing Department, or Medical Office to employees

Every employee working in the manufacturing division is reminded that steel-toed safety shoes must be worn at all times on the factory floor. This is a requirement of our insurance provider in compliance with OSHA regulations.

Training on emergency preparedness

From Human Resources, Manufacturing Department, Training Department, or Medical Office to employees

The Training Department will be conducting a series of training sessions on emergency preparedness during the first two weeks of April. Classes will include procedures to deal with mechanical failures, fire, spills, and electrical problems.

Every employee in the Manufacturing Department will be assigned to a specific session; assembly line managers will work with division heads to make assignments. We will schedule overtime and bring in temporary workers as necessary to allow regular production schedules to continue.

Training on emergency equipment shutdown

From Human Resources, Manufacturing Department, Training Department, or Medical Office to employees

During the week of August 12, members of the Training Department will conduct an emergency equipment shutdown drill once during each manufacturing shift.

The drill should take about fifteen minutes, and all employees are required to participate. Any member of staff who is absent because of vacation, personal day, illness, or other reason will be asked to meet on an individual basis with a representative of the Training Department to review emergency shutdown procedures.

Quality control planning

From Human Resources, Manufacturing Department, Training Department, or Quality Control Department to employees

During the week of October 9 through 13, consultants from an outside quality assurance company will be on-site to meet with managers and production line workers. The consultants are part of our ongoing commitment to improving the quality of our product and reducing costs wherever possible.

We encourage all employees to share their ideas and experiences with the consultants. No one knows our business better than our own staff; the role of the consultant company is to help analyze that hard-earned experience.

Nominations for manufacturing quality awards

From Human Resources, Manufacturing Department, Training Department, or Executive Office to employees

I am pleased to announce that Consolidated Intergalactic will once again honor three employees from the Manufacturing Department as High-Quality Heroes.

Division managers and supervisors are asked to nominate members of the CI team who have demonstrated the highest commitment to quality in their manufacturing work. Nomination forms are posted on the Human Resources Web site and can be filled in and submitted online.

Winners of the award will be announced on December 1.

Policy on employee-generated product suggestion program

From Human Resources, Manufacturing Department, or Executive Office to employees

Our best ideas for new products, services, and improvements to procedures come from those who know the company best: our team members.

Consolidated Intergalactic encourages all employees to submit suggestions that will improve our product, our efficiency, or our workplace. Each month, the Chairman's Office selects one suggestion for special honors; winners are also included in the group from whom the Employee of the Year is selected.

Letter of award for suggestion of product improvement

From Human Resources, Manufacturing Department, or Executive Office to employees

I am writing to thank you for your excellent suggestion for a change in manufacturing process. You are the winner of the Bright Idea of the Month.

I hope you'll make good use of the special bonus that will be included in your paycheck this week. And please keep the bright ideas coming; we always have room for more.

Change in part specification

From Manufacturing Department or Procurement Office to customers

At Consolidated Intergalactic we are constantly seeking to find ways to improve the quality and durability of our products.

We are pleased to announce that we will now be using anodized aluminum parts in the construction of metallic wind shifters; this should extend the life cycle of this critical industrial geegaw in applications with exposure to the elements.

Availability of same-day priority shipment and delivery

From Shipping Department to Sales and Marketing Departments

At the request of sales and marketing, we are pleased to announce the introduction of a special program for same-day shipment and delivery of certain of our most popular products.

The purpose of this program is to allow us to help out our customers with urgent need for standard products.

The CI Instant Response program will begin on September 1.

Here's the way the plan will work:

- The Warehouse Department will make it a high priority to keep in stock a week's supply of our top fifteen to twenty-five products in their most commonly ordered configurations and colors.
- Eligible customers must be located within 75 miles of our warehouse in Lumbertown, and must be able to accept shipments as late as 5:30 P.M.
- Customers that have established accounts with Consolidated Intergalactic and good credit records will be eligible to place orders under the program.
- Customers must place orders directly through their account executive (not online, and not through the general Customer Service desk), and orders must be received no later than 12 noon.
- Account executives must determine that ordered products are in stock and confirm acceptance of the order before confirming same-day delivery to customers.
- Orders will be assessed a $200 priority handling fee, plus shipping costs calculated at $5 per mile from our loading dock to the customer.
- All items will be priced at contract rates. No further discounts or special offers can be applied to Instant Response orders.

As we introduce this new program, it is important for all sales and marketing personnel to familiarize themselves with its details and to advise customers that we cannot guarantee same-day ordering and delivery until and unless we confirm availability of product.

From Manufacturing Department to Suppliers and Third Parties

Solicitation for bid for products

From Manufacturing Department, Procurement Office, or Office Services to outside company

Consolidated Intergalactic is soliciting bids for the provision of the following products:

Twelve (12) tons of 100 percent zinc pyrithione, delivered once per month in one-ton containers.

260,000 sixteen-ounce styrene bottles and closures, delivered in 5,000-bottle lots once per week.

The successful bidder must agree to deliver the supplies within a three-day window set each month by our Procurement Office.

We would like to invite you to submit a bid for the job. Full specifications for the job, and details of the bidding process, are available through the Procurement Office.

All bidders must fully comply with state and federal environmental safety laws. In addition, successful bidders must provide evidence of workers compensation and other required insurance and bonds for delivery drivers as stated in the bid specification.

The deadline for submitting a written bid is June 1.

Request for clarification of bid for products

From Manufacturing Department, Procurement Office, or Office Services to outside company

We have received your bid for supply of zinc pyrithione in response to our posted request for bids. In order for us to properly evaluate the bid, we need you to clarify your response to indicate that the product will be provided in unadulterated 100 percent strength. This is an essential element of the specification.

Please provide clarification of your bid no later than June 1.

Request for bid for products, rejection of bid

From Manufacturing Department, Procurement, or Office Services to outside company

Thank you for submitting a bid to supply bottles and closures to Consolidated Intergalactic. At this time, we have decided to accept the lower-priced bid of another company.

We encourage you to bid again for provision of supplies in the future.

Request for samples

From Manufacturing Department, Procurement Office, or Office Services to outside company

We are considering purchasing floor tiling from your company for a renovation project. Would you please send a set of samples and a color chart from your Majestic, Regal, and Imperial lines?

Complaint about quality of product

From Manufacturing Department or Procurement Office to supplier

We would like to bring to your attention the fact that we have had an unacceptably high number of failures of reverse-thread brass couplers supplied by your company. This has resulted in significant expenditures in manufacturing, maintenance, and shipping costs.

Attached please find a report by our in-house Quality Control Department that details the problems we have experienced with products received from your company.

We will expect a credit to our account, in the amount of $1,223.76, before we place further orders from your company.

Complaint about quality of product, follow-up

From Manufacturing Department or Procurement Office to supplier

We continue to experience unacceptably high rates of failure with brass parts supplied by your company.

With this letter, we are advising you that any further problems of this sort will result in termination of our master contract with your company.

Terminating contract because of quality of product

From Manufacturing Department or Procurement Office to supplier

Effective immediately, we are terminating our master contract with your company.

We have experienced repeated failures of brass parts supplied to us in recent months, causing us significant unanticipated expense in making repairs to equipment before it is shipped or in maintenance calls to our customers.

Under terms of the contract, we are entitled to return any unused or failed parts to you for full refund, and we will be contacting you soon with details of our shipment to you.

Welcoming new supplier

From Manufacturing Department or Procurement Office to supplier

I wanted to write to welcome you as a new parts supplier for Consolidated Intergalactic.

Within the next week you should expect to receive a call from a quality control engineer at our company to discuss the details of our specifications for anodized aluminum parts.

We look forward to working closely with you as a partner.

35 Retail Sales

From Retail Sales Outlet to Customer

From Customer to Retail Sails Outlet

From Retail Sales Outlet to Customer

Special offer of free shipping

From retail store to customer

We already offer the best prices in town, with the convenience of online or telephone shopping. Now we've got an even better offer for our best customers: free shipping for all orders of $49 or higher throughout the month of May.

To receive this discount, enter the code FREESHIP in the special offers box on our Web site, or use the same magic words when you speak to a sales representative on the phone.

Items purchased using this special offer will be shipped by standard ground freight, with delivery usually within five to eight days. Buyers can upgrade to second-day or overnight shipping by paying applicable charges listed on the Web site or as quoted by telephone sales representatives.

Notice of online sale

From retail store to customer

We've got some special prices for our most special customers. Go to our Web site anytime between now and June 30, fill up your electronic shopping cart with items at our already-discounted prices . . . and then enter this special code in the offers box: 20PERCENTOFF

That's right: a 20 percent discount, good for the entire month of June.

The discount applies before tax and shipping charges.

Introducing Frequent Buyer Club

From retail store to customer

At Consolidated Intergalactic, our business is built upon our base of loyal customers who rely on us for all of their doodad needs. The time has come for us to show some special thanks to our most valued retail customers.

Beginning immediately, all retail customers who purchase online or who register their names at one of our company-owned retail outlets will accrue points in the CI Frequent Buyer Club.

Here's how it will work: for each $25 in purchases (before sales tax, shipping, and handling charges) you will earn one CI Point. Each time your account reaches ten points or higher, we'll send you a certificate by e-mail or mail. Use the points just like dollars: twenty points is worth $20 off your next purchase.

Our computers will take care of all of the accounting and the math. All you need to do is use your CI Frequent Buyer Club number whenever you shop for the finest in doodads.

Rewards for referral of new customers

From Sales Department to customers

Want to share the good news about the great deals and exceptional products available directly from Consolidated Intergalactic's online retail Web store . . . and earn free gifts while you're at it?

We're pleased to introduce our Share the News bonus program.

Here's how it works: Ask your friends and acquaintances to list your CI Frequent Buyer Club number in the "Bonus Code" box for any first-time order made at our online Web site.

Your friend will receive free shipping as a new customer, and you'll earn five CI Points for every referral. It's a win-win-win deal: Your friend won't have to pay for shipping, you'll earn $5 toward your next order, and we'll have the chance to introduce ourselves to a new customer.

Offer to accept returned goods at retail outlet

From retail store to customer

We have received your e-mail inquiring about the return process for a purchase you made through our Web site. For details on how to package and ship items back to us, please visit *www.returns.consolidatedintergalactic.com.*

As a valued customer, we'd also like to let you know that you can bring any of our products to one of our retail outlets to make a return without having to pay for shipping. Just bring the product and your invoice or receipt to the store and we'll credit the purchase to your credit or debit card or issue a check.

Confirming an online order

From retail store to customer

Thank you for your online order.

The details of your order and shipping address are listed below. Please check this information carefully; if you see any errors please respond to this e-mail or call us at our Customer Service line within twenty-four hours to make corrections.

We will advise you when your order is shipped.

Confirming shipping of an online order

From retail store to customer

Thank you for shopping at our online store. Your order is packaged and ready to leave our distribution center.

Your shipping confirmation number is 6SJ7-AEIOU979. Shipment will be made by Combined Parcel Service; depending on packaging materials the order may be delivered in one box or multiple boxes. In most cases an entire order will arrive on the same day, although it is possible that orders made up of multiple boxes may arrive on different days.

Within twenty-four hours of receiving this e-mail, you may track the status of your order by visiting the Consolidated Parcel Service site at *www.tracking.cps.com* and entering the above shipping confirmation number on the tracking page.

Thank you again for choosing Consolidated Intergalactic Direct. We hope to serve you again soon.

Confirming pick-up of damaged item

From retail store to customer

Reference: Order number 78237987-01

We have received your request for replacement of a damaged item shipped from our online site.

We apologize for any inconvenience. We have already shipped a replacement for the damaged product; please refer to the shipping confirmation number you received to track its expected delivery date.

Your Return to Manufacturer Number is CONSOL654-IRMA.

Please place the damaged item in its original packaging along with a copy of the original invoice or a letter that lists your name and address and the above RMA number.

You can expect Combined Parcel Service to pick up the package within the next three days; the driver will have a preprinted, prepaid label to attach to the outside of the package. For your own protection, we recommend that you examine the label to make sure it includes the RMA number listed on this notification.

Thank you for your business.

Confirming shipment of a replacement for damaged item

From retail store to customer

Please accept our apologies for any inconvenience because of the damage in shipping on your recent order.

We will ship to you today a replacement for the damaged item. Your shipping confirmation number is 6SJ7-QWERTY997. Shipment will be made by Combined Parcel Service, and you can expect to receive the package within five to eight days.

Within twenty-four hours of receiving this e-mail, you may track the status of your order by visiting the Consolidated Parcel Service site at *www.tracking.cps.com* and entering the above shipping confirmation number on the tracking page.

You can also expect to receive an e-mail from us advising you how we plan to arrange for pick-up of the damaged item; we will pay all costs for the return.

Thank you for your business.

Returning an item not purchased from store

From retail store to customer

We are returning to you an item sent to us for credit on May 15; a copy of your letter is also enclosed.

This item was not purchased from our store or through our online Web site. We regret that we are unable to accept it for credit.

We hope you understand that we cannot help you with items that we did not sell, and that you will continue to make purchases at our stores.

Response to complaint about service charge applied without advance notice

From online sales Web site to individual

Thank you for your recent order, number 234-234-001.

We have received your letter about the $10 handling charge that was applied to this shipment.

This was indeed an error on our part. We do apply a special handling charge to all orders for fragile items such as porcelain birdbaths but somehow that notice was left off the page that described the product. We have corrected that error on our Web site.

In the meantime, though, we have refunded $10 to your credit card. We apologize for any inconvenience and hope that we will have the opportunity to serve you again in the near future.

Response to complaint about shipping and handling costs

From online sales Web site to individual

Thank you for your thoughtful letter about our shipping and handling costs for online purchases.

We agree with you that at the end of the day the bottom line (the total cost of product, shipping, and handling) is what really matters. However, we also find ourselves in a highly competitive marketplace where there are no rules requiring every vendor to display their total prices in the same way.

Companies that offer "free" shipping have to make their profit in other ways. They either build the cost of shipping and handling into the price or push to get the consumer to purchase accessories or maintenance plans they may not need.

It is our philosophy that we want our customers to have all of the information at hand to make an informed decision.

We believe our prices for products are very good, and we work hard to make sure that we are able to properly package and ship items in such a way that they arrive quickly—and undamaged—at the homes of our customers. The prices we charge for shipping and handling accurately reflect our costs.

I hope we can continue to earn your business in the future.

Response to request for refund after published deadline

From online retail sales Web site to customer

We have received your letter in regard to your request for a refund for returned items that were part of order #RRJ-3247.

Our "no questions asked" guarantee clearly states that cash refunds will be given for any item returned within thirty days of purchase. The offer goes on to say that we will accept back—for store credit only—any unused, undamaged items of clothing returned as much as a year after purchase.

The items you returned were received by us on March 12, which was forty-five days after the date of purchase.

However, because we value you as a customer, we will make a one-time exception to our returns policy; we have voided the store credit we sent you and have instead posted $64 to your credit card.

We hope to serve you again soon.

From Customer to Retail Sales Outlet

Asking for advice on returning damaged item

From customer to Sales Department

Regarding order number 78237987-01

I recently received an order of six nonmetallic oiled olive boats from Consolidated Intergalactic's online retail store. Unfortunately, two of the boats were damaged—one was chipped and the other was almost completely destroyed.

Please advise how I can obtain replacements and what you want me to do with the two damaged items.

Complaint about service charge applied without advance notice

From individual to online sales Web site

Regarding order 234-234-001

I am writing to complain about a $10 handling charge that was applied to my recent order from your company.

I purchased twenty-four miniature porcelain birdbaths for installation in dollhouses I am building for a community organization. The cost of the product, as listed on the Web site, was $5.95 with "free shipping" for orders of more than $100; my order totaled $142.80.

Nowhere on the product information page or the shopping cart did it indicate that a handling charge would be applied.

I am hoping that this was an error on your part and not an intentional attempt to deceive. I would appreciate a refund of the $10 handling fee.

Objecting to excessive shipping and handling charges

From individual to online sales Web site

I have placed a number of orders over the years from your company and have always been pleased with the quality and variety of products you offer.

However, I have recently noticed a steep increase in the cost of handling and shipping charges applied to all orders. In some cases, these charges exceed the cost of the products ordered.

As an online shopper, all that really matters to me is the bottom line: How much does it cost to purchase a product and have it shipped to me? I am concerned that your pricing structure is intended to confuse buyers.

Objecting to store credit instead of refund

From customer to online retail sales Web site

I recently returned two skirts purchased from your online Web site; they did not fit me properly and I was not satisfied with the styling. I have enclosed a copy of the invoice for order #RRJ-3247.

I have just received a notice from your store notifying me that I have received store credit in the amount of $64 for the returned items. This is not acceptable to me. I want a refund for the cost of the items as promised under your "no questions asked" guarantee.

I am hoping that this is an error on your part that will be quickly corrected. I would like to continue placing orders through your company, but will only do so if I receive a refund for the returned items.

Request for refund of shipping costs because of error in advertising

From customer to online retail sales Web site

Regarding order #57890-23089

Enclosed please find a claw hammer, returned for refund. As I explained to your Customer Service representative on the telephone, the hammer you shipped does not match the image that was posted on your Web site. I am very particular about my tools, and this hammer does not meet my needs.

Because of the error on your Web site, I am asking for a refund of the purchase price plus shipping, and reimbursement of the cost to me for returning the item. The amount charged to me was $27.95; the cost to me to ship the hammer back was $4.05.

Please post $32.00 to my credit card.

36 Customer Service: To Employees and Customers

From Customer Service to Employees

From Customer Service to Customer

From Customer Service to Customer, Repair and Warranty Issues

From Customer Service to Employees

Policy on handling of customer complaints

From Customer Service to employees

As a reminder, effective immediately all staffers in the Customer Service Department are now asked to immediately notify a supervisor if they are not able to resolve a complaint to a customer's complete satisfaction.

As part of our Extra Mile program, we will be asking Customer Service representatives to make follow-up calls to all customers within three days after they call with a complaint. Although we realize that we're not going to be able to make everybody happy every time, that is going to be our goal.

All of our jobs—in management, sales, manufacturing, shipping, and Customer Service—depend upon finding and satisfying our customers.

Memo regarding complaint about specific employee

Specific complaint from customer about employee

One of our customers, Copperhead Creations, has complained about the handling of a recent complaint she filed about the quality of a recent shipment of gadgets. According to Bob Zimmer, the sales representative assigned to this account, his contact at Copperhead said you were unwilling to make an adjustment to their order.

I have reviewed the records of the order and your handling of the complaint, and although I do not feel that you violated any of our established procedures, in the spirit of our Extra Mile program I think you should have asked for the involvement of a supervisor to seek a solution that would satisfy Copperhead Creations.

Please plan on meeting with me and with Bob in my office today at 2:30 P.M. to discuss a way to remedy the situation and to help you develop strategies to deal with this particular issue as well as any similar situation that might arise.

Memo regarding complaint about department

From Customer Service to specific department

We have received four complaints in the past two weeks from customers who ordered (and paid for) express overnight delivery of widgets required for emergency repairs.

In each case, the order was sent to the Shipping Department close to—but not after—our cutoff time of 4:30 P.M. That cutoff time was chosen because it still allows one hour to arrange for pick-up by our overnight delivery carriers, and the Shipping Department is also authorized to make special arrangements to bring packages to overnight carriers at their airport hubs as late as 6:30 P.M.

When we let down a customer in this way we are not only hurting our own business but also our clients who make promises of their own.

Effective immediately, any salesperson who books an order that includes express overnight delivery is instructed to confirm by telephone or e-mail that the Shipping Department has made proper arrangements for shipment.

At the same time, the Shipping Department is reminded that it is company policy to guarantee overnight delivery anytime an order is placed by 4:30 P.M. The department is instructed to make all such orders its top priority; under no circumstances is an express order to be put off for a day without approval from the Shipping Department head, following notification to the Sales Department head.

Policy to employees on handling customer requests

From Customer Service to employees

At Consolidated Intergalactic our customers run the company. There is no such thing as a bad idea when it comes in the form of a request from a client.

It is our policy to treat every request for a new product, a modification to an existing product, or a new service as the best sort of market research available.

If a current or potential customer asks for a product or service we currently do not offer, please pass along full details to our Marketing Department: the company, the name of the caller, telephone number, and information about the request. Please tell the customer that we will respond within one business day to discuss ways in which we can meet their needs.

Obviously, we cannot guarantee that every idea will be adopted by CI; some ideas are brilliant but not practical or affordable. However, we always want our first response to questions from customers to be: "Yes."

Policy on handling praise from customers

From Customer Service to employees

When a customer or client has something nice to say about you, we want to hear about it.

If you receive a phone call praising your work, please do not feel shy about asking the caller to pass along the same comments to the Chairman's Office. You can transfer the call to extension 3333 or suggest a written comment be sent.

If you receive a letter or e-mail thanking you for your work, you can send a copy to the Chairman's Office.

We do this for two reasons: We want to know when our customers are happy, and we want to reward employees who go the extra distance. All comments are included in our decision making for the Employee of the Month and Employee of the Year awards.

From Customer Service to Customer

Thank-you to new customer

From Manufacturing Department or Customer Service to customer

On behalf of all of us in the Manufacturing Department—the men and women who build the fine products of Consolidated Intergalactic—I want to welcome you and your company as a new customer.

Although this may be the first and last time you hear from those of us on the factory floor, I want you to know that we appreciate your business and promise our best efforts.

Response to customer complaint about quality of product

From Manufacturing Department or Customer Service to customer

We are sorry to hear of the difficulty you experienced in using a recent supply of chromium-plated wind shifters. We aim for 100 percent satisfaction for all of our customers, and in this case we have to admit that we missed; two lots of product produced earlier this month have fallen short of our quality standards because of problems with the quality of lubricant in gearbox assemblies.

I know that you have already been contacted by our Customer Service Department to alert you to the expected shipping date for a full set of replacement products. In the meantime, please accept my personal apology for the inconvenience we caused.

Letter to customer regarding RTM (return to manufacturer) policy

From Customer Service or Shipping Department to customer

We have received your request to return an order to Consolidated Intergalactic. We apologize for any inconvenience.

In order to allow for proper credit for returns, we ask that all customers request an RTM (return to manufacturer) number from the Shipping Department and display that number prominently on all shipping labels as well as on the packaging itself.

Acknowledgment of merchandise returned for credit

From Customer Service, Shipping Department, or Repair Department to customer

We have received your returned merchandise (RTM #6SJ7) and will be issuing a credit in the amount of $2,348 within the next seven days. We apologize for any inconvenience we may have caused, and look forward to future orders from you.

Acknowledgment of merchandise returned for repair

From Customer Service, Shipping Department, or Repair Department to customer

This is to confirm the receipt of a CI Model 50 impresser, returned for repair. Our technicians have begun analyzing the unit and will prepare an estimate for parts and labor; we will contact you within seventy-two hours to discuss the cost.

In some situations it may be more cost-effective to replace a failed unit that is out of its warranty coverage with a new model. Depending on the estimated cost of repair, your sales representative may offer special pricing on a replacement unit.

Announcing recall of product

From Customer Service, Sales Department, or Marketing Department to customer

Consolidated Intergalactic has issued a voluntary recall of its entire current line of Nickel-Dedoo nickel-plated reverse-screw filbert widgets because of a defect that could result in an uncontrolled acceleration in certain rare circumstances.

All customers are advised to stop using recalled products immediately.

The only products affected by this recall are those produced between December 1, 2007, and April 12, 2008. The widgets are marked with a lot number that ends with the four letter code of ABBA.

Older Nickel-Dedoo widgets and those produced after April 12, 2008 are not affected by this quality issue.

Consolidated Intergalactic will be contacting all affected customers to arrange for replacement of the defective units with re-engineered substitutes.

There have been no known incidents of failure of devices related to this defect, but CI has chosen to make this recall out of an abundance of caution. We apologize to all of our customers for any inconvenience caused by this recall.

Acknowledging receipt of recalled product

From Customer Service, Sales Department, or Marketing Department to customer

We have received your shipment of Nickel-Dedoo units, returned to Consolidated Intergalactic because of the current recall of these widgets.

Your replacement order of re-engineered widgets was shipped to you three days ago and should arrive today. An engineer from our Quality Control Department will be contacting you this week to find out if there is anything else we can do to assist your company at this time.

Once again, we apologize for any inconvenience caused by this recall.

Apology and replacement for damaged goods

From Customer Service, Sales Department, Marketing Department, or Shipping Department to customer

We have shipped a full replacement of your recent order (#ABEL2345).

We apologize for the inconvenience caused by damage in shipment. The freight carrier will be contacting you to pick up the original order; please retain all packaging, packing material, invoices, and damaged items for collection by the trucking company.

Apology for damaged goods, partial credit issued

From Customer Service, Sales Department, Marketing Department, or Shipping Department to customer

Please accept our apologies for the problems with your recent order (#ABEL2345). Several of the items were not properly assembled or were lacking attachment points.

We understand that your company was under deadline pressure and there was not enough time to allow us to ship a replacement order. You were forced to make your own repairs and adjustments to some of the chromium inverse involuters.

As we discussed, we have issued a credit in the amount of 50 percent of your total order before shipping.

We value you as a customer and hope not to disappoint you again.

Apology for delay in shipment of goods

From Customer Service, Sales Department, Marketing Department, or Shipping Department to customer

On behalf of all of us at Consolidated Intergalactic, please accept our apology for the delay in shipment of your recent order.

Quite frankly, we dropped the ball. We greatly underestimated the response to our special free shipping offer to valued customers and our production line was overwhelmed even as we worked round-the-clock.

One thing on which we will never compromise is the quality of our product. We were pushing the widgets as fast as we could, but unfortunately there were a number of customers whose orders were delayed five to ten days past promised shipment dates.

Requesting advice on shipment method, split order

From Customer Service to customer

Thank you for your recent order, number 6SJ7-309408.

Most of the items you ordered are ready for shipment at this time, but there will be a delay of two to three weeks before we are able to ship your orders for nonmetallic inverse wind shifters.

If you would like to reduce the cost of shipping, we can hold your order until all of the items are available.

Otherwise, we can ship the available items now and the back-ordered items when they are ready. This will add approximately $365.30 in shipping costs.

Please advise us of your preferred shipping method.

Requesting advice on shipment method, express option

From Customer Service to customer

Thank you for your recent order, number 6SJ7-309408.

Your items are being packaged now and will be ready to ship on March 1.

Standard shipping costs for an order of this size are $212.50, and you can expect delivery within five to eight business days.

We also offer an express shipment option, which would deliver your order within two to three business days after it is shipped. The cost for express shipping is $296.

Please advise your preferred shipping method; if we do not hear from you before March 1, we will send your order by standard shipping.

Requesting advice on shipment method, nonstandard shipping company

From Customer Service to customer

Thank you for your recent order, number 6SJ7-309408.

Your items are being packaged now and will be ready to ship on March 1.

We note that you have requested express delivery by United Big Box Service. We do not ordinarily use that company for deliveries. However, if you have an account with UBBS and would like to arrange for pick-up at our loading dock and direct billing for shipping, please contact me at extension 2398, and we would be happy to work with you.

Offering credit for delay in shipping

From Customer Service to customer

Regarding your recent order, number 6SJ7-2348983, we apologize for the delay between shipping from our factory and arrival at your business.

You paid for express delivery and the packages should have arrived within two to three business days. According to the delivery company, the packages were misdirected in their system resulting in a delay of ten days.

At this time we are crediting your account with a full refund for the shipping costs. We apologize for any inconvenience caused by this late delivery; we hope you understand that the problem was not of our making.

Acknowledgment of letter of praise from customer

From Customer Service or Executive Office to customer

Thank you for your letter about the exceptional service you received from the Consolidated Intergalactic installation team. We are very happy that you were pleased; our corporate mission statement puts the customer at the center of our universe.

Response to praise about quality of product

From business organization, Sales Department, Marketing Department, or Customer Service to customer

Thank you for your comments about the new and improved nickel-plated screw reverser. We're always looking for ways to make our products better, and it is very gratifying to hear from our customers when they are pleased with our efforts.

Response to praise about quality of service

From business organization, Sales Department, Marketing Department, or Customer Service to customer

Thank you for passing along your appreciation for the work of Paul W., one of our best maintenance engineers.

He was just doing his job . . . but we are very proud of our team.

Paul is a regular contender for Employee of the Year, and we will keep your letter—and others—in our files for consideration for that important award.

Response to complaint about quality of hotel

From travel agency to customer

Please accept our apologies for your disappointment with one of the hotels we booked for you on your recent twenty-one-day trip to China and Tibet.

As I'm sure you can understand, sometimes the information we are provided by hotels—especially when it comes to far-distant places—is not always completely accurate. That certainly seems to be the situation here.

We have e-mailed the management company for the hotel and have requested a credit for your four-day stay; we have informed the company that we will no longer book our clients at that hotel or any other they manage if we do not receive a satisfactory response.

As of today, we have not received a reply from the management company, but we want you to know how much we appreciate your business. Therefore, we are issuing you a credit in the amount of $525—the full cost of the four nights at the Happy Golden Fortune—that you can use on the next trip you book through our agency.

I hope this is satisfactory, and we look forward to the next time you plan to go away.

Response to complaint about service not provided

From travel agency to customer

We were very disappointed to learn that one of our travel providers did not meet its obligation on your recent cruise from London.

We contacted Black Watch Cab Company, and they told us their driver had become stuck in traffic coming to the airport to pick you up; they claim that he arrived at 8:30 A.M. and could not locate you.

We have credited to your charge card the $150 cost of the prepaid transfer.

Please accept our apologies; we hope you understand that this was a situation beyond our control.

Follow-up to response about service not provided

From travel agency to customer

I have received your second letter about the problem you encountered at Heathrow Airport on your recent cruise from London.

We very much value you as a customer and hope you will continue to book trips through our agency. We are therefore offering you a credit in the amount of $100 that you can apply toward your next booking with us; this is in addition to the refund to your credit card in the amount of $150 for the airport transfer that was not delivered.

Thank you again for the opportunity to help you plan your vacations.

Asking for comments on service

From travel agency to customer

Welcome home. We hope your trip exceeded your expectations; thank you for the opportunity to assist you in making arrangements.

To help us help you, and other clients, in making plans for future trips we would appreciate any comments you might have about airlines, hotels, and excursions we set up. Did anyone deliver exceptional service? Did anyone disappoint you?

As a token of our appreciation, please accept the enclosed atlas to help you plan your next vacation.

Response to detailed complaint about quality of product

From business organization, Sales Department, Marketing Department, or Customer Service to customer

First of all, on behalf of all of us at Consolidated Intergalactic, please accept my apologies for the substandard quality of your recent shipment of reversers.

We are committed to the highest level of quality in all of the products and services we provide. I wish we could claim 100 percent success, but that would be unrealistic; all of our products are highly complex in design and manufacture, and despite our best efforts, some less-than-perfect units manage to get out our doors.

We have assigned one of our quality control engineers to investigate the history of your particular order and to recommend steps we can take to improve the quality of that product.

In the meantime, I have issued a credit to your account for the full purchase price of your recent order. Please use the reversers that meet your own standards; we will arrange to pick up any that you reject.

I will personally oversee your next order from Consolidated Intergalactic, and you have my promise that we will try even harder to meet your needs.

Response to complaint from customer with courtesy adjustment without accepting liability

From Customer Service to customer

We have received your request for a credit related to the performance of some specialty parts produced for you by Consolidated Intergalactic.

At the time of your order, we advised you that we did not endorse the use of nickel-plated inverse expellers in your particular industrial application. Our Engineering Department recommends instead the use of chromium alloy coatings.

As a courtesy to a valued customer, we are issuing a credit for the parts that failed and for the unused items returned to us under RMA #1170BYA.

Response to complaint from customer, denying refund for cause

From Customer Service to customer

We have received your request for a credit related to the performance of some specialty parts produced for you by Consolidated Intergalactic.

At the time of your order, we advised you that we did not endorse the use of nickel-plated inverse expellers in your particular industrial application. Our Engineering Department recommends instead the use of chromium alloy coatings.

We are sorry for the problems you encountered. However, we hope you understand that we cannot warranty performance of products that are not used as recommended by our engineers.

We are unable to refund the purchase price of any parts that have been put into service by your company. However, as a courtesy to a valued customer, we will accept for credit any unused parts still in their original packaging. Please return such parts marked under RMA #1199BYA.

Response to complaint about quality of service

From business organization, Sales Department, Marketing Department, or Customer Service to customer

As I said on the phone earlier today, please accept my deepest apologies for the unacceptable level of service you received from Consolidated Intergalactic recently.

I trust that the repair crew we dispatched today met your expectations. I spoke personally with the director of Repair Services, and he informed me of the work that was performed to bring your machine back up to standards.

We have credited your account for the full cost of the first repair call and will not be charging you for the make-up visit.

I hope you will consider this incident a one-time problem and continue to put your trust in Consolidated Intergalactic.

Response to complaint about treatment by Customer Service

From business organization, Sales Department, Marketing Department, or Customer Service to customer

On behalf of Consolidated Intergalactic, please accept my apologies for the poor Customer Service you received in your call to inquire about pricing on Order #2344-6SJ7.

Although it is a fact that any price that is quoted is subject to change until an order is actually placed, our valued customers deserve better treatment than you received, and I will personally speak to the agent involved.

Unfortunately, because many of our products require use of natural commodities from some of the far corners of the planet, our prices do change from to time. We try to absorb minor fluctuations, but in the instance of the chromium-plated detanglers our costs for damiana extract have quadrupled since the start of the year because of a crop failure in Mexico.

In fairness to other customers, we are unable to adjust the price on orders placed after a price increase. However, as a courtesy to a valued customer I have credited your account $250, which can be used on your next purchase of products or services from CI.

Declining future orders

From Sales Department to customer

We apologize for your recent problems with orders from Consolidated Intergalactic.

We have issued refunds and credits five times in the past two months for problems you have encountered. It is our company policy to always do everything possible to meet the needs of our customers.

However, it is our opinion that the complaints you have made about our products are not reasonable. Unfortunately from time to time there is a mismatch between a supplier and a customer, and at this time we have decided that we can no longer accept future orders from your company.

From Customer Service to Customer, Repair and Warranty Issues

Letter to customer regarding warranty service policy

From Customer Service, Repair Department, Service Department, or Warranty Department to customer

Your standard warranty coverage for heavy equipment from Consolidated Intergalactic (including all impellers, expellers, molders, and grinders) includes a free annual checkup and tune-up.

We recommend you call to set up an appointment for this preventative maintenance service. Doing so will help prolong the usable life of your equipment and also allow us to apply updates and upgrades to your devices. You may also be offered discounted extended warranty coverage for machines with records of proper preventative maintenance.

Letter to customer offering warranty extension

From Customer Service, Repair Department, Service Department, or Warranty Department to customer

The standard warranty period for your CI Deluxe Impeller (Model 6SJ7, put into service on May 1, 2006) will come to an end on April 30.

It is Consolidated Intergalactic policy to support owners and offer repairs and maintenance on all of its products for a minimum of five years after sale.

If you would be interested in purchasing extended warranty coverage for this unit, please contact Customer Service. Coverage must be put into effect before the expiration of standard warranty coverage.

Letter to customer denying warranty repair because expired

From Customer Service, Repair Department, Service Department, or Warranty Department to customer

Our Repair Department has received your CI Deluxe Impeller, shipped to us for maintenance and repair.

This unit is no longer covered under its original warranty. We need your authorization to proceed with diagnosis of problems with its operation. Our standard fee for diagnosis is $250. If you choose to have the unit repaired, this amount will be applied against the total cost of labor.

Please contact us to discuss how you would like to proceed.

Letter to customer recommending against repair

From Customer Service, Repair Department, Service Department, or Warranty Department to customer

Based on our examination of your CI Deluxe Impeller, we estimate the cost of repairs to be approximately $1,520 including $520 in parts.

If you authorize the repair, we expect to be able to return the unit within ten days. CI will warranty the new parts for ninety days after the unit is put back in service. The diagnostic fee of $250, already billed, will be applied toward the total cost of repairs.

Offer of discount on new purchase by customer with equipment not repairable

From Customer Service, Repair Department, Service Department, or Warranty Department to customer

Although your ten-year-old CI Deluxe Impeller can be repaired, we do not recommend this course of action. The ordinary life cycle for a piece of industrial equipment of this sort is about five years, and we would expect additional costly repairs in future years.

An equivalent current model, capable of at least 25 percent faster operation, would cost about $2,250 delivered and installed. As a courtesy to our long-time customers, we would apply the $250 diagnosis fee to the cost of the new unit.

We look forward to hearing from you soon.

Letter to customer denying warranty repair for cause

From Customer Service, Repair Department, Service Department, or Warranty Department to customer

We regret to inform you that we will be unable to honor the warranty for repair of your CI Deluxe Impeller.

Inspection by our technicians shows that the crankcase has been filled with 10W40 automotive oil instead of the recommended high-viscosity synthetic oil. Use of the proper lubricant is a specific requirement for all warranty repairs.

The estimated cost for repair of the seized bearings and cleaning of the entire system is $625, including $150 in parts. The repaired unit would be returned to service with a ninety-day warranty on repaired or replaced parts.

Letter to customer offering trade-in on outdated or unrepairable item

From Customer Service, Repair Department, Service Department, or Warranty Department to customer

For a limited time, Consolidated Intergalactic is offering a trade-in program for owners of older models of CI Express Macerators.

Please contact your sales representative for details of the program, which allow for credit of as much as 25 percent of the original purchase price of CI equipment traded in for purchase of new machines.

37 Customer Service: From Customers

Request for return authorization

From customer to Customer Service or Shipping Department

I am writing to request an RTM (return to manufacturer) number for the return of Order #6SJ7. As we discussed, the sprocket holes in the new design for the nickel-plated gadgets do not align with our present geegaw design.

We have placed an order for a replacement unit.

Complaint about treatment by Customer Service

From customer to business organization, Sales Department, Marketing Department, or Customer Service

I am extremely unhappy with the treatment I received recently in a telephone call to your Customer Service department. The woman I spoke with identified herself as Judy.

I called in regard to Order #2344-6SJ7 to inquire about a pricing discrepancy between a price quote we received on March 20 and the actual cost that was billed in the order that was placed on April 2.

I was told, "Don't you know that prices are subject to change?"

Yes, I do know that prices change. But I object to the tone taken by your representative, and I also feel that we should have been notified at the time that we placed the order that prices for chromium-plated detanglers had nearly doubled in the two weeks between my inquiry and the date of the order.

Praise about treatment by Customer Service

From customer to business organization, Sales Department, Marketing Department, or Customer Service

I wanted to let you know about the extra effort shown by one of your Customer Service representatives in dealing with us.

I called this morning to inquire about an item that has been on back-order for several weeks; this item is a critical element in our own manufacturing process and we are down to a ten-day supply in our own warehouse.

Your customer representative Marjorie Passaj went out of her way to assist us. After she had confirmed that the product was still unavailable, she put us in touch with a manufacturing engineer at Consolidated Intergalactic who helped us develop a work-around that substituted bronze parts for sections of our product line that are inside the case and reserved chromium-plated parts for those that are display. In addition to reducing our cost of manufacture, this substitution will allow us to extend our supply of chromium parts to last thirty days.

Meanwhile, Ms. Passaj was conveying our situation to your procurement department. She just called to inform me that we have a confirmed shipment date for chromium parts in fifteen days.

Ms. Passaj represents your company very well, and we are grateful for the assistance.

Request verification of warranty status

From customer to Warranty Services, Repair Department, Marketing Department, or Customer Service

Regarding the six CI impellers currently installed in our factory (see attached list of serial numbers), would you please verify the remaining warranty coverage for each device? I would also appreciate a quote on an extended warranty and preventative maintenance contract.

Requesting status and payment of rebate

From customer to Warranty Services, Repair Department, Marketing Department, or Customer Service

It has been six weeks since we submitted the paperwork for a rebate on our purchase of twelve non-metallic inverse impellers. We have not received the rebate of $1,200 that was offered by Consolidated Intergalactic at the time of purchase.

Would you please confirm receipt of the rebate request and advise us when we can expect payment?

Documenting second request for status and payment of rebate

From customer to Warranty Services, Repair Department, Marketing Department, or Customer Service

Regarding our recent request asking about the status of a rebate, enclosed please find copies of the invoices, rebate forms, and bar codes from all twelve devices purchased from Consolidated Intergalactic on March 15.

We would appreciate your immediate attention to this matter.

Detailed complaint about quality of product

From customer to Sales Department, Marketing Department, or Customer Service

I am writing to complain about the quality of the product we recently received from Consolidated Intergalactic.

Our order AUG3109-1005 included six gross of nickel-plated screw reversers. We have ordered this component a number of times in the past; it is an important visual element of our Refrigerated Portable Cake Box line of products.

We have been quite satisfied with the quality of the CI products we have purchased in the past. However, the most recent shipment included several dozen reversers that were not fully sanded and polished.

We have set aside the faulty units and have asked our assembly line workers to individually inspect each reverser before any are installed in our products.

I would appreciate a call to discuss this situation.

Complaint about quality of service

From customer to Sales Department, Marketing Department, or Customer Service

I am writing to tell you of my unhappiness with a recent service call by Consolidated Intergalactic. (The repair ticket and invoice for the call are attached.)

There is hardly anything to praise about the entire service call.

Although your Service Department called the day before to confirm the appointment, the repair person showed up four hours late; we had adjusted our work shift for the day to avoid down time but that is exactly what happened.

The computer-guided internal scraping device that is at the heart of CI's maintenance procedure for non-metallic inverse impellers kept breaking down. Your technician was forced to disassemble the scraper three times to clear obstructions before he could even begin work on our equipment. Even more annoying, the job ticket for the maintenance call included those ninety minutes as billable time.

And finally, we were greatly displeased with the quality of the work that was actually performed. Based on our calculations of throughput, the impeller seems to be operating about 20 percent slower than it had been before the maintenance visit. Our manufacturing team believes that some of the internal parts may have been improperly installed or are defective.

Demand shipment of product for order submitted

From customer to Sales Department, Marketing Department, or Customer Service

Regarding our order #9089-GZRN, it is now three weeks past the promised shipment date. I understand that the product was out of stock at the time I placed the order, but at this point I need to know if Consolidated Intergalactic is going to be able to fulfill the order within the next two weeks.

Please advise the status of this order.

Demand refund for unshipped order

From customer to Sales Department, Marketing Department, or Customer Service

Regarding order #9089-GZRN, please cancel that contract and credit our account for any associated charges.

I understand that the product is out of stock; we are unable to wait any longer for these necessary parts and will seek replacements from other suppliers. Please confirm receipt of this cancellation.

Demand cancellation of unshipped order

From customer to Sales Department, Marketing Department, or Customer Service

Regarding order #9089-GZRN, please cancel that contract.

At this time, we will have to seek a different supplier for this essential component of our product line. Please confirm receipt of this cancellation.

Praise quality of product

From customer to Sales Department, Marketing Department, or Customer Service

We are very pleased with the improvements you have made to the nickel-plated screw reverser. In our opinion, Consolidated Intergalactic has made its best product even better.

Praise quality of service

From customer to business organization, Sales Department, Marketing Department, or Customer Service

We recently received a service call from Paul W. as part of regular preventative maintenance on a CI Turbocharged Chromium Extractor.

The work performed by Paul was, as always, of the highest professional quality.

More importantly, though, he responded to a question from a member of our manufacturing crew that led him to examine another CI product in our shop, a nonmetallic inverse impeller. In doing so, he determined that this critical element of our operations was in imminent danger of failure because of a dried gasket; that simple repair, which was not on his work ticket for the day, probably saved our company tens of thousands of dollars in lost production from a catastrophic failure.

Letter accompanying return of product for credit

From customer to Customer Service

Enclosed please find three vanadium inverse impellers purchased for use in our craft and hobby shop. We have determined that the units do not meet our needs.

As offered in your "no questions asked" thirty-day return policy, please issue a credit for the three units and shipping to our location.

Thank you.

Response to praise about treatment by Customer Service

From business organization, Sales Department, Marketing Department, or Customer Service to customer

Thank you so much for letting me know about the excellent Customer Service provided to you by Marjorie Passaj.

This is exactly what we expect from all of our Customer Service representatives: We tell them we want them to "own" any problem brought to them.

Ms. Passaj was Employee of the Month in December, and as we can see, she has not let up in her efforts since.

Letter accompanying return of product for repair under warranty

From customer to Customer Service

Enclosed please find a CI Turbocharged Chromium Extractor, submitted for repair under standard warranty coverage.

As we discussed on the telephone, several of the compacting blades have developed cracks. In addition, the rubber gasket that holds the feed tube is not sealing properly, resulting in leaks at operating temperatures above 200 degrees Fahrenheit.

Please advise us when we can expect to receive the repaired unit or a rebuilt replacement.

Letter accompanying return of product for repair not under warranty

From customer to Customer Service

Enclosed please find a CI nonmetallic wind shifter, model BRON-6SJ7. As we discussed on the telephone, the device has recently developed a noticeable skew to the west.

You suggested that we send the unit to your attention for evaluation and an estimate of the cost of repair of the unit. Please call me when you have that estimate; we will decide at that time whether it makes sense to repair the device or to purchase a new model.

Response to message about changes to schedule

From customer to travel agency

I received your telephone message left at my hotel here in Rome about the proposed changes in my flight schedule for May 14.

Of the options you listed in your phone message, I would like to take the Northeast Airlines flight from Rome that departs at 7 A.M. on May 14 and goes directly to Chicago; from Chicago, any available flight that will get me to Lumbertown or Eumonia that evening would be acceptable.

I understand there may be some charges assessed by the airlines and cancellation fees from the hotels; I purchased a trip cancellation insurance policy through your agency to handle just this sort of situation and will be seeking your assistance in recouping any costs after I return home.

Please respond by e-mail or fax to the hotel with confirmation of my flight changes. Thank you for your assistance.

38 Academic Institutions: To Organizations and Individuals

From Academic Institution to Organization

From Academic Institution to Individual

From Academic Institution to Organization

Response from college acknowledging development of new course and seeking assistance

From educational institution to Employment Office

Thank you for your thoughtful letter about the need for special training on organic chemistry as a prerequisite for hiring at your company.

This is exactly the sort of role we seek as a community college; we want to provide education to local students and educated students to local employers.

Based on the information you have provided, we have determined that we could set up a curriculum of six academic credits (two courses over two semesters) that would specialize on the material you seek. A class load of fifty students would involve the part-time involvement of two professors and two lab assistants.

If Consolidated Intergalactic can commit to enrolling fifty students per year for at least two years, at standard credit hour rates, we would be able to deliver the courses you have requested.

Please give me a call at (727) 555-8888 extension 1234 to discuss this proposal in more detail. If we decide to go forward, we would like to set up a task force—including representatives of Consolidated Intergalactic as well as academic deans—to design the courses and recruit professors and lab assistants.

Request for permission to use copyrighted material in academic class

From academic institution to individual or company

(NOTE: Check with your legal department or outside legal counsel if you have any concerns about proper use of this release form.)

I am a professor at Lumbertown Community College, teaching a course about industrial quality control.

I am writing to request permission to reproduce and distribute the following copyrighted material to students in my class: (*Describe requested material, including name of publication, date of publication, and page or pages of material to be copied or otherwise distributed.*)

This material will be used as follows: (*means of reproduction, number of copies to be produced, and the dates the material will be distributed*)

I warrant that this material will only be used for the above-stated purpose, that I will not resell this material or make any charge other than the actual cost of reproduction, and that any requested copyright notice will be included on all copies.

I would appreciate it if you would indicate your permission by signing the following permission form and returning it to me at the address on this letter.

Thank you.

Grant Of Permission

Regarding the above request for authorization to make use of copyrighted material, we grant permission for the stated use. I certify that I am an authorized representative of, or the actual copyright holder, and have permission to give such authorization.

Name of person granting permission:

Signature of person granting permission:

Title of person granting permission:

Requested copyright credit to be published:

Date of permission:

Requesting participation in job fair

From community organizations to Human Resources or Employment Office

On behalf of Lumbertown Community College, we would like to invite Consolidated Intergalactic to participate in our annual Job Fair.

This year's event is scheduled for Saturday, May 12, in Archbold Gymnasium on the main campus, beginning at 9 A.M. and continuing until 3:30 P.M.

Each year we usually see more than a thousand eager jobseekers. Although attendees are free to visit any company at the fair, we do offer prescreening at the registration desk to try to best match applicants and employers.

There is no charge to companies to participate in the fair; we provide booths and offer assistance in traffic control.

I look forward to hearing from you soon. The deadline for inclusion in the listing of companies that will be published in the Lumbertown Times and in our own on-campus media is May 1.

From Academic Institution to Individual

Inviting executive to serve as associate professor or instructor

From educational institution to individual

Linda English, senior publicist
Consolidated Intergalactic
Media Relations Department

Dear Linda:

I have enjoyed working with you on many community projects here in Lumbertown and have always been highly impressed with your professionalism as a public relations specialist.

I'm writing to invite you to consider a part-time position as an associate professor at Lumbertown Community College. We are hoping to expand our journalism courses to include copywriting, media relations, and public relations.

We would be very pleased to add you to our faculty, and I am certain you would enjoy meeting and working with our bright and eager students.

I look forward to hearing from you.

Offering services as associate professor or instructor

From individual to educational institution

Robert J. Kensington
Dean of Academic Affairs
Lumbertown Community College

Dear Dean Kensington:

As I approach my twenty-fifth year as a copywriter in the Media Relations Department of Consolidated Intergalactic, I have decided I am finally secure in my position.

It is about time for me to try to offer some help to some of the people who may one day replace me in a public affairs or media relations job. I'd like to offer my time to Lumbertown Community College as an instructor or associate professor.

I'd be willing to teach a course on copywriting, media relations, or corporate communications. I'd be available for night and weekend classes beginning this coming fall or next spring.

I have a B.A. in journalism from Syracuse University and am a member of the executive Board of the National Association of Public Relations Specialists.

I look forward to hearing from you.

Response to request for work experience to be applied toward degree credit

From educational institution to individual

Thank you for your letter inquiring about applying your work experience as a quality control engineer toward an advanced degree in environmental engineering.

We would be happy to work with you to explore this option. Here is what we will need:

- A complete resume showing your academic and work experience;
- A copy of your job description for your current position and any other relevant jobs you have held; and
- A detailed letter from your immediate supervisor describing your assignments and accomplishments as a quality control engineer.

Once we have this material, we will be able to determine if your work experience matches a necessary curriculum component for the degree you seek. If it does, we may ask you to prepare a thesis or take an oral or written examination to demonstrate your competence in this field.

We look forward to hearing from you.

Response to complaint about teacher

From educational institution to individual

I have read your letter about Mr. Claren and his eighth-grade social studies class. I am sorry that you are not happy with the nature of this class.

The title of the class is "Seminar in Contemporary American Issues" and it is purposely set up as a discussion group that reacts to the news of the day. Mr. Claren has led this class for eight years, and we have found that, in general, it appeals very much to students who do not require or do not want a great deal of structure. In many ways it is an advance peek at a college seminar course.

Since this is an elective course and not a requirement for graduation, I would be happy to arrange for your son to drop the class from his schedule; we could substitute an independent reading course or a directed research project. Please let me know if this is what you want.

Response to complaint about student behavior

From educational institution to individual

On behalf of the Lumbertown School District, let me first of all apologize for the inconvenience caused you by having the school bus stop in front of your home.

I have asked our bus coordinator to look into the situation and see if we can make a change to the location of the bus stop; the problem with using the small park you wrote about is that it is past the point where the bus makes a left turn toward the school and would add about ten minutes to the bus route because of rerouting. In addition, we do try to minimize the number of busy roads that our students must cross to get to the nearest bus stop and this would add a major intersection.

In the short term, I have asked that one of our bus monitors come to your location several times a week to attempt to deal with the problem. Unfortunately, the school district's ability to control or discipline students begins and ends when they are on our property (including the school bus) but does not extend to private property.

I hope to have a more complete solution to your problem within ten days.

39 Academic Institutions: From Organizations and Individuals

From Organization to Academic Institution or Employees

From Individual to Academic Institution

From Parent or Guardian to Academic Institution

From Organization to Academic Institution or Employees

Requesting assistance in setting up courses to support available jobs

From Employment Office to educational institution

I am writing to seek your assistance in dealing with a shortcoming we have noticed in applicants for entry-level engineering jobs at Consolidated Intergalactic.

It is our experience that four-year and two-year college graduates lack sufficient background in organic chemistry with a specialization on South Pacific nuts, oils, and byproducts.

Knowledge of these substances is essential for our product line, and we have found it necessary to search for employees from places as far away as New Guinea and Indonesia, or to send new hires to college courses in that part of the world.

We would like to explore the possibility of sponsoring a curriculum at Lumbertown Community College to enhance the skills of applicants for employment at our company. We typically hire fifty to seventy new engineers each year.

Announcing new academic course to support company goals

From Human Resources to employees

We are pleased to announce the launch of a new sequence of courses on organic chemistry at Lumbertown Community College, developed in cooperation with Consolidated Intergalactic.

It is our hope that these courses will allow more advancement opportunities for existing employees at CI as well as opening the door to new hires from the community. Our unique product line requires special background in nuts, natural oils, and related products not ordinarily taught as part of a college curriculum.

The two-course, six-credit sequence at LCC is specifically tailored to our needs.

Any employee interested in taking the courses can register for tuition reimbursement through the Benefits Office. Priority will be given to staffers in the research, engineering, and manufacturing divisions, but we also seek applications from employees in sales, marketing, and other areas of the company.

From Individual to Academic Institution

Requesting transcript as former student

From individual to educational institution

> I am a graduate of Lumbertown High School (Class of 2006, student ID number 6SJ7-0689). I am writing to request a certified copy of my grade transcript and graduation status for use in application for a job training program.
>
> If there are any charges, I would appreciate it if you would send an invoice along with the transcript to avoid delays.

Thank you.

Granting permission to third party to request transcript

From individual to educational institution

> I hereby grant permission to authorized officials of Consolidated Intergalactic to request a certified copy of my college transcript and confirmation of the granting of academic degrees.
>
> I graduated from Lumbertown Community College in May of 2007, with an associate degree in quality control engineering. My former student number was 1609-1107.

Requesting verification of academic degree as former student

From individual to educational institution

> I am a graduate of Lumbertown Community College, class of 2004. As part of my application for a research grant, I require a formal certification of the associate's degree in quality control engineering I received from LCC.
>
> I would appreciate it if you would send me a letter or certificate as soon as possible. If there are any charges, please send an invoice along with the letter to avoid delays.

Granting permission to third party to verify academic degree

From individual to educational institution

> I hereby grant permission to the National Academy of Nonmetallic Inverter Manufacturers to request certification of my academic degree.
>
> I graduated from Lumbertown Community College in May of 2007, with an associate's degree in quality control engineering. My former student number was 1609-1107.

Responding to inquiry about availability as associate professor or instructor

From individual to educational institution

Robert J. Kensington
Dean of Academic Affairs
Lumbertown Community College

Dear Dean Kensington:

Thank you for your letter inquiring about my availability to teach a course on copywriting at Lumbertown Community College.

I am honored that you would think of me. To tell you the truth I had been considering exactly this sort of position as a capstone to my career; I will be reaching my twenty-fifth anniversary at Consolidated Intergalactic in July.

I'd like to accept your offer to come to the campus and meet with you and other members of the department to discuss my possible involvement as an instructor. I'd also like to take about two weeks to draw up an outline for a course or two; I will give you a call within that period to set an appointment.

Thank you again for your offer.

Declining offer of post as instructor

From individual to educational institution

Robert J. Kensington
Dean of Academic Affairs
Lumbertown Community College

Dear Dean Kensington:

Thank you for your letter inquiring about my availability to teach a course on copywriting at Lumbertown Community College.

I am honored that you would think of me.

I am very interested in sharing my experiences and knowledge with students, but at this time I have to decline your offer. My current work assignments leave me no opportunity for outside engagements; I travel nearly every week and could not possibly commit to a regular schedule of classes.

I would be happy to visit with your students during a class sometime this spring, and I promise to be in touch with you at a later date when (I hope) my schedule becomes a bit less fully packed.

Request for information on scholarships or grants

From individual to educational institution

I am considering applying to Lumbertown Community College for the coming fall semester.

I intend to study marine biology and aquaculture. I graduated from Lumbertown High School in 2003 and have spent the last four years in the U.S. Coast Guard.

Would you please send me information about available scholarships or grants that would be appropriate for my background and interests?

Thank you for your assistance.

Request for information on off-campus housing

From individual to educational institution

I plan to attend Lumbertown Community College in the fall. Could you please assist me in finding off-campus housing within walking distance of the school? I am willing to consider sharing an apartment or rental home.

Request for information on work-study plans

From individual to educational institution

I am excited to be an accepted student at Lumbertown Community College for the coming fall semester.

I would like to find out about any available work-study, assistantship, or part-time job opportunities on campus. I am willing to work in any capacity that is appropriate for my skills and background; my previous job experience includes customer support in a computer software company, forklift driver at a lumber processing yard, and preschool athletics coordinator.

Request for transfer of credits from former school

From individual to educational institution

I am preparing to enroll at Lumbertown Community College for the coming fall semester.

I would appreciate it if you would prepare a certified copy of my transcript from Eumonia Junior College and copies of the course descriptions for the associated classes. I attended EJC from the fall of 2005 through the end of the spring semester in 2007; my student number was 3939-0202.

Please send the materials to me at my address as listed above. If there are any charges for preparation of the transcript, please advise. I can pay fees by debit card, or send a check in response to an invoice.

Thank you for your assistance.

Request for transfer of credits into existing program

From individual to educational institution

Enclosed please find a certified copy of my transcript from Eumonia Junior College along with detailed descriptions of the courses from the college catalog and documents distributed by professors.

I am applying to transfer the fifteen credits listed on this transcript toward a degree in quality control engineering I intend to pursue at Lumbertown Community College.

Please let me know if there are any questions about my academic or personal background.

Asking for work experience to be applied toward degree credit

From individual to educational institution

I have applied for acceptance to Lumbertown Community College for the fall, seeking a graduate degree in environmental engineering.

I am currently a quality control engineer with Consolidated Intergalactic in Lumbertown, a position I have held for six years. I have received professional certification from the International Association of Gadget Quality Control Assessment.

I would like to explore ways in which my experience at CI could be applied toward some of the necessary credits required for a degree. I would appreciate a call or letter to discuss my options.

Providing requested information seeking credit for work experience

From individual to educational institution

Thank you for your letter about the necessary steps to my apply work experience toward an advanced degree in environmental engineering.

I believe that my six years as a quality control engineer at Consolidated Intergalactic are very appropriate as a component of the necessary elements for an advanced degree in environmental engineering.

Enclosed please find a current curriculum vitae with my academic and work experience and the names and telephone numbers of supervisors.

I have also attached a copy of my current job description as well as two earlier job descriptions for positions I have held with Consolidated Intergalactic.

Under separate cover, you will be receiving a letter from Bill Kennedy, department head of the Quality Control Department. Mr. Kennedy will address your question about my assignments and accomplishments.

Thank you for your consideration. I look forward to hearing from you soon.

Request for meeting with principal or dean

From individual to educational institution

Dear Dean Arnold:

I will be enrolling at Lumbertown Community College in the fall. I would appreciate the opportunity to meet with you sometime between now and registration; I have been away for four years while serving in the Coast Guard, and I want to make the most of my return to college.

I would appreciate your guidance in selection of a major and course schedule and advice on making the most of my experience in preparing for a career.

Request for meeting with guidance counselor for college prep

From individual to educational institution

I would like to schedule a meeting to discuss my preparations for college and the application process.

As you suggested in an earlier meeting, I have been studying college catalogs and Web sites for schools that grant degrees in aquaculture. At this time I am considering Syracuse University, Boston University, Northeastern University, and Lumbertown Community College.

I am available to meet with you any afternoon; my last class ends at 2:45 P.M. My parents have also asked if they may attend.

Letter of praise about teacher

From individual to educational institution

I am writing to tell you how much our daughter, Chelsea Peers, has enjoyed and benefited from her semester of eighth-grade social studies with Mr. Claren.

According to Chelsea and several of her friends, Mr. Claren is the best teacher they have had at Lumbertown Middle School. They tell me that he encourages the class to learn about and become involved in all of the important issues of the day, directing them to develop their own opinions and solutions.

To tell you the truth, this is the first time that our daughter has ever praised one of her teachers. We're not saying that her other instructors were not very good at what they do, but Mr. Claren seems to be able to break through to students in a way we have not seen before.

Letter of complaint about student behavior

From individual to educational institution

I am writing to seek your assistance in controlling the behavior of a group of about twenty Lumbertown Middle School students who gather in front of my house each morning to wait for the school bus.

To begin with, the students make a great deal of noise at 7:15 in the morning. There are at least half-a-dozen senior citizens who live on our block, and this sort of wake-up alarm is not appreciated. I am also sorry to report that many of them are smoking cigarettes and others bring food; they leave behind a mess of litter every morning.

There is a small park about 300 feet away that has benches, trash cans, and more space for the students to gather. It would make much more sense to me to move the bus stop there.

Offer to volunteer services at school

From individual to educational institution

According to an article in the *Lumbertown Gazette*, the school district is looking for volunteers to teach "classes in real life" at the high school.

I worked as a claims investigator for a major insurance company for more than twenty years before retiring two years ago. I would be happy to come back to school to meet with students and talk about my job experiences.

From Parent or Guardian to Academic Institution

Personal letter asking for early release of child

From individual to educational institution

Please release my son, Henry Kensington, from school today at 1:30 P.M.; he has a doctor's appointment that could not be scheduled after the regular end of the school day. I will pick him up at the front office at 1:30 P.M.

Letter of explanation for absence of child

From individual to educational institution

Please excuse my son, Henry Kensington, for his absence from school on November 5 and 6. He had a fever, and his doctor recommended bed rest and advised against his return to school while he might still be carrying a contagious disease.

Letter of explanation for late arrival of child, family obligations

From individual to educational institution

Please excuse my daughter, Kelsey Kensington, for her late arrival at school today. We had an important family obligation to attend to this morning and as a result she missed her first class period.

Letter of explanation for late arrival of child, medical appointment

From individual to educational institution

Please excuse my daughter, Kelsey Kensington, for her late arrival at school today. She is undergoing a series of allergy shots and her first appointment required an examination by her doctor; we expect that future injections can be scheduled for after-school hours.

Requesting permission for third party to pick up child from school

From individual to educational institution

I am writing to grant permission for our nanny, Marjorie Norris, to pick up our son Henry Kensington any time when my husband or I are not able to do so personally.

I understand school regulations that require Ms. Norris to provide proper identification to the front office for this purpose, and further that permission for a nonfamily member to pick up a student must be renewed at the start of each month of the school year.

Letter explaining extended absence because of family matter

From individual to educational institution

Please excuse Henry Kensington's absence from school from February 2 to 7. Our family had to travel to Florida to visit a close relative who had been hospitalized for an emergency surgery.

Henry kept current with his studies, and we have contacted his teachers to seek make-up homework assignments.

Letter of permission for after-school or out-of-school activity

From individual to educational institution

I hereby give permission for my son, Henry Kensington, to participate in after-school activities including intramural soccer and the computer club.

We understand that a family member, or a third party previously identified to the school, must pick up Henry at 4:30 P.M. on any day when he does not take the bus home.

Letter to school nurse explaining medication for child

From individual to educational institution

Our son, Henry Kensington, is recovering from a heavy chest cold. He has been cleared by Dr. Perole to return to school, but he needs to take an antibiotic three times a day for the next week.

The attached package includes five capsules; per the attached instructions from Dr. Perole, would you please arrange for Henry to take one capsule each day along with his lunch?

Please let me know if there are any questions. Thank you.

Letter to school nurse requesting excuse for swimming class

From individual to educational institution

Our son, Henry Kensington, is recovering from a heavy chest cold. He has been cleared by Dr. Perole to return to school, but we were advised that he should not participate in vigorous physical education classes, including swimming lessons, for the next week.

Would you please arrange for an alternative activity during his third period P.E. class from today through March 14?

Please let me know if there are any questions. Thank you.

Letter of complaint about teacher

From individual to educational institution

I am writing to express my concern about the educational practices of Edward Claren, eighth-grade social studies teacher at Lumbertown Middle School.

According to my son, Henry Kensington, Mr. Claren conducts most of his classes as open forums without any structure. Students are free to bring up any subject in the news of the day and many times the discussions become quite heated.

The "textbook" for the class is the daily newspaper, and the only assignments for members of the class is a midterm essay and a final term paper on subjects chosen by the students. I fail to see how this sort of loose classroom provides a proper education on social studies.

I have heard the same complaint from several other parents of students in Mr. Claren's class.

40 Personal Business: Services

From Individual to Service Provider or Seller

From Individual to Landlord

From Individual to Individual

From Individual to Service Provider or Seller

Request for bid for catering in home

From customer to business organization

I am writing to solicit bids for catering of a reception to be held at my house in Lumbertown.

We are planning to host twenty-four to thirty people from 5 P.M. to 7 P.M. on May 1 for a preshow fundraising event for the Lumbertown Repertory Theatre.

We would like to serve hot and cold hors d'oeuvres and finger sandwiches, along with a cash bar for drinks. In addition to the food, we would require set-up, butler service, a bartender, and clean-up.

If you are interested in providing this service, please contact me no later than April 1 with a price list.

Follow-up on bid for catering in home

From customer to business organization

Thank you for your bid to provide catering and staffing for a fundraising function at my home on May 1. We are considering your bid and will be in touch within the next week.

Meanwhile, can you please provide evidence of workers compensation and liability insurance as well as appropriate licenses from the state or town health department.

Acceptance of bid for catering in home with details

From customer to business organization

We have decided to accept your bid to provide catering and staffing for a fundraising function at my home on May 1.

Attached is the order form for the various appetizers we would like served. Based on RSVPs already received, we expect to have as many as thirty-six people at the reception, and therefore we have increased the size of the food and drink order accordingly.

Please draw up a contract based on the order form and send it to me for final approval and signature.

Request for credit for problem with catering in home

From customer to business organization

Regarding your recent services at a fundraising reception held in my home on May 1, I am writing to request credit in the amount of $100 because you were unable to provide two servers, as specified in the contract.

We were lucky enough to have several volunteers who pitched in to help bring food to the guests.

Request for bid for family event

From customer to business organization

I would like to receive a bid from your company to provide the following services for a wedding celebration to be held at my home on June 15:

Hot and cold appetizers to be served at a reception on the lawn, from 12:30 P.M. to 2 P.M.;

Salad, entrée, and soup to be served course-by-course at tables in the tent, from 2 P.M. to 4 P.M.;

A dessert buffet bar to accompany a wedding cake (supplied by a specialty bakery of our selection); and

An open bar for the predinner reception and wine and champagne service during dinner.

We have contracted with Lumbertown Party Planners to provide for a tent, food preparation area, tables, and chairs. According to my contact there, Jerry Hudson, they have worked with your company in the past and would be able to coordinate their set-up and supplies with your needs.

Follow-up on bid for family event

From customer to business organization

We have received your bid to provide catering services for a wedding at my home.

You offered a steak and salmon option for entrees. Could you please also offer vegetarian and chicken dishes, and provide prices for those meals?

In addition, we are considering purchasing our own wine and champagne instead of selecting from your list of available bottles. Would you please provide a price that includes serving alcohol at the dinner in the tent?

Thank you for your assistance.

Acceptance of bid for family event

From customer to business organization

Thank you for your bid to provide catering for the wedding reception at my home on June 15. We have decided to hire your company for this important event.

Please prepare a contract based on the selections indicated on the attached order form. We will provide all alcohol for the predinner reception and the dinner itself; we will require a bartender and servers for drinks and food.

Please also provide copies of current workers compensation and liability insurance as well as applicable state and local health department licenses.

Request credit for problem with services at family event

From customer to business organization

I am writing to request a refund in the amount of $625 from the amount paid for the June 15 wedding reception and dinner served at my home by your company.

We ordered and paid for 100 lobster salads as an appetizer (at $6.25 per person). Instead, our guests were served an ordinary romaine and tomato salad.

Attached is a copy of the order form and contract for the dinner which clearly shows the charge for the lobster salad.

Requesting copy of old invoice or contract for tax purposes

From customer to business organization

I would appreciate a copy of the invoice for installation of an oil burner and tank at our residence in October of 2003. According to my bank, we issued checks totaling $8,250 to your company at that time.

We are requesting this information as part of the calculation of the cost basis for our home for tax purposes.

Asking new car dealer to bid for your business

From individual to automobile dealer

Barney Olds, sales manager
Lumbertown Auto Megamall

Dear Mr. Olds:

I want to purchase a new car, and I'd like to make the process as direct and painless as possible for me and for your dealership.

I am ready to buy a 2008 Haidatsu Quadrawheel XLT. I have attached a printout from Haidatsu's Web site that shows a model fitted out with all of the equipment I would like; I am not interested in any additional add-ons such as pinstriping, undercoating, or special wheels. I will accept any available color, although my preference would be blue or red.

One other essential element of the bid: We will not accept a vehicle with any dealer's logo attached to the body of the car.

According to my research, this model, as equipped in the printout, has a manufacturer's suggested list price of $27,834, and the dealer's invoice cost is $26,442. We are aware of several current manufacturer's incentives to dealers, and therefore we would expect your selling cost to be at or below the "invoice" price.

I would like to hear from you with your best price for sale of this model. I'm not interested in spending a lot of time haggling or playing games: I am sending this same letter to several area Haidatsu dealers, and I plan on accepting the best offer.

I look forward to receiving your written or e-mailed bid; we will consider all offers received by 5 P.M. on Friday, August 15.

Responding to bid on purchase of new car

From individual to automobile dealer

Barney Olds, sales manager
Lumbertown Auto Megamall

Dear Mr. Olds:

I have received your e-mailed bid for the sale of a 2008 Haidatsu.

The model you have proposed to sell does not come close to matching the one I asked about in my previous letter. Among other things, we specified a four-wheel-drive model, and we do not have need for expensive gadgets like a GPS mapping system or chrome wheels.

I have attached a second copy of the specifications for the model we are interested in purchasing. If you are interested in bidding for our business, please respond in writing or by e-mail no later than 5 P.M. on Friday, August 15.

Responding to bid on purchase of new car, rejecting price

From individual to automobile dealer

Barney Olds, sales manager
Lumbertown Auto Megamall

Dear Mr. Olds:

We have received your bid for sale of 2008 Haidatsu Quadrawheel XLT.

In my original letter, I included the results of my research which showed that this model, as equipped in the printout, has a manufacturer's suggested list price of $27,834 and a dealer's invoice cost of $26,442.

We were expecting a bid close to or below the invoice price, taking into account several available manufacturer's rebates to the dealer.

Your bid price was considerably higher than those we have received from other dealers in the area. At this time, we intend to accept an offer from another dealer unless you are interested in submitting a new bid that is much more competitively priced.

We will consider all offers received by 5 P.M. on Friday, August 15.

Responding to bid on purchase of new car, accepting price

From individual to automobile dealer

Barney Olds, sales manager
Lumbertown Auto Megamall

Dear Mr. Olds:

I am pleased to accept your bid for sale of a 2008 Haidatsu Quadrawheel XLT, priced at $26,441 and equipped as stated in your e-mail.

We will arrange for obtaining a title and license plates from the Registry of Motor Vehicles in Lumbertown; please exclude from the bill of sale the $150 charge for obtaining the title and plates.

Please prepare a bill of sale and registration papers based on the stated price plus the applicable 6 percent sales tax; we will pay exactly $28,027.46.

As stated in our original request for bids, please ensure that the vehicle does not include any dealer's logo applied as a decal or attached metal plate. We will accept only a removable dealer's license plate frame if you choose to offer one.

I look forward to hearing from you when the paperwork and the vehicle are ready for us.

Responding to bid on purchase of new car, considering financing

From individual to automobile dealer

Barney Olds, sales manager
Lumbertown Auto Megamall

Dear Mr. Olds:

I am pleased to accept your bid for sale of a 2008 Haidatsu Quadrawheel XLT, priced at $26,441 and equipped as stated in your e-mail.

In your e-mail you inquired about whether we would be interested in financing the vehicle through your dealership. We have been offered a rate of 6.5 percent for a forty-eight-month loan through the Lumbertown Automobile Association; if you can improve on that rate for the same term, we would be happy to consider obtaining a loan through your lender.

I look forward to hearing from you when the paperwork and the vehicle are ready for us.

Requesting information on available real estate properties

From individual to real estate agency

Bylow Real Estate
Neil's Harbour, Nova Scotia

I am considering purchasing a vacation home in your area and would appreciate receiving listings of properties that meet my interests. My wife and I plan to spend two weeks in Nova Scotia in July and will be able to look at properties at that time, but we want to narrow down the possibilities before we make the trip.

Here is what we are looking for: a three- or four-bedroom house with a lake or ocean view and at least an acre of land. The home should be new, or a well-maintained and fully updated older home; we are not interested in a "fixer-upper" or a house that otherwise needs a lot of work before it can be occupied.

Based on my research, it appears that the price for homes of this sort in your area runs from about $400,000 to $1,000,000 (Canadian), and we are prepared to make an offer in that range.

We will be in contact after we have had a chance to review listings you send us by mail or e-mail.

Asking for further details about specific real estate property

Requesting additional information on a specific real estate property, real estate agency

Bylow Real Estate
Neil's Harbour, Nova Scotia

Thank you for sending on the set of listings of properties that meet our interests in Nova Scotia.

Of the fifteen you sent, we are most interested in MLS numbers 27, 43, 56, 78, and 79.

For each of these properties, please provide the following additional information: current property taxes, the total of heating and electrical bills for the past twelve months, and details of any other special assessments or association costs.

We will be in touch before June 15 to set appointments. Please advise us if any other similar properties come on the market.

Thank you for your assistance.

Seeking proposals for real estate listing

From individual to real estate agency

Lumbertown Superior Properties
Lumbertown

I am considering putting my home up for sale in the next six months. The property, at 225 Rolling Meadow Drive in Lumbertown, is a well-maintained two-story contemporary house with five bedrooms and three bathrooms; it is set on an acre of land with sweeping views of Lake Lumbertown.

At this time I am interested in hearing proposals from area real estate agents about services they can offer to assist in the sale of my home. I'd also be interested in recommendations about the best time of year to place the home on the market and other suggestions to obtain the highest possible price.

Please call me to make an appointment to discuss the above questions.

Thank you.

Requesting analysis of long distance telephone usage and plan

From individual to communications company

Lumbertown Telephone and Telegraph Company
Lumbertown

Regarding account 7275550121-222

I am considering making a change to my long distance telephone plan, including the possibility of subscribing to a new plan with Lumbertown Telephone and Telegraph Company or changing to a new provider for some or all of my telephone service.

I would appreciate it if you would review my recent phone bills as an example of typical usage and make recommendations for any plans that would reduce my costs.

I note, as a point of comparison, an offer from the Lumbertown Cable Television Company that offers voice over Internet telephone service with unlimited local and long distance calls for $34.95 per month.

I look forward to hearing from you soon.

Requesting analysis of cell phone plan

From individual to communications company

Regarding account 7275550122

I have been a customer of Lumbertown Cellular for five years. In recent months, my cell phone bills have been higher than I expected when I first signed up for the plan, and I still own the same cell phone I purchased when I first signed up with your company.

I would appreciate it if you would review my recent cell phone bills and make recommendations for adjustments to the monthly plan that will result in a lower monthly cost.

As a point of comparison, I have been offered a plan from Z-Mobile Zellular that would give me a new digital phone, 1,000 minutes of service, and free nights and weekends for $45.99 per month.

I look forward to hearing from you soon.

Seeking bids from landscaping company

From individual to service provider

I am soliciting bids from area landscaping companies for lawnmowing, fertilizing, and trimming services for my property at 225 Rolling Meadow Drive in Lumbertown.

We have approximately half an acre of grass, and simple plantings along the exterior of the home. I am not interested at this time in a complete reworking of the landscaping for the property.

I look forward to receiving your bid for services. We expect to make a decision on a landscaping company by May 1.

From Individual to Landlord

Notice of intent to move, apartment lease

From individual to landlord

As required by the lease I signed on August 1, 2007, I am writing to inform you that I will be vacating Apartment 3A on July 31, 2008.

The apartment will be available for inspection beginning July 15.

Notice of intent to move before end of lease

From individual to landlord

As required by the lease I signed on August 1, 2007, I am writing to inform you that I will be vacating Apartment 3A on March 31, 2008.

I understand that because I will be leaving the apartment before the end of the term of the lease, I must pay a month's advance rent and forfeit my security deposit as penalty.

The apartment will be available for inspection beginning March 15.

Asking for return of security deposit, apartment lease

From individual to landlord

It has now been thirty days since I vacated Apartment 3A at the end of my one-year lease. As required, the apartment was clean and all keys were returned.

As of this date, I have not yet received the return of my security deposit; according to terms of the lease, you hold $750 in an interest-bearing escrow account and the funds are to be returned to the lessee within thirty days after the end of the term.

I look forward to receiving the deposit soon.

Request for references about landlord

From individual to Better Business Bureau

I am considering entering into a lease at Evergreen Estates in Lumbertown.

I would like to know if your records include any complaints or judgments regarding Evergreen Estates Leasing Company or Roger Clement, owner of the company.

Thank you for your assistance.

Requesting change to proposed lease

From individual to landlord

Thank you for sending the application and proposed lease for the apartment. I enjoyed meeting you and I like the apartment very much.

I do have a few questions about the lease.

- Section 4 of the lease says that you can raise the rent at any time with thirty days notice. I've never seen this in a lease; I am perfectly willing to commit to pay you the agreed-upon monthly rental for twelve months, but I am concerned that I am being asked to sign a contract with a price that is undefined.

Can we change the lease to include a fixed monthly rent for the twelve-month period of the agreement?

- The lease says that I would be responsible for any damage caused by frozen pipes. I understand that it is my responsibility to maintain a proper level of heating in the apartment, and will do so. But can I make a small change to that section of the lease to add the words, "unless frozen pipes are caused by failure of the heating system"?

I hope you don't mind my questions. I can see that you are a very careful landlord; I intend to be a very careful tenant.

Transmittal of signed lease and security deposit

From individual to landlord

Enclosed please find the signed lease for the apartment at 225 Rolling Meadow Drive in Eumonia. I look forward to moving in on June 1.

I have also included two checks. The first, #4253 in the amount of $1,000, is the refundable security deposit for the apartment, and according to the lease it is to be deposited in an interest-bearing savings account with quarterly reports supplied to me. The second, #4254 in the amount of $750, is the first month's rent for the apartment.

I am very excited about the apartment, and look forward to a successful year (or more) in Eumonia.

Notice of intent to sublet apartment

From individual to landlord

I am writing to notify you that I will be subletting my apartment for the summer while I am traveling out of the country. The apartment will be occupied in July and August by Marv Chapin, a graduate student at Lumbertown Community College.

Under terms of the lease, I am attaching the executed sublease contract signed by Mr. Chapin along with the required $100 check for such amendments to the principal lease.

I understand that as the signatory to the original lease it remains my responsibility to pay the monthly rent for the term of the lease, and I have made arrangements to do so. Further, I have made it clear to Mr. Chapin that he is to otherwise follow all of the terms of the lease for the two months he will occupy the apartment.

Notice of intent to vacate apartment at end of lease

From individual to landlord

My lease for Apartment 3 at 225 Rolling Meadow Drive in Eumonia expires on May 31, and I have decided to move to a location closer to my place of work in Lumbertown. Therefore, under terms of the lease, I am giving the required thirty-day advance notice that I will not be renewing the agreement.

I have enjoyed the apartment very much, and I have found you to be a responsible and cooperative landlord. Thank you for your consideration over the past year.

Notice of intent to vacate apartment before end of lease

From individual to landlord

I regret to inform you that I must vacate my apartment at 225 Rolling Meadow Drive in Eumonia on April 30, one month before the end of the lease.

I am moving back east to take care of personal matters.

I understand that under terms of the lease, the landlord is entitled to keep, as liquidated damages, $25 per day up to a maximum of $750 as a penalty for the early termination of the lease.

You currently hold my security deposit, which now amounts to about $1,045 with accumulated interest, and I understand that the termination fee will be deducted from this amount. I would appreciate return of the remaining funds of about $295 as soon as possible; my new mailing address is listed on this letterhead.

I have enjoyed the apartment very much, and I have found you to be a responsible and cooperative landlord. Thank you for your consideration over the past year.

From Individual to Individual

Receipt for payment for items sold

From customer to individual

RECEIPT

Date:

This is to acknowledge receipt, on this date, of the amount of $3,250 (three thousand two hundred and fifty dollars) as full payment for purchase of a 1975 Plymouth Duster, VIN#6SJ7AJRKEK.

The goods are sold to: (name, address)

The seller is: (name, address)

The seller warrants to be the legal owner of the goods, and that the goods are free of any and all liens or encumbrances. The seller makes no express warranties about condition, and the buyer takes the goods as is.

Seller's signature _____

Date _____

Buyer's signature _____

Date _____

Receipt for payment for services rendered

From individual to individual

Date:

This is to acknowledge receipt, on this date, of the amount of $150 (six hundred and fifty dollars) as full payment for the installation and configuration of a personal computer system in your home.

Services are provided without warranty, and acceptance is indicated by the signature of the purchaser below.

Client: (name, address)

Client's signature: _____

Date: _____

Services provided by: (name, address)

Provider's signature: _____

Date: _____

Confirming oral agreement to purchase

From individual to individual

This is to confirm our telephone conversation of earlier today in which I agreed to purchase your used Abacus Model 5100 personal computer, equipped with 1MB of RAM, a 250GB hard disk, and a CD/DVD drive. The agreed-upon full purchase price was $150, which I will pay by cash or bank check when I pick up the machine on Thursday, May 18 at 3 P.M. at your home.

Basic invoice for sale of products

From individual to individual

INVOICE

Invoice Number:

Date:

To: (customer name, address)

Contact Name: (name)

Contact Phone Number, E-mail: (phone number, e-mail addresse)

From: (seller of product, address)

Contact Phone Number, E-mail: (contact information)

Detailed Description of Products Provided:

Dates of shipment or delivery of product:

Detailed prices and total billed amount:

Reference to contract or purchase agreement:

Due date for payment:

Notes about method of payment, penalties for late payment:

Basic invoice for services

From individual to individual

INVOICE

Date:
To: (customer name, address)
Contact name: (name)
Contact phone number, e-mail: (contact information)

From: (provider of service, address)
Contact phone number, e-mail: (contact information)
Detailed description of services provided:

Dates of provision of service:

Detailed prices and total billed amount:

Reference to contract or purchase agreement:

Due date for payment:

Notes about method of payment, penalties for late payment:

41 Personal Business: Financial and Government

From Individual to Financial Institution or Insurance Companies

From Individual to Government Agency

From Individual to Financial Institution or Insurance Companies

Contesting credit card charge

From customer to financial institution or credit card company

Regarding account number: 28280-XX-9287

My Name
My Address
My City, State, and ZIP Code
Today's Date

I am writing to dispute a charge in the amount of $225, posted on August 19, 2007, from the Hot Springs Motel and Spa.

The charge represents one day's lodging at this motel. However, I cancelled the reservation at 5 P.M. on August 17, 2007. According to the motel's published policy, a full refund of reservation charges will be made when cancellations are made at least 48 hours in advance of 6 P.M. on the check-in date.

When I cancelled the reservation, I spoke with "Mary" and received a confirmation code of 4320. Please deduct the charge from my bill.

Adding name to credit card account

From customer to financial institution or credit card company

Adding name to credit card account

Regarding account number: 28280-XX-9287

(Name)

(Address)

(City, State, and ZIP Code)

(Date)

Please add my daughter, Wanda Spendmore, as an authorized user of the above-named account and issue her a credit card in her name. I agree to be responsible for valid charges made on the account.

Notification of change of address on credit card account

From customer to financial institution or credit card company

Regarding account number: 28280-XX-9287

Please change the mailing address for statements and notices related to the above account, as follows:

Former Address:

(Name)

(Address)

(City, State, and ZIP Code)

New Address:

(Name)

(Address)

(City, State, and ZIP Code)

Written confirmation of telephone report of loss of credit card

From customer to financial institution or credit card company

Regarding account number: 28280-XX-9287

I am writing to confirm the loss of the above credit card on May 1, 2007; I made a telephone notification of the loss of this card on May 2.

The card was apparently stolen from my wallet while traveling in Rome, Italy. I had made no charges using the card while in Italy.

I understand that I may be asked to sign an affidavit of loss. Please send any related paperwork to my address of record.

Written confirmation of request to cancel credit card account

From customer to financial institution or credit card company

This is to confirm my telephone request to cancel my Left Bank of the Mississippi credit card number XXX-XXXX-9828 which was stolen on May 1 in Rome, Italy.

Please issue a replacement card, with a new account number.

Requesting old credit card statement

From customer to financial institution or credit card company

Regarding account number: 28280-XX-9287

Please send me copies of my credit card statements for the periods that include September 1 through November 30, 2006. I need to document spending for improvements to my home.

Requesting old checking account statement

From customer to financial institution

Regarding account number: 5894-908-N1256

Please send me a copy of all statements included in the period that covers May 1, 2006, through April 30, 2007. I understand that there is a charge of $3 per statement, and I authorize deduction of that amount from my account.

Requesting copy of cleared check

From customer to financial institution

Regarding account number: 5894-908-N1256

Please send me a photocopy of check number 1287, dated March 1, 2008, written from my account to Lumbertown Stump Removal Service. My statement indicates that the check was cashed, but the merchant claims not to have received the payment.

Requesting old statement from investment company

From customer to financial institution

Regarding account number: 6SJ7-8498989898

Please upload to my account for online viewing the statements that cover the period from January 1, 2004 through December 31, 2004. I need these for tax accounting purposes.

Requesting calculation of cost basis

From customer to financial institution

Regarding account number: 6SJ7-8498989898

I am writing to request assistance from an analyst in calculating the cost basis for my holdings of Intercontinental Widgets (Symbol: ICW). According to my records, I have held shares in this company since February of 2003 and have made periodic reinvestments of dividends and interest in shares; there was also a stock split in 2005.

Confirming telephone request to stop payment on check

From customer to financial institution

Regarding account: 79878-990890

This is to confirm my telephone request to stop payment on check #4509 issued on March 5 to Wanda Spendmore in the amount of $56.89.

Documenting claim to homeowner insurance carrier

From customer to insurance company

Regarding policy number: 28451825

Enclosed please find copies of invoices related to repair of our home for damages caused by a windstorm. I have also attached a copy of the appraiser's report produced by your company on October 5, 2007 immediately following the storm.

The total cost of repairs to the home for damage caused by the windstorm was $7,896.52.

Please keep me posted on the progress of my claim.

Cancelling auto insurance because of sale of vehicle

From individual to insurance company

(NOTE: Some states may require license plates to be returned to the motor vehicle department before an insurance policy may be cancelled.)

Regarding policy #6SJ7-231489

Please cancel the above auto insurance policy effective immediately. I sold that car on March 12, 2008.

The license plates for the vehicle, N89JK, were returned to the state motor vehicles department on the date of sale. A copy of the receipt for the return of the plates is attached.

Please issue a check for any refundable portion of the insurance to my address, as listed below.

Asking for insurance analysis

Individual to insurance agency

Mark Hackett
Lumbertown Halfstate Insurance Company

Dear Mark:

The renewal dates for my homeowner's, automobile, and personal umbrella liability policies are all upcoming within the next ninety days.

I would appreciate it if you would review each of my policies to see if the coverage amounts should be increased (or decreased) and whether there are any lower-cost carriers I should be considering.

I look forward to hearing from you after you have had a chance to examine our coverage levels.

From Individual to Government Agency

Requesting change in personal property assessment

From individual to government agency

(NOTE: Consult a lawyer, real estate agent, or other expert for advice on any tax matter.)

Regarding: (Address)
                    (Tax parcel number)

I am writing to request a reappraisal of the valuation of my home as part of the 2008 tax assessment for the town of Lumbertown.

In comparing the valuation placed on my home to those of surrounding homes, as published by the town clerk, I believe that an error has been made. My home, with three bedrooms and two baths on a one-acre plot of land is valued $125,000 higher than two nearby homes that have four bedrooms and three baths and equivalent land. All three of the homes are also of the same approximate age.

With this letter I am formally requesting a reappraisal and adjustment of my tax assessment. Please contact me with any questions.

Requesting correction of mistake on tax bill

From individual to government agency

(NOTE: Consult a lawyer, real estate agent, or other expert for advice on any tax matter.)

Regarding the current Town of Lumbertown property tax bill—a photocopy of the bill is attached—please correct the stated information so that it matches the deed that is on record with the town clerk.

The correct captioning for the ownership of the property is as follows: (Insert information)

Requesting copy of official document, tax bill

From individual to government agency

I am writing to request a duplicate copy of my 2007 town property tax bill. This is in regard to
(Address)
(Tax location number)

Requesting information about government program

From individual to government agency

I am writing to request information about and an application for the town's Senior Citizen Property Tax Reduction Plan. I currently reside at
(Address)
(Tax location number)

Requesting application for government program

From individual to government agency

Following up on our phone conversation of earlier today, I am writing to request an Application to Operate a Home-Based Business. As we discussed, I plan to set up a tutoring service in my home, and my insurance company alerted me to the need for a license from the town.
Please send the application to the address on this letterhead.

42 Personal Job-Related Communications

From Organization to Employee or Employees

From Employee to Staff

From Individual to Business Contact

From Organization to Employee or Employees

Letter of condolence

From Executive Office, Human Resources, or Communications Office to individual

Dear Marjorie:

I was so sorry to hear of Tim's passing.

On behalf of all of us here at Consolidated Intergalactic, please allow me to convey our condolences.

I want you to be the first to know that we have established a scholarship fund in Tim's memory. The Tim Hatch Scholarship will be awarded each year to a child of any company employee who best exemplifies the commitment to excellence shown by your husband.

With my best regards,

Announcement of death of employee or former employee

From Executive Office, Human Resources, or Communications Office to employees

It is with sadness that we report the passing of Tim Hatch, a long-time and valued member of the Consolidated Intergalactic family. Tim, who retired in 2007 after thirty-seven years with the company, began as a clerk in the mailroom in 1970 and rose to become vice president of shipping and fulfillment.

Former CEO Rob Edwards said this about Tim Hatch: "Tim was one of the best of our best for four decades."

Please join me in passing our heartfelt condolences to his wife Marjorie and their sons and grandchildren.

For those who are interested in attending the memorial services or sending their own remembrances, please see the attached memo about memorial services for Mr. Hatch.

Best wishes to ill employee

From Executive Office, Human Resources, or Medical Office to employee

On behalf of all of us at Consolidated Intergalactic, I am writing to extend our best wishes for your recovery. I know that Human Resources has been in contact already, but I wanted to add my personal offer to do whatever we can to help you and your family get through this difficult time.

Letter to staff about coworker in hospital

From Executive Office, Human Resources, or Medical Office to employees

Bob Heller, executive vice president of personnel and departmental supervisor for Human Resources, underwent emergency surgery Thursday night.

According to his family, Bob is recovering well but will likely be away from his desk for six to eight weeks. I hope you'll join me in wishing him well.

Best wishes to employee with illness in family

From Executive Office, Human Resources, or Medical Office to employee

I was informed by your supervisor that you have taken a leave to assist with the care of your mother. Please allow me to extend our best wishes to her, and to offer you whatever assistance we can during this difficult time.

Welcome back to employee returning from sick leave

From Executive Office, Human Resources, or Medical Office to employee

I'm sure your coworkers are expressing the same sentiments today, but I wanted to add my personal best wishes to you as you return to work after your extended illness.

Welcome back.

Letter of congratulation (marriage)

From Executive Office or Human Resources to employee

On behalf of Consolidated Intergalactic, please accept our congratulations on your marriage. We wish you and Betty all happiness.

Letter of congratulation (childbirth)

From Executive Office, Human Resources, or department head to employee

On behalf of all of us at Consolidated Intergalactic, congratulations on your joyous event. We wish you, Betty, and little Sarah health, happiness, and success.

In keeping with a custom that goes all the way back to the founding of our company, we are pleased to inform you that we have opened a bank account for Sarah with an initial contribution from the company of $250.

Letter of congratulation (promotion)

From Executive Office, Human Resources, or department head to employee

Congratulations on your promotion to vice president of Employee Benefits. I'm very pleased that you have accepted this offer, and especially happy that we were able to promote from within.

I'm certain you will do a fine job in this important post.

Letter of congratulation on employment anniversary

From Executive Office, Human Resources, or department head to employee

On behalf of Consolidated Intergalactic, congratulations on reaching your twenty-fifth anniversary as an employee. I am proud to welcome you to a greatly valued elite club: the CI Silver Achievers. I look forward to hosting you for lunch in the Board of Director's dining room on June 1.

Letter of best wishes on retirement

From Executive Office, Human Resources, or department head to employee

On behalf of the entire Consolidated Intergalactic family, I want to wish you the very best in retirement. You have been a loyal and productive employee for twenty-three years, and we appreciate your services.

We hope you enjoy this next stage in your life.

We hope you will make use of our retirement specialist in Human Resources for any questions you have about benefits. Again, thank you for your contributions over the years.

From Employee to Staff

Letter of farewell from departing employee

From employee to staff

As you may have heard, I will be leaving Consolidated Intergalactic effective May 1 to take a new position as chief executive of Amalgamated Motors in Detroit.

I want you all to know that this was a very difficult decision for me and my family. I have greatly enjoyed my time here, and I share with you a great deal of pride over our accomplishments.

I hope to be able to personally bid farewell to each of you over the next few weeks. Please know that I wish you, and Consolidated Intergalactic, the best of luck and success.

Personal letter about retirement

From employee to coworkers

As you may know, I will be retiring from Consolidated Intergalactic on October 31. I wanted to take this opportunity to thank all of my coworkers—past and present—for the privilege of being on the CI team with them.

We've all accomplished a great deal in building and maintaining this company, and I wish all of you the best of luck in the future.

Mary and I, and our children, expect to remain active in community organizations here in Lumbertown and I hope to see all of my friends regularly.

Response to letter of condolence

From individual to Executive Office or department

Thank you for your kind letter of condolence. Tim was a very special man, and as devoted as he was to his own family, he considered his coworkers at Consolidated Intergalactic a second family.

Response to letter of congratulations (marriage)

From employee to Executive Office, Human Resources, or department head

Thank you so much for your letter wishing us well. Betty and I are just settling in to our marriage, but we are so pleased with all of the expressions of love and support from friends, family, and the good people at Consolidated Intergalactic.

Response to best wishes on retirement

From employee to Executive Office, Human Resources, or department head

Thank you for your kind letter of best wishes. I will always think well of Consolidated Intergalactic and the people I worked with over the years.

Letter of condolence from employee to individual

From employee to individual

Dear Barbara:

I was saddened to hear of the passing of your sister. I know how close the two of you were, and I am certain this is a very difficult time for you.

Please know that you are in my thoughts. If there is anything I can do to assist you, please let me know.

Letter of congratulation from coworker (promotion)

From employee to individual

Congratulations on your promotion!

Consolidated Intergalactic is very lucky to have you as a member of the team, and you are very deserving of this new recognition of your skills and background.

Letter of congratulation to coworker (retirement)

From employee to individual

Best of luck in retirement. We will miss you around here; I hope you'll keep in touch and allow me to buy you dinner sometime soon—I owe you at least that for all of the help you've given me over the years.

And please pass along my congratulations to Susan who will finally have you all to herself.

Forming a car pool

From employee to individual

I thought you might like to know that we're putting together a car pool from Holliston to Lumbertown. I know you live a few miles from Holliston; if you're interested in joining us please give me a call.

The company will be providing a subsidy to workers who car pool to work, and it will also save us the cost of gas and upkeep. I think it's a great deal.

From Individual to Business Contact

Request for career advice

From individual to business contact

You have been my most valuable mentor over the years. I was hoping you would you be willing to spare a few minutes in the next week or so to give me some advice on my career. I have a few decisions I need to make about some advancement opportunities, and I would greatly value hearing your perspective on them.

Request for personal advice

From individual to business contact

Jane and I are considering moving to a new home not far from where you live. I was hoping you would spare a few minutes to give me your opinion of real estate, schools, and the commute to Lumbertown. If you don't mind, here's my home phone number: (343) 555-0123. We're available all weekend and most nights from about 6 to 10 P.M.

Thanks.

Thanks for a gift (within business context)

From individual to business organization

Thank you so much for the commemorative plaque celebrating Consolidated Intergalactic's fiftieth anniversary of membership in the Lumbertown Chamber of Commerce. We have already enshrined the tablet in a place of honor in our front lobby.

Declining a gift (for business ethics reasons)

From individual to business organization

Thank you for your recent gift of a floral display in celebration of Consolidated Intergalactic's sixtieth anniversary.

We appreciate your company's recognition of our birthday. However, it is against CI policy to accept gifts from any of our suppliers. For that reason we have delivered the flowers to the Lumbertown Home for Adults.

43 Personal Legal Matters

From Individual to Attorney or Government Agency

From Individual to Organization or Third Party

From Individual to Attorney or Government Agency

Requesting costs for legal services

From individual to attorney or Legal Office

I am in need of the following legal documents for my wife and myself:

- A simple will, conveying interest in our home and financial investments to our children and their successors in the event of our deaths;
- A health care proxy, giving permission to our children to make necessary medical decisions in the event both of us are incapacitated or otherwise unable to make decisions; and
- A Durable Power of Attorney giving permission to our children to make necessary financial and legal decisions in the event both of us are incapacitated or otherwise unable to make decisions.

Could you please tell me the cost for preparation and court filing (where necessary) for these forms? Thank you for your assistance.

Notification of loss of state-issued identification card

From individual to government agency

Regarding personal identification card PID-23048-2323

I am writing to notify you that my state-issued identification card, along with other personal identification, was stolen while on a trip in Rome, Italy.

I have filed a police report with Italian authorities, but would like to put on record with the state the fact that my PID card was taken and block any attempt at misuse of the card by any unauthorized person.

I am currently still in Europe, but upon my return I will be applying for a new PID with a changed identification number.

Submission of power-of-attorney forms to government agency

From individual to government agency

(NOTE: Consult with your attorney or legal advisor for advice on drawing up and filing power-of-attorney and other basic legal forms. Be aware that if you grant such powers to another you may be giving up some or all control over important financial and other matters.)

Regarding: Ben Adams
Account: 225 Rolling Stone Drive, Holliston, NY

Enclosed please find certified copies of a Durable Power of Attorney granted by Ben Adams to me, granting me authority to act on his behalf in all personal business and real estate matters.

Although Mr. Adams retains ownership of the above-listed home in Holliston, please send all tax notices, sewer and water bills, and other correspondence to my attention at the address listed below. I will be paying all bills and managing Mr. Adams affairs on his behalf.

Please contact me if you have any questions about this matter.

From Individual to Organization or Third Party

Authorizing guardian to approve medical care for minor

From individual to school or other third party

I am the parent (or legal guardian) of the following minor child:

Child's name:

Permanent address:

Date of birth:

I hereby give full authorization and consent for the following person to act as temporary guardian for my child, and to make necessary decisions on behalf of my child for medical or dental care as recommended by a qualified doctor, medical practitioner, or dentist:

Temporary guardian's name:

Address:

Date of birth:

Social Security number:

The temporary guardian is authorized to sign any insurance forms or medical release forms necessary for services provided. Further, I grant permission to the temporary guardian to pay necessary medical, dental, or living expenses related to the care of my child.

This temporary authorization shall be in effect from (DATE) to (DATE) only.

Parent or legal guardian's name:

Signature:

Date of Birth:

Social Security number:

Today's date:

Authorizing guardian to approve academic decisions for minor

From individual to third party

I am the parent (or legal guardian) of the following minor child:

Child's name:

Permanent address:

Date of birth:

I hereby give full authorization and consent for the following person to act as temporary guardian for my child, and to make necessary decisions on behalf of my child for academic and recreational activities as required by authorized school, camp, or recreational group officials.

Temporary guardian's name:

Address:

Date of birth:

Social Security number:

The temporary guardian is authorized to sign any necessary permission or legal release forms. Further, I grant permission to the temporary guardian to pay necessary fees or expenses related to the care of my child. This temporary authorization shall be in effect from (DATE) to (DATE) only.

Parent or legal guardian's name:

Signature:

Date of Birth:

Social Security number:

Today's date:

Authorizing third party as power of attorney for specific business purposes

From individual to third party

(NOTE: Consult an attorney before using this form for any complex or high-value business purpose.)

Name of Grantor of Permission: _____

Address of Grantor of Permission: _____

Date of Birth: _____

Social Security Number: _____

I hereby appoint (NAME OF THIRD PARTY) as my Attorney-in-Fact to act in my place for the specific purposes stated below.

Name of Attorney-in-Fact: _____

Address of Attorney-in-Fact: _____

Date of Birth: _____

Social Security Number: _____

Permitted Activities for Attorney-in-Fact: _____

This limited power of attorney takes effect on the following date (STARTING DATE) and continues in effect until (ENDING DATE); it may also be terminated in writing by me at any time for any purpose.

The Attorney-in-Fact may make decisions and enter into contracts related to the above-mentioned permitted activities, and I declare that I will ratify all lawful acts performed in exercising these powers.

Any person, business, agency, or organization who receives or is given a copy of this limited power of attorney may act under it for the limited purposes listed above. I agree to indemnify any third party for any claims that arise against it because of reliance on this power of attorney for the performance of any lawful service or delivery of any lawful product within the scope of the purposes listed above.

If this power of attorney is revoked, such revocation will only be effective upon a third party after they have received notification of such withdrawal of permission.

Signed:

This _____ day of _____, 20xx

State of: _____ County of: _____

Signature of Grantor (principal): _____

Printed Name of Grantor: _____

Signature of Attorney-in-Fact: _____

Printed Name of Attorney-in-Fact: _____

Witnessed by: _____

Notarized by: _____

Submission of power-of-attorney forms to financial institution

From individual to bank or financial institution

(NOTE: Consult with your attorney or legal advisor for advice on drawing up and filing power-of-attorney and other basic legal forms. Be aware that if you grant such powers to another you may be giving up some or all control over important financial and other matters.)

Regarding: Ben Adams
Account: 6SJ7-34310-21

Enclosed please find certified copies of Durable Power of Attorney forms that give me permission to make the specified decisions regarding the finances of Ben Adams.

Please notate your files to indicate that I have been granted power of attorney for Mr. Adams and please add my name and address to your records and issue second copies of all bank statements and correspondence to me.

I expect to take over the management of Mr. Adams' checking and savings accounts to pay bills, make transfers, and perform other banking tasks while he is incapacitated.

Please feel free to contact me if you have any questions about the paperwork I am submitting.

44 Personal Medical Matters

From Individual to Insurance Company

From Individual to Medical Office

From Individual to Insurance Company

Documenting claim to medical insurance carrier

From customer to insurance company

Regarding member number: 123098567

Enclosed please find documents to support my claim for reimbursement of medical expenses incurred while traveling away from my home.

As indicated on your Web site, I am providing the following documents:

An invoice showing expenses paid to an emergency medical facility in Chillicothe, Ohio;

A detailed doctor's report from the emergency medical facility, including diagnosis, services performed, and medications prescribed;

A receipt for prescription medications related to this illness; and

Copies of hotel and airline ticket receipts that document the starting and ending date of this trip away from home.

The total amount for out-of-home-area medical expenses was $1,546.23.

I have also included a signed copy of your medical claim form. Please keep me posted on the progress of my claim and advise me of any questions related to this claim.

Request to medical insurance company for formal written ruling on claim

From individual to insurance company

Regarding policy #459801020
Policyholder name: Thomas Poster
Claim #H4-2361A

August 12, 2007

I am writing to request an update on the status of my claim for reimbursement for medical expenses incurred while I was on a trip in Europe. I submitted the claim and necessary forms more than five weeks ago, on July 5, 2007.

I would appreciate a statement of coverage and a check as soon as possible so that I can submit a claim to a secondary medical insurance company.

Contesting primary medical insurance claim denial

From individual to insurance company

Regarding policy #459801020
Policyholder name: Thomas Poster
Claim #H4-2361A

August 12, 2007

I am writing to formally contest your company's denial of my claim for reimbursement of expenses incurred on an international trip.

According to your representative in a telephone conversation on July 30, 2007, my insurance policy should cover all out-of-area medical expenses minus a copay of $500. I was given the following confirmation code for our telephone conversation: AMGUIEH.

Please advise me of the progress of my reinstated claim as soon as possible.

Transmittal to secondary medical insurance company of claim

From individual to insurance company

Regarding policy #ST02929
Policyholder name: Thomas Poster

August 12, 2007

I am a policyholder in your Worldwide Travel Plan Insurance. Enclosed please find a statement of coverage and claims paid by my primary health insurance company for medical expenses incurred while I was on a trip in Europe. Also included is the claims form from your company and an affidavit of the circumstances of my illness and the dates of travel away from my home area.

I am now requesting your company accept my claim for the portion of my expenses that were not covered by my primary insurance carrier.

Notifying insurance company of change of address

From individual to insurance company

Regarding policy #459801020
Policyholder name: Jeremy Stein
Date of birth: April 3, 1916

Please change your records to indicate my new permanent address, listed below.

Former address: (Address)
New address: (Address)
Telephone: (Telephone number)

Notifying life insurance company of death of policyholder

From individual to insurance company

Regarding policy #459801020
Policyholder name: Jeremy Stein
Date of birth: April 3, 1916

I am writing to request necessary forms to file a life insurance claim for the above policy. Jeremy Stein died on May 15, 2008, at Lumbertown Community Hospital. Mr. Stein was my uncle, and I am listed with your company as a beneficiary; I also am listed on Mr. Stein's records as an attorney-in-fact under a Durable Power of Attorney.

(Name)
(Address)
(Phone number)

Notifying life insurance company of change of name

From individual to insurance company

Regarding policy #459801020
Policyholder name: Maribeth Plame
Date of birth: April 3, 1986

Please change your records to indicate a change of name; I was married June 5, 2007, and have taken my husband's name as part of my own.

Former name: Maribeth Plame
New name: Maribeth Plame-Kineck
Address: (Address)
Telephone: (Telephone number)

Notifying insurance company of changes to policy because of divorce

From individual to insurance company

> Regarding policy #459801020
> Policyholder name: Maribeth Plame-Kineck
> Date of birth: April 3, 1986

Please change your records to reflect the following changes which are due to a decree of divorce that was granted June 4, 2008. A copy of the final decree is attached.

> Former Name: Maribeth Plame-Kineck
> New Name: Maribeth Plame
> Address: (Address)
> Telephone: (Telephone number)

Please also remove David Kineck as one of the beneficiaries on my policy. At this time it is my intent that any proceeds from my policy will go to my parents Jack and Jill Plame, who are currently listed on the policy as secondary beneficiaries.

From Individual to Medical Office

Requesting transfer of medical records from one doctor to another

From individual to doctor or medical institution

(NOTE: Some doctors or medical institutions may require use of their own forms to request transfer of records. You can seek release of your records with your own letter, but they may respond with a form for you to fill out.)

I hereby authorize (name of doctor or medical organization) to release to (name of new doctor or medical organization) a copy of the full set of my medical records in your possession.

> Please send the files to:
> (New medical provider)
> (Address)
> (Phone number)

_____   _____
(Your name printed)   (Your signature)

_____   _____
(Date)   (Subscriber number or Patient ID)

Requesting transfer of dental records to new dentist

From individual to doctor or medical institution

(NOTE: Some dentists or dental groups may require use of their own forms to request transfer of records. You can seek release of your records with your own letter, but they may respond with a form for you to fill out.)

After more than fifteen years in Lumbertown, I will be moving next month to Eumonia. I appreciate your assistance over the years. I am writing to request transfer of my dental records to a dentist near my new home.

I hereby authorize (name of dentist or dental group) to release to (name of new dentist or dental group) the full set of my dental records in your possession.

Please send the files to:
(New medical provider)
(Address)
(Phone number)

_____   _____
(Your name printed)   (Your signature)

_____   _____
(Date)   (Subscriber number or Patient ID)

Filing power-of-attorney and legal and medical proxies with doctor

From individual to doctor or medical institution

Enclosed please find a certified copy of the following legal documents related to your patient, Jeremy Stein:

- Durable Power of Attorney
- Health Care Advance Directive
- Living Will

Please include these documents in your medical records for Jeremy Stein. I will be assisting Mr. Stein as necessary in making medical and other decisions.

Submission of power-of-attorney and health care proxy forms to nursing home

From individual to nursing home:

(NOTE: Consult with your attorney or legal advisor for advice on drawing up and filing power- of-attorney and other basic legal forms. Be aware that if you grant such powers to another you may be giving up some or all control over important financial, medical, and other matters.)

Regarding: Ben Adams

Account: 225 Rolling Stone Drive, Holliston, NY

Enclosed please find copies of a Durable Power of Attorney and Health Care Proxy granted by Ben Adams to me.

Please notate your files to indicate that I will be assuming responsibility for managing Mr. Adams's financial affairs and that I have also been authorized to make any and all medical decisions on his behalf. I have included my day, night, and cell phone numbers below.

Please also note that in keeping with Mr. Adams's express wishes, the Health Care Proxy includes a Do Not Resuscitate notice. We have discussed this matter with Mr. Adams and his attorney, and ask that his wishes in the event of a medical crisis be respected.

Granting permission to third party to discuss medical status

From individual to doctor or medical institution

I hereby grant permission to (name of doctor or medical facility) to verbally discuss with the below-named person or persons the following medical and billing information about me:

- Medical information, including my symptoms, diagnosis, medications, and treatment plan
- Lab, X-Ray, or test reports
- Scheduled appointments for assessment, treatment, or procedures
- Billing and payment information.

Such information may be disclosed to

(Name)

(Address)

(Telephone)

(Name)

(Address)

(Telephone)

This permission may be revoked by me at any time by written notice.
This permission is given by

(Your name)

(Your address)

(Your phone)

(Your Patient ID or Medical ID number)

Submission of power-of-attorney form and medical directive to doctor

From individual to doctor

(NOTE: Consult with your attorney or legal advisor for advice on drawing up and filing power-of-attorney and other basic legal forms. Be aware that if you grant such powers to another you may be giving up some or all control over important financial, medical, and other matters.)

Regarding: Ben Adams
Account: 225 Rolling Stone Drive, Holliston, NY

Enclosed please find copies of a Durable Power of Attorney and Health Care Proxy granted by Ben Adams to me.

In keeping with Mr. Adams's wishes, the proxy includes a Do Not Resuscitate notice.

Further, the proxy gives express permission for any and all medical practitioners to disclose and discuss all medical conditions, procedures, and test results with me and to allow me to make informed decisions on behalf of Mr. Adams.

Please notate your files to indicate this Health Care Proxy as well as the Durable Power of Attorney that allows me to manage Mr. Adams's financial affairs.

I have included my day, night, and cell phone numbers below.

45 Personal Travel

From Individual to Travel Agency or Service Bureau

From Individual to Airline

From Individual to Travel Service Provider

From Individual to Travel Agency or Service Bureau

Request travel agency trip planning

From customer to travel agency

Thank you for your time on the phone today. As we discussed, my wife and I are interested in a trip to the Mediterranean this spring.

We have three weeks available for the trip, and have tentatively chosen the period from May 1 to May 22. We can adjust our schedules to be able to travel as much as three days earlier or later if a better price or better arrangements are available.

We would like to visit the following places, spending about four or five days at each stop: Rome, Florence, Valletta, and Paris. It does not matter to us in which order we visit these places; please make your recommendation based on the best available airfares and hotels.

I noticed an advertisement from the Malta visitor's bureau about a special archeological tour that is available from Valletta on May 10 and 11. We would like to include that excursion as part of our trip. I've enclosed a copy of the ad.

I look forward to hearing from you with details.

Hiring translator and guide for trip

From customer to tour agency

Thank you for your offer of translation and guide service on my upcoming trip to Shanghai. I have electronically attached to this e-mail a copy of my schedule in China.

I accept your offer of pick-up service at the airport and transportation to my hotel on September 5; my flight from Beijing is due to arrive at 3 P.M.

On September 6 and 7 your service will provide a car and guide for tours to Yangshuo and Guilin, and on September 8 you will provide transportation from our hotel to the airport in Shanghai.

Please confirm the details of this schedule and the cost for all services and method of payment for the deposit.

Thank you.

Making adjustments to vacation plans

From customer to travel agency

We have received your proposed schedule for our trip to Italy and Malta in May. The plans generally look fine; we would like to make a few adjustments.

On the basis of our own research, we have found that the museums in much of Europe are closed on Mondays; we would like to adjust the trip dates so that we travel on Monday whenever possible.

Please send a revised itinerary.

Request travel insurance

From customer to travel agency

Thank you for your assistance in planning our upcoming trip to the Mediterranean.

I would like to find out about the availability of trip cancellation and emergency medical insurance for our travels.

We need to cover only the nonrefundable portions of airline and hotel reservations, and we would like to purchase a secondary medical insurance policy that would provide protection for expenses, including emergency repatriation, that are not included in our standard medical plan.

Please also provide information about insurance plans that would cover us for a full year and multiple trips, rather than an individual policy that applies only to this upcoming trip.

Complaint about the quality of the hotel

From customer to travel agency

Thank you for your assistance in planning our recent trip to Tibet. We enjoyed our travel very much.

However, I do need to tell you that one of the hotels you booked for us—the Happy Golden Fortune in Shanghai—was a great disappointment. This was listed in your itinerary as a four-star lodging and it was described as "recently renovated rooms, in a location within walking distance of the Bund."

This hotel was in no way a luxury hotel, and if there has been any renovation of rooms, the three we saw were certainly not included. The quality of this hotel was well below that of any place we have stayed in recent years and significantly worse than the two- and three-star hotels you arranged for us in other cities on this trip. We asked the front desk to give us a better room, and after considerable resistance we were eventually shown two other rooms which were in even worse repair. And as far as the distance to the Bund, someone somewhere may consider 10 miles to be walking distance, but not us.

I feel that we are owed a credit for the cost of our four-night stay at this hotel.

Asking credit for service not provided

From customer to travel agency

We have just returned from our cruise from London to Barbados. The trip was one of the best we have taken; thank you for your help in making arrangements.

However, we did experience one problem with the prepaid transportation that was included in the package. On arrival at Heathrow Airport we were supposed to have been picked up by a car and driver for transportation to the cruise ship in Southampton. According to the documents you provided, the Black Watch Cab Company was supposed to be waiting for us at the exit from the customs hall at 8 A.M. on October 5.

Our plane was on time and we got through customs exactly as planned. But there was no representative of Black Watch at the exit. We waited for nearly an hour and then finally we decided we had no choice but to hire a taxi to drive us to the dock; if we had waited much longer we would have been in danger of missing the departure of our cruise.

The cost of the taxi was 100 pounds, or approximately $200.

Our prepaid transfer, arranged through your travel agency, cost $150.

I feel that we are owed a refund of the $200 in out-of-pocket expenses for the taxi we hired. I look forward to hearing from you on this matter.

Response to offer of credit for service not provided

From customer to travel agency

I have received your letter in which you responded to my complaint about a prepaid transfer that was not provided on our recent trip to London.

Our out-of-pocket expense for a taxi from Heathrow Airport to the docks in Southampton was $200. Your offer of reimbursement for our prepaid transfer was $150.

I feel that your agency should take responsibility for all services and reservations it makes on behalf of a client. We signed a contract for the trip, and one of the elements of the contract was not delivered.

I realize that $50 is not a huge amount of additional cost for us, but as a matter of principal we feel that we should not have had to pay more than the amount in the contract we signed. I hope you will reconsider your decision and that we will be able to continue to do business with your company.

E-mail requesting assistance in making changes to schedule

From customer to travel agency

I am currently in Rome on a trip booked through your agency. Because of an unexpected family emergency, I need to come back home about a week ahead of schedule.

My current itinerary calls for me to fly five days from now, on May 14, from Rome to Athens to spend a week in Greece.

Can you please change my reservations so that I can fly directly from Rome to New York and on to Lumbertown on May 14? Please also cancel hotel, excursion, and car rental reservations made for Greece.

I would appreciate it if you can handle this change in my schedule by response to this e-mail. Because of the time difference and my schedule it will be difficult for me to call you on the telephone for the next forty-eight hours. If you need to call me, you can try to reach me at the Grande Termini Hotel; the best time to reach me would be between 7 and 9 P.M. Rome time, about noon to 2 P.M. your time.

Thank you for your assistance.

From Individual to Airline

Requesting posting of frequent flyer miles

From individual to airline

Regarding Frequent Flyer Club Account Number: 100020200

Enclosed please find copies of four boarding passes for flights on AmericaUSNational Airlines for posting to my frequent flyer club account. These flights have not shown up on the last two month's statements.

Complaining about airline service

From individual to airline

I just returned from a flight on AmericaUSNational Airlines (Flight #328 from Circleville to Eumonia) on May 5, 2008. I am very dissatisfied with the service I received.

The flight was delayed at least six different times and did not depart until 6 P.M., four hours after its scheduled time. We were not given any explanation by the agent at the gate; her name tag was "Brenda." The weather was not a factor; it was a beautiful, clear day and all of the other airlines were flying on time.

Once we were on board the plane, we learned from the flight attendant that the reason for the delay was the fact that there were too few tickets sold for the 6 P.M. flight, and the airline had decided to combine the 2 P.M. and 6 P.M. passengers on one plane.

I find this explanation to be completely unacceptable. Your passengers have meetings and appointments and we have purchased tickets based on your published schedule. The fact that a particular flight is not profitable for you is a problem you should address after you have successfully delivered your passengers.

Documenting baggage loss or damage on airline

From individual to airline

Regarding claim # AJ347987

Enclosed is a list of the contents and replacement value of the contents of my suitcase that was lost by AmericaUSNational Airlines on Flight #328 on May 5, 2008. I have included a copy of the purchase receipts for several of the most costly items, including a new business suit and several pieces of electronic equipment.

According to your claims office, I can expect to receive payment for the suitcase and its contents within thirty days. Please keep me advised of the progress of my claim.

Complimenting service on airline

From individual to airline

Your new commuter jets on the Eumonia to Circleville route are a tremendous improvement to the quality of your service. We finally have first class service (at a reasonable price).

I hope you have great success with this enhancement of local service; I will recommend these new flights on your airline to all of my business acquaintances and friends.

Complimenting member of airline staff

From individual to airline

I wanted to let you know that one of your flight attendants, Mary Englund, went out of her way to assist me on a recent flight. I was returning to Eumonia from an overseas trip, and I was not feeling well.

Ms. Englund helped open a row of seats for me, collected blankets and pillows, and regularly checked on me throughout the flight. And on arrival, she arranged for a wheelchair and a special escort from the plane to the airport exit where my family was waiting.

I am aware of the fact that airlines help passengers whenever they can, but they usually require advance notice. Ms. Englund's uncommon level of courtesy was much more than I could have reasonably expected.

From Individual to Travel Service Provider

Seeking confirmation of hotel reservation

From individual to hotel

Please confirm receipt of my reservation deposit for a double room at your hotel, with arrival on Sunday, June 3, 2007 and departure on Tuesday, June 5. The confirmation code I received when I called was AEIOU07; I do not see a charge on my credit card account for the reservation and have not received any confirmation by e-mail or postal mail.

Cancelling hotel reservation and requesting confirmation

From individual to hotel

Please cancel reservation AEIOU07, in the name of Shepherd, for arrival on June 3, 2007. I would appreciate confirmation of the cancellation of this reservation and the refund of the deposit you hold.

Thank you.

Requesting verification of cancellation, requesting refund

From individual to hotel

Please confirm receipt of the cancellation for reservation AEIOU07, in the name of Shepherd, for arrival on June 3, 2007. I sent an e-mail cancelling this reservation on May 1, but have not received confirmation.

According to your posted reservation policies, cancellations made more than ten days before planned arrival date receive 100 percent refund of deposit. I have checked with my credit card company and as of this date no such refund has been given by your hotel.

Commending employee for special effort

From customer to hotel

I just returned from a vacation trip to Denver, staying at your hotel for four nights beginning May 5.

I want to let you know about the exceptional service provided by your concierge, Maria Maldonado. Soon after arrival I became ill, and Ms. Maldonado helped arrange for a doctor's call to my room and the delivery of prescription drugs from a pharmacy; over the next few days she checked in on me regularly, arranging for special room service and coordinating with the housekeeping department so that I was able to recuperate as best I could.

Ms. Maldonado went far beyond the ordinary in assisting me, and I am deeply appreciative.

Request to hotel for duplicate receipt

From individual to travel provider

I stayed at your hotel from August 29 to 31, 2007. When I returned home I was unable to find my copy of the receipt; would you please generate a new receipt and mail it to me at the address on this letter?

Thank you.

To auto rental company documenting insurance claim

Documenting insurance claim

Regarding rental agreement number MAR08-20849793US

Enclosed is a list of items stolen from my rental vehicle on March 8, 2008, along with replacement values for each. I have included receipts for my laptop computer and digital camera and estimates for lesser-valued items.

Under terms of the Theft and Breakage Insurance I purchased for the above-listed rental, I am requesting a total of $3,235 in reimbursement.

Please confirm receipt of this claim and advise me of the status of payment.

Index

How to Use the CD

1001 Business Letters for All Occasions and its accompanying CD was designed to serve as a comprehensive business resource, providing you with the letters you need to run your business in the real world. These letters will help you to manage your finances, close sales, track employee performance, and more.

If you wish to view or edit any of the letters on the enclosed CD-ROM, simply insert the disk, scroll through the sub-folers, and click on the specific letter you would like to view. Save the file to your desktop and begin working. You can then edit or manipulate the letters any way you like and then save them in any format that you choose.

Consult your word processing manual for information on viewing and editing documents saved as Rich Text Format.

About the Authors

Corey Sandler is the author of more than 180 books on business, history, travel, sports, and entertainment. Earlier in his career he worked as an executive for newspaper and magazine companies, managing staffs of more than a hundred. He also held a job as a mid-level manager for an agency of New York state government and an administrative post for a major university.

Janice Keefe is a researcher and author of business books. She has worked for several publishing companies as well as a state agency.

Among their bestselling books from Adams Media is *1001 Letters for All Occasions*. They also wrote *Performance Appraisal Phrase Book*, *Performance Appraisals That Work*, and *Fails to Meet Expectations*.

You can learn more about the authors and their other books and contact them through their Web site, *www.econoguide.com*.